STATISTICAL LITERACY
AT SCHOOL

Growth and Goals

STUDIES IN MATHEMATICAL THINKING AND LEARNING
Alan H. Schoenfeld, Series Editor

STATISTICAL LITERACY AT SCHOOL

Growth and Goals

Jane M. Watson
University of Tasmania

LEA
LAWRENCE ERLBAUM ASSOCIATES, PUBLISHERS
2006 Mahwah, New Jersey   London

Lawrence Erlbaum Associates, Inc., Publishers
10 Industrial Avenue
Mahwah, New Jersey 07430
www.erlbaum.com

Cover design by Tomai Maridou

CIP information for this book can be obtained by contacting the Library of Congress

ISBN 0-8058-5398-7 (cloth : alk. paper)
ISBN 0-8058-5399-5 (pbk. : alk. paper)

Books published by Lawrence Erlbaum Associates are printed on acid-free paper, and their bindings are chosen for strength and durability.

Printed in the United States of America
10 9 8 7 6 5 4 3 2 1

Contents

Preface

Statistical thinking will one day be as necessary for efficient citizenship as the ability to read and write (attributed to H. G. Wells).[1]

PURPOSE

The incorporation of probability and statistics as a significant part of most school mathematics curricula from the early 1990s[2] has necessitated the adoption of two new goals for educators: the preparation of *all* students to participate in decision making based on data and the preparation of *some* students for further study of formal statistics. This book is mainly about the former, termed *statistical literacy*, although the foundation laid will assist students following the latter path in making sense of the purpose of formal statistics. It is throughout the elementary and middle school years that intuitions and understanding about chance and data are refined. It is the premise of this book that the refinement can be best enhanced if educators appreciate that

- statistical literacy—the goal—incorporates content from across the school curriculum as well as wider contexts,
- there are many important connections among the ideas related to statistical literacy that require constant reinforcement, and
- development of understanding is observable in structural forms that suggest pathways to improvement, and

- suitable tasks and activities are able to assist in diagnosing levels of current understanding and in moving students to higher levels.

The content focus of this book is on the preliminary ideas of sampling, representation, summary, chance, inference, and variation, which are essential to later work in formal statistics. For those students who do not proceed to formal study, these concepts provide a basis for decision making or questioning when presented with claims based on data in societal settings. Not every school graduate needs to be able to perform statistical tests but everyone needs to be able to question statistical claims made without reasonable justification.

The first purpose of this book is to establish an overall framework for statistical literacy in terms of both the links to specific school curricula and the wider appreciation of contexts within which chance and data handling ideas are applied. This acknowledgment of context is sometimes forgotten when introductory definitions for probability and statistics are presented in text books.

The second purpose is to demonstrate, within the framework, that there are many connections among specific ideas and constructs. These links are highlighted in figures at the beginning of each chapter. Although it may not be possible to teach or assess the complete statistical investigation process at one time or with a single task, it is important to reinforce connections constantly.

To follow student development of understanding over time it is essential to have both a structure within which improvement can be gauged and tasks that are appropriate for the goals and allow students to display various levels of understanding. A third purpose of this book hence is to provide tasks, adaptable for classroom or assessment use that are appropriate for the goals of statistical literacy. The fourth purpose is to present extensive examples of student performance on the tasks, illustrating a hierarchy of achievement, to assist in monitoring gains and meeting the goals of statistical literacy.

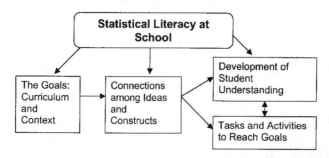

AUDIENCE

Who might be interested in this book?

- Educational researchers interested in cognitive development within the field or in devising tasks for classroom interventions or teaching experiments. Starting points provided include traditional curricular problems, as well as more holistic tasks written in a broader contextual setting, important for building skills to be used outside of school.
- Teachers who want to focus on the concepts involved in statistical literacy without the use of formal statistical techniques. These teachers may be specialist mathematics teachers but they may also be generalist teachers who see the need to incorporate statistical literacy across the curriculum. These teachers are more likely to be teaching at the elementary or middle school level, but may indeed be teaching "mathematics for society" courses at any level, including secondary, college, or adult education.
- Statisticians who are interested in the development of student understanding before students are exposed to the formal study of statistics. There are some in the statistics community who believe that all exposure to probability and statistics should be left until college so that incorrect ideas are not taken up.[3] It is the premise of this book that such a step would be much worse in that many intuitions are picked up outside of school and work in the classroom can redress fallacies. It would also be a huge disadvantage to those who never reach college-level statistics.

The book is structured around the aspects of chance and data that are the focus of the school curriculum in most western countries. This is because the book is intended as a complement to curriculum documents and text book series. It is consistent with the principles and standards espoused in the reform agenda of the National Council of Teachers of Mathematics.[4] It is intended to provide additional ideas for tasks, to indicate what is likely to be observed in terms of student outcomes, and to reinforce connections across the curriculum. Although a wide range of tasks and observed outcomes are presented, of course there are aspects that cannot be addressed in a single volume. The topics covered reflect the research studies in which the author has been involved. The two notable omissions are actual data collection and the use of technology. Although sampling, including sample size, sampling method, and sampling bias, is covered descriptively, there is virtually no discussion of tasks where students are required to design a sampling strategy and collect their own data. The one partial exception to this is when students are asked if they can determine which of several dice are fair and may choose to carry out trials of throwing the dice.

The use of technology is not a feature of this book for several reasons. One is the belief of the author that technology is a tool to assist in saving time in performing calculations and in preparing visual representations to aid in analysis. At the level of technical understanding required in the middle school before formal statistics are met, most investigations are not sufficiently complex to require more than a basic calculator and graph paper. In fact some statistical packages provide representations that are impossible for beginners to interpret. The development of software for beginners is currently taking place and new packages are appearing on the market appropriate for the middle school level.[5] A related issue, however, is the availability of technology in the classroom. Not only does a teacher need an appropriate software package but also the classroom needs computers that can be accessed on demand. Unfortunately many classrooms still do not have such access and it is not necessary to wait until it occurs to develop meaningful understandings about chance and data. Although a software package was used in a few instances in the author's research projects, it was felt that the space required to explain the simulation involved and its current lack of availability commercially to teachers or researchers, meant that the exercise was not warranted. Teachers and researchers who have access to and familiarity with software, will be able to adapt tasks presented here to include their packages. They should not forget the importance, however, of continuing to include "by-hand" sketches and "number play" to build intuitions.

OVERVIEW OF CONTENT

The focus of this book in terms of students is their observed levels of understanding with respect to the tasks presented to them. Although suggestions for classroom interventions are made based on these observations, these are not based on research-based trials. They are based on the experience of the author or anecdotal evidence provided by classroom teachers. Many of the suggestions have been trialed by me with teachers in professional development sessions and then by them in their classes with feedback returned to me. Although it has been demonstrated in related research studies that mean performances on surveys can be improved by classroom intervention,[6] it has not been possible to date to assist all students to the highest level of performance on all tasks (or even close to it). The realities of school and society suggest that this goal will be a long time coming and that teachers and educational planners still need to cater for all levels of understanding as starting points when students enter classes at any particular level. The aim of the book in this regard is to provide a rich description of what realistic expectations should be.

Chapter 1 sets out the purpose and foundations of the book, focusing on the four aspects noted at the beginning of the Preface: the place of statistical literacy historically and with respect to the school curriculum, the connections that are important within the school curriculum, the theoretical frameworks that are used to discuss the hierarchy of student understanding, and the background of tasks and data collection for the material presented in the book. There is also a section devoted specifically to variation, due to its importance to probability and statistics but its lack of exposure in curriculum documents and text books.

The next six chapters consider specific topics in the chance and data curriculum. Each chapter begins with a figure setting out the connections among the topics and other relevant features of the curriculum. The linear presentation of chapters should not suggest that statistical investigations proceed chapter by chapter. In fact with variation as the reason for all statistical investigation, Chapter 7 is intended as a review and tying together of the ideas in the previous chapters. Chapter 2 considers issues of sampling, beginning with an exploration of student understanding of the term. This is followed by discussion of context, sample size, method, fairness, bias, and the idea of being random. Chapter 3 looks at various graphical representations and the levels of understanding students display. Both creation and interpretation of graphs are considered, as are pictographs, graphs to show association, bar charts, pie charts, and stacked dot plots. Chapter 4 presents ideas associated with average. Because averages are the main summary statistics presented before formal statistics are encountered, it is important to follow students' understanding, particularly in terms of the links to colloquial ideas. The chapter also treats bias, problem solving, and inference related to measures of average. Chapter 5 deals with chance, developing several perspectives. These include the use of language associated with chance, the measurement of chance based on traditional probabilistic concepts, and issues related to luck, bias, and risk. Beginning inference is the focus of Chapter 6. Although formal statistical tests are not considered, the issues dealt with include predicting, hypothesizing, comparing data sets, considering associations, and questioning inferences. Building intuitions in these areas provides a foundation for later work in inferential statistics. Chapter 7 considers the underlying phenomenon of variation through an exploration of students' understanding of the term and four case studies that integrate concepts from the previous chapters.

Finally, Chapter 8 presents a summary of analysis of survey data that suggests a developmental hierarchy for students over the years of schooling with respect to the goal of statistical literacy. Six stages of sophistication are described, from idiosyncratic to critical mathematical. These stages reflect the expectations for students when they leave school or enter formal statistics courses. The aim is to create an awareness of likely observed degrees of student achievement in relation to the desired goals of educators.

As well as the Reference list of sources referred to in the endnotes that accompany each chapter, many others are listed under Further Reading and provide starting points for further reading and research.

PERSONAL ACKNOWLEDGMENTS

This book is the culmination of 10 years of research into school students' understanding of statistical concepts. The research had several antecedents and many contributors. As the author, I would like to explain a little of my personal history and thank those who have worked with me over the years.

My study of statistics and probability was through undergraduate and masters degree theoretical courses that were dependent on calculus rather than experimental trials. I tutored and taught undergraduate science and engineering students introductory probability and statistics courses[7] in a similar vein for 13 years in the Mathematics Department at the University of Tasmania with an occasional interest in investigating media reports involving conditional probability,[8] before moving to the Faculty of Education where my job initially was to teach mathematics to pre-service elementary teachers. At the time of the production of *A National Statement on Mathematics for Australian Schools*,[9] I was a consultant on the chance and data and measurement strands of the curriculum for the senior secondary level and when it came out I was head of the team to produce professional development materials for teachers to introduce the chance and data component of the new curriculum.[10] The dearth of research in this area on students' and teachers' understanding and on classroom-based intervention was readily apparent. Hence began a decade of research funded by the Australian Research Council on various aspects of learning associated with chance and data. At the same time there were three large government-funded professional development projects in conjunction with the Australian Association of Mathematics Teachers, Inc. led by Jeff Baxter, under the title, Learning the Unlikely at Distance Delivered as an Information Technology Enterprise (LUDDITE). These projects clarified some teacher needs and trialed information technologies including satellite television, nationwide video conferencing, a professional development course on CD-rom, and a Web site in conjunction with a newspaper.[11]

The research began in earnest in 1993 funded by a grant with Kevin Collis to employ his model of cognitive development (cf. Section 1.4) to analyze the responses of students in grades 3, 6, and 9 to tasks described in

Section 1.5. Grants followed in 1995–1997 to consider higher order statistical functioning when students worked in groups; in 1996 to profile teachers' understanding of the curriculum; in 1997 to collect longitudinal data following from 1993 and 1995; in 1998–2000 to consider the effect of cognitive conflict on statistical understanding; in 1999 to consider the provision of help in group-work situations; in 2000–2002 to investigate student understanding of variation and trial the teaching of chance and data with an emphasis on variation; in 2001 to investigate statistical literacy using Rasch methods; and in 2002–2004 to consolidate a model of statistical literacy using all data and resources. All of these studies have contributed to some degree to the outcomes presented in this book in relation to the development of student understanding. Outcomes associated with other research objectives are reported in journals available internationally and are not detailed here.

Kevin Collis provided both the reputation and the theory that helped the research get started and worked closely with the team until his retirement in 1995. Jonathan Moritz began as the research assistant for the first project and had some level of involvement with each of the later ones, as well as beginning his own doctoral research. Sharyn Lidster began working with me on the collaborative research, work which was continued admirably by Helen Chick. Rosemary Callingham, who completed a masters degree research project on teachers' understanding of average, was involved early in the group-work research and later with the Rasch analysis in relation to statistical literacy. Rob Torok began the variation research in his Bachelor of Teaching honors thesis and Ben Kelly took over the research assistance for the rest of that project. Annaliese Caney assisted projects by coding statistical literacy items and helping analyze "random" data. Many teachers in Tasmanian classrooms have been involved in various ways in the research, from organizing survey administration to teaching units of work or providing opportunities for students to trial tasks. Particular thanks, however, go to Sharyn Lidster in relation to teaching pie graphs, Denise Neal for work in early childhood, Neville Windsor in relation to work with sampling and the "hospital problem" with senior secondary students, and Pat Jeffery who was the project teacher at the elementary level for all lessons in the variation project. Overseas collaboration began with useful correspondence from Iddo Gal and Cliff Konold and many research task suggestions from Lionel Pereira-Mendoza, who visited Tasmania twice. Others to visit Tasmania included David Green, Cliff Konold, and Mike Shaughnessy, the last also coming twice. Sharing an interest in the place of variation in the data and chance curriculum and students' understanding of the concept, Mike was a substantial collaborator on the 2000–2002 project.

Thanks go to all of these people for their enthusiasm and in many cases patience in working as part of a team. Especially for the long hours and sometimes heated arguments leading to progress, I express gratitude to Jonathan, Helen, Rosemary, Ben, and Mike. Thanks for help with proof-reading and indexing to Ben. In the end it was Judith Deans who changed my handwriting into legible typescript with unending determination and patience, as well as working to satisfy the publishing guidelines. At Lawrence Erlbaum Associates thanks go to the various editors who worked on the manuscript and of course thanks to Alan Schoenfeld who accepted the book in his series, Studies in Mathematical Thinking and Learning. Finally I express gratitude to Gerald Johnston, my support through all of the years of research and writing.

ENDNOTES

1. Huff (1991), facing contents page. The original of this quote cannot be traced but Wells is quoted as saying something similar in Walker (1931), and Wells (1994) said, "A certain elementary training in statistical method is becoming as necessary for anyone living in this world of today as reading and writing" (p. 141).
2. Australian Education Council (1991); Ministry of Education (1992); National Council of Teachers of Mathematics (1989).
3. This must remain as "anecdotal" evidence, as although many colleagues have repeated such claims to me, none can provide a published reference or person willing to put the claim in writing.
4. Kilpatrick, Martin, & Schifter (2003); National Council of Teachers of Mathematics (2000).
5. Konold & Miller (2005).
6. Watson & Kelly (2002a, 2002c, 2002e).
7. Watson (1991).
8. Watson (1978, 1980).
9. Australian Education Council (1991).
10. Watson (1994b).
11. Watson (1996, 1997b, 1998c, 1998d); Watson & Baxter (1997); Watson, Baxter, Olssen, & Lovitt (1996). The Web site is now called 'Numeracy in the News' and is easily accessed through an internet search engine.

Purpose and Foundations

Beware the pushy fish-eater

MEN who eat a lot of fish are driven by ambition and the desire for success, British researchers claim.

Seven in 10 men who frequently eat canned tuna, sardines, salmon, mackerel or kippers admit to being ambitious, and one in two rate themselves as more successful than others.

The study, commissioned by John West Foods, reveals they are also thin-skinned types, with only 5 per cent of regular fish-eaters saying they coped well with criticism compared with a quarter of the non-fish eaters.[1]

Schoolgirls are smokers, drinkers

MORE than a quarter of 11 and 12-year-old Australian schoolgirls have smoked cigarettes . . .

This was revealed yesterday in a study by the National Health and Medical Research Council [which] suggests anti-drug campaigns may not adequately address the risk factors associated with drug use by girls.

The major influences identified by the survey included the behaviour of the girls' friends, their literacy level, and parental example . . .

Girls were more than seven times more likely to smoke if their friends did and 2.3 times more likely to smoke if their parents did. And girls with poor literacy rates were five times more likely to have smoked in the last month than girls with high literacy skills, the research found.

The national study surveyed 1,400 girls at 86 primary schools.

Twenty-six per cent reported having smoked at some stage in their lives and six per cent said they had smoked in the previous month.[2]

1.1   MOTIVATION AND PURPOSE

These two newspaper articles provide the starting points to motivate this book. The goal is for students to be able to read articles like these critically, to ask salient questions, and to make judgments about the veracity of the claims being made. Because the articles report on "studies," not only can their content be linked to the content of the school data and chance curriculum but also their settings illustrate the contexts required for statistical literacy outside of the school classroom.

"Beware the pushy fish-eater" should raise questions such as the following in the mind of the reader. Does the article claim that eating fish frequently causes men to be more ambitious? Why would a company that sells fish wish to conduct such a survey? How many people were involved in the survey and how were they selected? How were questions asked? How many categories of fish eating were used? Were women as well as men surveyed? How many people were in each category? How were the data presented to tell the story and summarized to support the conditional statement that "seven in 10 men who frequently eat canned tuna, sardines, mackerel, or kippers admit to being ambitious"? So many details are missing that a statistically literate reader is likely to dismiss all claims with a chuckle.[3]

In contrast to "Beware the pushy fish-eater," "School girls are smokers" presents enough information about a study by a reputable national body that many critical questions can be answered. The sample size and an indication of representativeness are given, although of course one could ask for more. The reporting of the observed percents of smokers and the conditions under which the percents were calculated are given. The reporting of relative likelihood in terms of multiples again involves conditional statements, for example P(girl smokes | parents smoke) = 2.3 P(girl smokes | parents do not smoke). Comparing the influence of parents and friends is possible in this fashion. Questions, however, do remain; for example with respect to literacy levels it would be important to know the overall levels for the entire group to compare with the smaller groups. Summary graphs would be useful in gaining a perspective on the variables measured. Just as in the case of the "pushy fish-eater," various categories are used to partition the sample but this time at least it is possible to gain a feel for the cell sizes with 364 having smoked at some stage and 84 in the last month. Whether one considers these values adequate for taking the claims about smoking influences seriously is still up to the reader but much more information is provided to assist in decision making.

In planning for action to make it possible for students to reach the levels of critical statistical literacy required to become informed citizens, there are four interrelated premises that form the foundation for this book. The first is that building of the appropriate understanding must take place within the school curriculum and in most parts of the world this means mainly the mathematics curriculum. This is a result of the extension of the mathematics curriculum to include topics in statistics and probability in the early 1990s.[4] In this context it is important to appreciate the history of statistics in the curriculum and the connections that can be made to reinforce and enhance learning. These connections are found among statistical ideas and between them and other mathematical concepts, as well as with contexts within which data and chance are found to apply.

The second premise is that statistical literacy, although based on concepts currently in the school curriculum, goes beyond them to be embodied in a complex construct that weaves together literacy skills, critical thinking, contextual understanding, and motivation to be involved in decision making. Although very recent, the emergence of discussion of statistical literacy as an important part of the quantitative literacy skills needed to enter the adult world provides part of the foundation for the goals of this book.

The third premise is that the development of statistical literacy understandings takes place over time and can be nurtured by an appreciation of the structural complexity of developing concepts and the increasingly sophisticated requirements of appropriate statistical thinking. In planning learning experiences it is essential to know where students are currently in their understanding and where it is desirable for them to be at the end of the experience.

The fourth premise is that appropriate tasks and activities are needed to build understanding in relation to the data and chance concepts in the school curriculum, in relation to the wider contextual goals of statistical literacy, and in relation to the increasing sophistication and structural complexity demanded to reach the goal of critical thinking. Throughout the book discussion is based on tasks that have been used in various research settings and that provide a means both of assessing students' current levels of understanding and of assisting in progression to higher levels of understanding.

The next four sections of Chapter 1 develop the ideas and history surrounding these four premises in preparation for the presentation in the following seven chapters. Chapter 1 ends with a discussion of variation, the fundamental notion that underlies all of statistics and probability.

1.2 HISTORY AND CONNECTIONS OF STATISTICS IN THE SCHOOL CURRICULUM

This section outlines the history and influences that have created the data and chance components of the school curriculum. As these components are the basic building blocks for statistical literacy, their profile in the mathematics curriculum is important. The section finishes with comments on the importance of building connections among these components and with other important ideas inside and outside the mathematics curriculum.

Although weighted mean problems have been used as part of the arithmetic or algebra curriculum for well over a century,[5] ideas associated with the process of statistical investigation gained official recognition in the mathematics curriculum only near the end of the twentieth century.[6] The following extract from the rationale presented by the famous Indian statistician, Radhakrishna Rao in 1975, for the inclusion of statistics in the secondary school curriculum illustrates the views of the statistics community. He hoped that by starting early, the connections between his discipline, barely a century old, and those it served, could be more naturally established for the benefit of all.

> The subject matter of statistics may be broadly defined as information gathering and information processing. As such, it is basic to all scientific inference for the advancement of natural knowledge and decision making in technology and practical life. . . . Statistics ceases to have a meaning if it is not related to any practical problem. There is nothing like a purely statistical problem which statistics purports to solve. The subject in which a decision is made is not statistics. It is botany or ecology or geology and so on. Statistics can flourish only in an atmosphere where it is in demand and it can develop only in trying to solve problems in other disciplines.[7]

In some places probability, from a theoretical perspective, received attention first in the school curriculum, as part of pure mathematics, often associated with numerical techniques such as the calculation of permutations and combinations.[8] In 1980, Peter Holmes summarized a framework that has been the basis of the structure of the school statistics curriculum in the major curriculum documents.[9] He considered the five components that comprise the stages of statistical investigations based on potential questions of interest:

- Data collection, including use of a census, types of data, sampling, and obtaining data;
- Data tabulation and representation, including tabulation and pictorial representation;
- Data reduction, including measures of location, measures of dispersion, other summarizing statistics, and regression and correlation;
- Probability, including assigning probabilities, manipulating probabilities, and modeling and probability distributions;
- Interpretation and inference, including inferring from tables and diagrams, trends and projections, data comparison, parameter estimates, variability estimates, test statistics, and type I and II error.[10]

This framework was the basis for the suggested statistics curriculum for the last 5 years of compulsory education in England and Wales.

Although the place of probability as a component of statistical investigation has engendered some debate,[11] it has remained an integral part of the curriculum in most places. The concept maps devised to elucidate the basic model have become increasingly complex as people attempt to include the essential associated concepts. Figure 1.1 contains the model for statistical investigations suggested in a project for teachers at the University of North Carolina.[12] It is quite detailed and whereas it does not impose exactly the same major organizers as Peter Holmes did, for example including the posing of a question, the same ingredients are present somewhere in the figure. The lack of a major position for probability in Fig. 1.1 reflects the dilemma associated with the use of formal inference procedures based on probability at the school level. Hence in Fig. 1.1 probability is associated with sampling in terms of collecting data but not with interpreting the results. This is a reasonable model before the senior years of schooling and the question posed to begin an investigation may very well be based in a chance context. The basic notions of probability, building from subjective and frequency-based intuitions, however, need to be included in the elementary and middle school curriculum as a foundation for later more formal usage of probability in inferential reasoning.

Working from the perspective of how statisticians operate when they are solving a problem using a statistical process, Chris Wild and Maxine Pfannkuch suggested a complex four-dimensional model for statistical investigations that encompasses the ideas previously noted and others that are more general in nature.[13] The four dimensions are associated with the investigative cycle, the types of thinking required, the interrogative cycle, and the dispositions required. These are amplified within the context of a formal statistical investigation. The investigative cycle is similar to what is seen in the school curriculum related to data and chance but the other three dimensions have parallel aspects in the broader goals of the mathematics curriculum.

The investigative cycle includes grasping and defining the *problem, planning* for what is needed, collecting and managing *data,* carrying out *analysis,* and interpreting and communicating *conclusions.* These major points are those in the dark boxes of Fig. 1.1. The second dimension of the model expands on the types of thinking involved in a statistical investigation. The general types of thinking described are relevant across the mathematics curriculum: strategic (planning, anticipating), seeking explanations, modeling, and applying techniques. The specific types of thinking fundamental to statistical investigations are recognition of the need for data, transnumeration (changing representations), consideration of variation, reasoning with statistical models, and integrating the statistical and contextual.

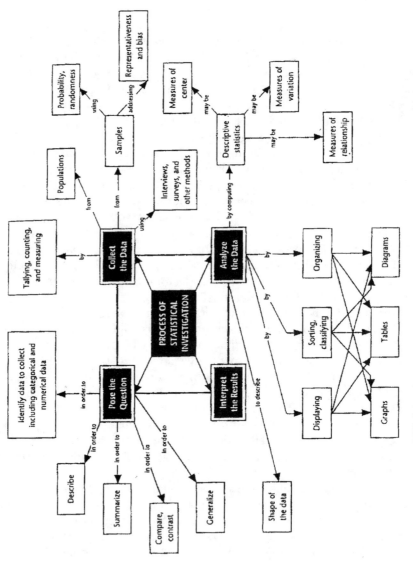

FIG. 1.1. Concept map of the process of statistical investigation.

Making these types of meta thinking explicit is important, as for example in Fig. 1.1 they do not receive specific mention.

Although the interrogative cycle is again devised with reference to a statistical investigation it has relevance to the area of statistical literacy generally. It again has five components: *generate* plans, explanations, models; *seek* internal and external information; *interpret* by seeing, translating, comparing, and connecting; *criticize* by checking reference points; and *judge* in making decisions. In evaluating reports created by agencies or others within society, these are the ingredients needed to interrogate claims made. Related to the interrogative cycle is the fourth dimension of dispositions: skepticism, imagination, curiosity and awareness, openness, a propensity to seek deeper meaning, being logical, engagement, and perseverance. Sometimes taken for granted, these traits of disposition are important both within the classroom and outside.

Working on the same premises as these models, the National Council of Teachers of Mathematics' *Principles and Standards* at the beginning of the twenty-first century suggest the following Data Analysis and Probability Standard:

> Instructional programs from pre-kindergarten through grade 12 should enable all students to—
>
> • Formulate questions that can be addressed with data and collect, organize, and display relevant data to answer them;
> • Select and use appropriate statistical methods to analyze data;
> • Develop and evaluate inferences and predictions that are based on data;
> • Understand and apply basic concepts of probability.[14]

These points cover exactly the major categories of Peter Holmes and are reflected in Chapters 2 to 6 in this book.

The collaboration of statisticians and mathematics educators in the 1980s produced the Quantitative Literacy series, which provided curriculum materials for the high school level in anticipation of the first NCTM *Standards* document in 1989.[15] This series reflected the aims of Peter Holmes and others based on investigations, starting with surveys and samples[16] and investigations in probability.[17] It also went further in introducing hands-on simulation experiences[18] and later developing links to the measurement part of the mathematics curriculum.[19] These were the precursors of many curriculum materials developed in the 1990s and of the use of the phrase "quantitative literacy" that was taken up again more generally in mathematics at the turn of the twenty-first century.[20]

Similarly at the elementary level, the *Used Numbers* series of books aimed to introduce appropriate pre-statistical ideas to students as young as kindergarten age. The activities suggested often introduced links to other parts of the mathematics curriculum. Emphasizing the use of "real data in the classroom," the focus across the early and elementary years ranged across counting data,[21] sorting data,[22] measuring data,[23] considering the shape of data,[24] summarizing data,[25] and predicting from data.[26] As appropriate statistical ideas were built up across the years, the statistical aspects suggested by Peter Holmes were successively covered. These materials were subsequently integrated into curriculum materials with a wider affiliation across the mathematics curriculum and have had a considerable influence in consolidating connections across the curriculum.[27] Other materials with similar aims have been developed, some particularly with context in mind, making connections outside the classroom with social topics leading to skills in statistical literacy.[28]

Because data and chance did not have a noticeable place in the school mathematics curriculum until around 1990,[29] many school districts, school mathematics departments and teachers at all levels believe that the topics cannot be as important to students as the other traditional parts of the mathematics curriculum. It is not at all unusual to find the units on data and chance placed in the time table at the end of the academic year, either to fill in time with activity when students and teachers are tired and winding down, or to be deleted as unnecessary if more time is needed for other topics such as algebra or trigonometry. What is missed in these views is an appreciation of the part that understanding of data and chance play in public and private decision-making when students leave school.[30] For many students statistical understanding will be as essential, if not more so, than algebra or trigonometry in everyday life. Not a large percent of school students use their school mathematics to study college mathematics and subjects that require it as a co-requisite. All students, however, potentially enter a society where everyday decisions are argued and made on the basis of data analysis in the face of uncertainty.[31] If the school curriculum is meant to prepare students for this world, then there must be an acknowledgement of the importance of statistical thinking. Although this can and should take place across the school curriculum, the mathematics curriculum provides the logical foundation and structure that is the natural starting point for understanding. Context can be added both within the mathematics classroom and across many other subject areas if collaboration takes place.[32]

Although the connections of statistical thinking to other areas of the school curriculum may seem obvious through experimentation in science, surveying groups in social science, or considering risk in health, the many connections of data and chance to other topics in the mathematics curriculum are often ignored or missed completely. Proportional thinking, for example, which is a fundamental topic in the middle school mathematics curriculum,[33] is essential in working with samples, probabilities and averages, as are part–whole ideas generally. The connection is not only in one direction, however, for these topics in data and chance provide excellent examples of the usefulness and application of the theoretical concepts. Being tied to self-contained text book chapters may prevent such connections being exploited to the full and this book provides many examples to encourage a deeper appreciation of how reinforcement of concepts across the mathematics curriculum can occur. Each chapter begins with a type of concept map that suggests the links that are associated with the statistical theme of that chapter. These include other topics in data and chance, as well as mathematics generally, and topics and issues important across the curriculum because of the need to develop decision-making skills.

Two perspectives are taken on the importance of data and chance for the school curriculum in this book. On one hand it is essential to provide a broadly based mathematics curriculum for all students to be useful to them when they leave school and begin to take part in society as knowledgeable citizens. An important part of this is being statistically literate. On the other hand it is also necessary to provide a foundation for the development of formal statistical understanding for students who choose to do advanced courses at the senior secondary or college level. The often-heard complaint that statistics courses are dry and full of formulas might cease to be heard if students came into these courses with appropriate intuitions, for example about variation, and an appreciation of what decision-making based on data is all about. These two perspectives are particularly important in environments where emphasis on "essential learnings" or "new basics" may cloud conventional curriculum boundaries and some topics are at risk of being left out.[34]

1.3 THE PLACE OF STATISTICAL LITERACY

The creation of links from the school statistics curriculum to statistical literacy in a general sense began soon after the introduction of revised mathematics curricula in the early 1990s. In some countries, for example New Zealand,[35] there was specific mention in the mathematics curriculum document of the need to apply understanding in the context of statistical reports that appear in contexts outside of school. "Interpreting statistical reports" is one of three themes in the Statistics part of the New Zealand mathematics curriculum, the other two being "Statistical investigations" and "Exploring probability." Among the suggested learning experiences is "Investigating ways in which statistical information is presented in the media and other sources, and recognizing and identifying sources of deception in misleading graphs and their accompanying statements."[36]

In her 1992 Presidential Address to the American Statistical Association, Katherine Wallman chose the topic of statistical literacy. In her brief definitional summary she focused on the application of understanding of the type developed during the school years for people as users rather than creators of statistics.

> 'Statistical Literacy' is the ability to understand and critically evaluate statistical results that permeate our daily lives—coupled with the ability to appreciate the contributions that statistical thinking can make in public and private, professional and personal decisions.[37]

More recently in summarizing the current state of understanding concerning adult statistical literacy, Iddo Gal suggested that the requirements are contained in the following two components:

(a) people's ability to interpret and critically evaluate statistical information, data-related arguments, or stochastic phenomena, which they may encounter in diverse contexts, and when relevant,

(b) their ability to discuss or communicate their reactions to such statistical information, such as their understanding of the meaning of the information, their opinions about the implications of this information, or their concerns regarding the acceptability of given conclusions.[38]

The goals for statistical literacy intersect with the wider goals of adult literacy as it was defined in several English-speaking countries during the 1990s. When the United States, Canada, and Australia set out to assess the literacy levels of their adult citizens a scheme was devised to assess *prose* literacy, *document* literacy, and *quantitative* literacy.[39] Although it is not possible to claim that all of the elements of statistical literacy are contained in these three dimensions of adult literacy, there are certainly many examples given across them that are related to statistics, in particular the interpretation of graphs and tables within document literacy and the further use of graphs and tables, along with appreciation of percents and averages, within quantitative literacy. To provide evidence of links such as these, from statistical literacy to adult literacy outside of the classroom, is helpful in advocating links to literacy within the school curriculum.

Another link from statistical literacy to wider aspects of literacy is found in recent attention and debate associated with quantitative literacy more generally. In the United States in 2002, quantitative literacy was the focus of attention from a National Research Council forum of 100 scientists, mathematicians, educators, and policy leaders.[40] Issues stressed included quantitative literacy being about the democratization of mathematics, making it available to the poor as well as the rich, girls as well as boys, the plebeian as well as the elite. How this could happen if schools created two different tracks, one consisting of algebra, trigonometry, and calculus for the elite college-bound, and a second consisting of quantitative literacy for the others, most of whom are poor or minority, was considered another dilemma. The forum claimed that such a system would be a disservice to the calculus-bound students because they would receive a much narrower foundation in mathematics. If, however, mathematics were taught as it should be—for reasoning rather than the mastery of algorithms—there would be little need for a distinction between mathematics and quantitative literacy.[41]

Although some students, often those who are proficient with the symbolic aspects of mathematics, baulk at the literacy requirements of meeting statistics in context, the extract in the previous section contends it is precisely the context embedded in description that is the reason for the existence of statistics.[42] After many years of diminished interest, the importance of context is being recognized at both the college and the school level.[43] The link to context within the formal curriculum is a step in the direction of using the statistical understanding developed in order to comment on situations where statistical reasoning should apply outside of the classroom and where the observer has not been involved in the investigation from the beginning. This is where those like Iddo Gal, with his emphasis on adults,[44] would like to see students operating by the time they leave school.

In terms of the relatively short history of statistics in the school curriculum, the interest in statistical literacy at the school level is very recent indeed. This book is an effort to continue placing the issues in front of teachers and curriculum designers, in particular by reinforcing the connections among all parts of the curriculum. Similar to the view that mathematics and numeracy should be complementary aspects of the school curriculum,[45] so statistics and statistical literacy should be complementary and integral aspects of the mathematics curriculum.

Although the data and chance curriculum covers the overall process of carrying out a statistical investigation in detail, reflecting what statisticians do, documentation focuses on individual manageable components. This book follows a similar format by devoting five chapters to what are nearly universally considered the stages of a statistical investigation. Doing this is necessary in order to focus on the development of student understanding at significant points in the process and to highlight particularly difficult ideas. It also helps in documenting the links that are so important in making sense of the relationships involved. Having done this, however, it is then necessary to consider statistical literacy more generally, particularly in terms of the expectations when students leave school. This would be considered by many to be part of the wider consideration of quantitative literacy but makes up a significant component of it.[46]

Statistical literacy is the meeting point of the data and chance curriculum and the everyday world, where encounters involve unrehearsed contexts and spontaneous decision-making based on the ability to apply statistical tools, general contextual knowledge, and critical literacy skills. Although some cur-

riculum documents make reference to objectives related to applying statistical understanding in social contexts,[47] it is difficult for published classroom
materials to provide current examples. Teachers must hence take on the responsibility of using current affairs to challenge students to develop critical
skills in this area. Teachers across the curriculum, not just in mathematics,
share this responsibility. Throughout the book, examples are presented that
link the specific statistical topics to media-based examples to assist in developing critical thinking and questioning skills. In Chapter 8 student performance across a wide range of tasks is examined to suggest a hierarchy of development. This development weaves together the skills from the curriculum,
the context of the tasks, and the critical thinking necessary in some tasks to
question authority.

1.4   DEVELOPMENT OF UNDERSTANDING—
THEORETICAL FRAMEWORKS

Building on the premise that data and chance are essential components of
the school and mathematics curriculum, it is important to document the
development of student understanding of topics associated with data and
chance. Although it might be considered a positivist view of mathematics
teaching to plan lessons that present the correct construction of the topic
under consideration and then assist the students to adopt this construction,
or perhaps reconstruct it for themselves, research has shown across the
mathematics curriculum that this view may be naïve. From the extensive research into young students' basic understanding of arithmetic operations[48]
to research into older students' understanding of other areas of the mathematics curriculum,[49] studies have shown that misconceptions are difficult to
eradicate and that some students have in-school beliefs about mathematics
that conflict with their out-of-school beliefs.[50] Particularly in areas associated with chance, conflicting views related to luck and remembered personal experience are likely to be retained long after a student has learned
and perhaps forgotten a formula to calculate a probability. These views may
be hidden from a teacher but may influence decision-making if they are
seen as divorced from the completion of a theoretical mathematical task.

Although many mathematics educators have advocated for some time
that teachers must begin classroom activities from the "current" understanding students display, there is a suspicion that recent trends to achieve
test outcomes may put pressure on teachers to rush ahead without thoroughly exploring students' starting points. This may achieve short term success but is likely to be detrimental to some students in the long term.[51]

In discussing students' developing understanding in this book, the purpose is to describe a hierarchy that categorizes observed outcomes and
from which steps can be inferred that can be taken to help students move

from one level of performance to a higher one. This hierarchical development is seen both in individual tasks completed and overall in combining skills appropriate to statistical literacy generally. Although appreciating that many factors influence student learning, including home environment, socio-economic status, peer pressure, classroom strategies, and intrinsic motivation, it is the cognitions that are the observable and measurable outcomes in terms of curriculum content documents. These are the outcomes that governments want their citizens to possess and so attempt to measure. Setting aside at the moment measurement issues, the overall aims of this book are consistent with those of educators who want to see curriculum goals met and achievement reached. In reaching the goals, however, it is the contention of this book that account must be taken of where students start and how they progress.

Two types of framework were used in analyzing the responses of students reported in this book, one related to the structure displayed and the other to the statistical appropriateness of the answer. Both frameworks are hierarchical and in some situations complement each other.

Since the work of Jean Piaget, many variations on the stage theory of cognitive development have emerged in the field of educational psychology.[52] The Structure of Observed Learning Outcomes (SOLO) model devised and modified in the 1980s and 1990s by John Biggs and Kevin Collis was used in helping analyze much of the data reported in this book.[53] It is a useful model because it stresses that it is what is *observed* in students' responses that is analyzed, not what the observer thinks the student might have meant. Such an approach does not label the student as high or low on a scale but places the observed response at that point in time on a scale. There is always the acknowledgment that at a different time a different response may be observed. Responses are considered snapshots in time that can be useful in deciding what activities can be presented to assist students in further development.

Another useful aspect of the model is the meaningful terminology used in defining levels of response, terminology that naturally reflects the structure of the response given. Within different modes of development, similar to Piaget's stages, the model posits three levels of progression in observed learning outcomes. At the first level, termed *unistructural*, responses employ single elements related to the task set. If the task requires more than one element for success, then it is unlikely that success will be achieved. At this level it is also possible that more than one single element may be employed but that these will contradict each other and the contradiction will not be recognized. As an example, it is not unusual for elementary school students to state that "all dice are fair" and yet "one comes up more for me." Each is a single statement about the context of the task but the child shows no indication that they are not consistent.

At the second level, called *multistructural,* responses display two or more elements related to the task set, usually in sequence. Again the requirements of the task determine if success is possible at this level. An example of success is comparing two small numerical data sets of the same size by totaling the values. The summing of the values in the first set is repeated in the second set and then a comparison is made to see which total is larger. At this level when conflict is encountered, it is usually recognized but not resolved. For example if two numerical data sets of unequal size are compared, a student may recognize that it is not fair to compare the totals but may not have another strategy to use.

The third level of response, *relational,* includes responses that integrate the multiple elements of the task to achieve closure with respect to the expectation of the task set. If conflict arises during the completion of a task, it is likely to be resolved. Sometimes responses display relational understanding of processes by achieving a numerical answer to a problem, whereas at other times it is the structure of a description that determines its level. When asked for the definition of the term "sample," for example, students may answer in a unistructural fashion with "a small piece" or "a taste." They may put two elements together providing a multistructural response, such as "a part of a whole" or "a bit, a taste." Finally they may integrate elements to show the purpose of having a sample, "a small bit of something to show what it is like," which is considered a relational response.

If a response does not use any element related to the task, it is considered *prestructural.* For example, in defining a term like "sample," a student may become confused with another term, like "simple: not very hard, the cake was simple to make." Sometimes when students are unfamiliar with the requirements of the task they may resort to imaginative storytelling. Such responses are sometimes termed *iconic* because of the use of visual or mythical associations.

One of the problems of judging observed responses is that it may be difficult to tell if they are optimal, the best that the students can give, or functional, at a lesser level perhaps because the student lacks the motivation to try harder. In the previous example defining the term *sample,* because there is no final numerical answer to tell students that the response is finished, they may stop with "a taste" thinking it is an adequate answer. In a survey this is likely to be the end of the story, whereas in an interview it is possible to probe further and see if the student can expand the response. The observed outcomes, however, are the basis for determining follow-up interventions with students, not wishful thinking about what they might have said.

The concrete symbolic mode is the mode described in this model that encompasses most of the learning that takes place during the school years. Symbolic learning, such as related to numbers and language, is often built from the use of concrete materials. The formal mode, where abstract ideas become the elements of tasks for manipulation in a unistructural, multistructural, or relational manner, may come into play at the senior secondary grades when theoretical statistics is introduced. Most of the responses described in this book, however, are placed in the concrete symbolic mode. This is because they are based on concrete referents that can be manipulated, such as data, graphs, or dice. The SOLO model suggests that the unistructural-multistructural-relational process takes place within each mode of functioning and at some point there is the opportunity to move from the relational level of one mode, say concrete symbolic, to the unistructural level of the next, say formal. The length of time students are in school and the complexity of the concrete symbolic concepts in the curriculum make it likely that two or even more unistructural-multistructural-relational cycles may appear in the concrete symbolic mode as ideas are built up, consolidated, and then applied in other contexts. An example of this phenomenon is the development and then application of the idea of average or arithmetic mean. A first cycle may occur in the progression of thinking of average as "normal," "a total or an algorithm," and then "an algorithm that produces a value that represents a data set." Once this idea is consolidated as a tool, it can then be used as an element in more complex contexts, perhaps in making decisions about differences in two or more data sets. It then becomes part of another cycle, often still within the concrete symbolic mode because of the nature of the task. Throughout this book levels of response are presented in the descriptions of ideas presented by students. Sometimes it is possible to distinguish easily the unistructural, multistructural, and relational nature of the responses, but if not, there is always an implied hierarchy that can be inferred from careful reading of responses. Detailed descriptions are given in the associated research papers listed in the endnotes and references. The starting points in the analysis of responses to different tasks are likely to be different relative to each other. It hence not possible to claim that multistructural levels of response should necessarily be expected across all tasks if observed on one task. The relationship among levels of response to tasks is illustrated in Chapter 8.

It is of course possible for a student to give a response that is structurally complex but inappropriate to the task set. Sometimes contradictions appear and are unresolved, as just described for the multistructural level of the SOLO model. In the light of the goals of the school curriculum and the statistical literacy skills required for adults, a complementary Statistical Literacy Hierarchy was developed for use in planning and assessing student understanding in statistical contexts.[54] The hierarchy is described in tiers, to separate it from the levels and modes of the structural model.

The first tier of statistical literacy involves the development of appropriate terminology to be used for statistical decision-making. The basic understanding of probabilistic and statistical terms is essential if they are to be used in context. As noted previously the development of understanding of terms such as average may take place in stages and is not as easy as memorizing a formula. It has been found that students who can parrot the add-and-divide algorithm may have little idea of what the final number represents in terms of a data set.[55] Within Tier 1 of the Statistical Literacy Hierarchy it is likely that teachers will observe a SOLO-like cycle of increasingly complex responses building to acceptable meanings for terms like *average* and *sample*.

Other examples of terminology encompassed in the first tier of statistical literacy include more specific average references like mean, median, and mode; indicators of spread like range and outlier; terms related to chance like events, independent, and conditional; and kinds of graphs like bar, pie, stem-and-leaf, and box-and-whisker. Obviously more than words are needed for the development of terminology. In statistics visual aspects of many terms are very important and often do not attract the classroom attention they deserve. In planning activities for Tier 1 development, teachers may be aware of the need to motivate students with contextually-based examples. This leads naturally to the aim of the second tier of the hierarchy, an understanding of probabilistic and statistical language and concepts when they are embedded in the context of wider social discussion. The further overlap with literacy skills is clear because of the need to unpack the implications of sentences and paragraphs that contain statistical language. The fact that many students see such tasks as far removed from the traditional computational and symbolic ethos of the mathematics curriculum is a challenge for teachers. Students must be helped to realize, however, that reading, interpreting, and writing about mathematics when it occurs in non-symbolic contexts is part of the training required for when they leave school. Understanding statements about risk is a case in point and issues surrounding risky behavior and likelihood statements could provide a basis for classroom debate. Developing the ability to interpret terminology in context is also likely to occur in SOLO-like steps of increasing complexity as literacy and general reasoning skills improve with respect to Tier 2.

The ultimate aim of such engagement with context, the third tier of the Statistical Literacy Hierarchy, is for students to possess the ability and confidence to challenge statements they meet that are made without proper statistical foundation. It is common, for example, to hear people quote reports they have read in the newspaper or heard on television as fact without any doubt or caution being expressed. Sometimes such trust is not warranted and students need to develop detective-type skills that make them suspicious of all claims until presented with the evidence to support them. Finding errant uses of basic mathematics, such as inaccurate percents or means, is a starting point to make students aware that slips occur, sometimes inadvertently. More subtle reporting, for example of voluntary surveys or of samples without details of size, needs to be the focus of further study and analysis. Finding and debunking media reports can be a motivating experience for teenagers who enjoy challenging authority.

Although the Statistical Literacy Hierarchy is indeed a hierarchy of sophistication of involvement with context, it is not necessary to achieve complete mastery of a tier before being introduced to the goal of the next. In fact, starting with a challenging scenario from Tier 3 can motivate an interest in finding out the appropriate statistical meaning of a term used (Tier 1) and how it makes sense in the context presented (Tier 2). Sense-making and possible challenge to claims can then be addressed. Consider for example the newspaper article in Fig. 1.2.[56] Although subtle in its reference, the issues associated with samples and populations are highly significant and can be used to help students become aware of the need to ask behind-the-scenes questions about a supposedly straightforward report.

Just as it is possible to observe levels of development in association with the first two tiers of statistical literacy, so it is with the third tier as students become increasingly aware of the issues involved in questioning claims. At the unistructural level single ideas of a global type may be expressed: "How can that be true?" or "Could people be lying?" At the multistructural level perhaps questions about methodology arise: "What was the sample size and who were the people sampled?" At the relational level it may be possible to question associations: "Is it really true that beer causes crime[57] or could there be some other lurking variable that is associated with both of these factors?"

Bands must learn the art of business
By Jody Scott

ONLY 21 bands who released debut albums in the US last year made a profit. By comparison, 25 people were struck by lightning.

These statistics were thrown at more than 100 young musicians by Phil Tripp, publisher of the Australasian Music Industry Directory, to show how elusive music business success can be.

FIG. 1.2. Article illustrating the need for statistical literacy.

It is hence the interaction of structural complexity and statistical appropriateness that determines the hierarchical categories of response that are reported throughout this book.[58] The relationship of the structural levels of responses and their statistical appropriateness in terms of the Statistical Literacy Hierarchy depends on the nature of the task presented. The highest level or category of response depends on appropriateness as well as structure. A response to a task asking for analysis of a media article for example may result in a complex response addressing the context of the article but which does not observe the inappropriate claim. Such a response would be placed at a lower level than a response of a simpler nature that focused directly on the issues related to the errant claim.

The increasing sophistication associated with the categories of response reinforces the importance of teachers knowing where their students are in order to assist them to perform at higher levels. Sometimes the examples of responses given in the following chapters are from naïve students who have not been yet "taught" the topics about which they are questioned. Although this may cause some readers to dismiss their responses as not relevant once the curriculum has been implemented, it is dangerous to take such a view. Many naïve views were expressed by grade 9 students with at least limited exposure to many of the topics canvassed. As many teachers are aware, not all students in a class absorb the knowledge imparted by their teachers on the first, or even the second time it is presented. It is likely that teachers will be surprised at the variation in performance of their students on some of the tasks presented in this book, even if they are used for post-instruction assessment.[59]

1.5   TASKS AND DATA COLLECTION

One of the issues in assisting students to progress through a hierarchy of development is related to decisions about which tasks are appropriate for various purposes. Tasks are required to assess both starting and finishing points. Some tasks are appropriate to build understanding. Some tasks potentially provide cognitive conflict that can dislodge inappropriate beliefs and intuitions. Although some tasks appear to require only a mental exercise and written comment, they may form the basis of a lengthy classroom discussion and debate, or the basis of a hands-on activity involving experimentation, hypothesis formation, and/or inference drawing. Almost every task presented in this book can be adapted for various purposes, depending on the aims of the researcher, classroom teacher, or curriculum developer.

Moving from traditional textbook-based problems to open-ended tasks is perhaps more important to the development of data and chance understanding than it is to any other part of the mathematics curriculum.[60] Suggestions are made throughout the book on how tasks might be used in the classroom. The big step for some teachers is to take the chance, acknowledge the risk, and move to hands-on activities and class discussion that is more than regurgitating answers. Moving from "How did you solve that problem?" to "Why do you believe that experimental outcome is the appropriate one?" can be challenging for some teachers.

The tasks chosen to explore student understanding in the research reflected the five components of the school statistics and probability curriculum as outlined by Peter Holmes[61] as well as the overall importance of variation[62] and critical thinking skills.[63] They were also consistent with standards advocated in national curriculum documents in the United States and elsewhere.[64] The tasks were used in three different settings: written surveys, individual interviews, or collaborative settings with groups of three students. The following chapters focus on the student outcomes from these tasks and the development of understanding displayed. Often it is quite clear from the task description whether it is from a survey or interview and the distinction is rarely made in order not to disrupt the flow of the text.

Two surveys were originally developed to take about 45 minutes each to complete by grade 9 students.[65] One survey consisted of 20 items gathered from earlier researchers[66] and related specifically to aspects of the curriculum. Items were either multiple-choice, often with explanations requested, or short-answer in nature. For grade 3, classes only 10 of the basic items were used, those involving less reading and less sophisticated ideas. The second survey contained 10 items based on extracts from newspapers, and required interpretation, looking for unusual features, and in one case sketching a graph. Students below grade 6 did not answer this survey and grade 6 students answered fewer questions than grade 9. Later a third survey was developed using some items from the earlier two surveys, as well as others to assess aspects related to variation in data sets.[67] As with the earlier surveys, a subset of questions was asked to grade 3 students with more questions attempted in each of grades 5, 7, and 9.

Longitudinal data were collected after two and four years for the first two surveys and after two years for the third survey, and the numbers of students involved in various years and grades are reported in Table 1.1. In subsequent years (1995, 1997, and 2002) some students were surveyed who were in the same schools but were not surveyed in 1993 or 2000. The numbers reported in Table 1.1 do not distinguish longitudinal data from new data collected in subsequent years because they are not relevant to the discussion in Chapters 2 to 8.[68]

Individual interviews of approximately 45 minutes were conducted with 62 students in grades 3, 6, and 9 in 1993 and with 30 students in grades 3, 5, 7, and 9 in 1994. The interview consisted of nine protocols based on creating and interpreting a pictograph, manipulating and interpreting a bar

TABLE 1.1
Numbers of Students Completing the Three Surveys
in Different Grades and Years

				Grade				
Year	3	5	6	7	8	9	10	11
Survey 1—Data and Chance Curriculum								
1993	322		312			393		
1995	305	465	340		377	371		249
1997	237	231	237	318	187	105	299	52
Survey 2—Media Items								
1993			312			393		
1995			340		377	371		249
1997			237		187	105	299	52
Survey 3—Subset of Surveys 1 and 2 plus Variation								
2000	175	183		187		193		
2002		180		241		88		61

graph, determining the fairness of dice, suggesting relative chances of outcomes involving two or more dice, comparing two data sets, discussing samples, discussing average, considering random events, and considering conditional probabilities. Again these protocols were adapted from tasks related to the topics used by earlier researchers,[69] as well as including original components. Not all protocols were completed by all students due to time constraints and interviewer decisions about student appreciation of the topic, particularly for younger students.[70] In 1997, 42 of the students interviewed earlier were interviewed again using the same protocols.[71] In 2000, 60 new students in grades 3, 6, and 9 were interviewed using the same protocols including video extracts from responses of the earlier students that presented cognitive conflict in relation to suggestions made by the new students.[72] Also in 2000, 66 different students in grades 3, 5, 7, and 9 were interviewed using four different protocols and the protocol on comparing two data sets from the previous interviews. The other four protocols focused on variation in a probability sampling situation, variation in the weather, variation in spinner outcomes, and definitions related to variation.[73] At this time 7 six-year-olds in a pre-grade-1 class were interviewed with the protocols on pictographs, bar graphs, probability sampling, and the weather.[74]

Between 1994 and 1997 various groups of students in grades 3, 5, 6, and 9 worked collaboratively in groups of three in either isolated or classroom settings on extended problem-solving tasks related to the data and chance curriculum. One of the tasks was based on 16 data cards that presented information on several variables for which students were asked to formulate hypotheses and produce a poster of evidence to support.[75] Outcomes related to this project work are discussed at appropriate points throughout the chapters.

1.6 THE PLACE OF VARIATION

Without variation there is no need for statistics. It is variation that distinguishes statistics from most other parts of the mathematics curriculum. For some it is the uncertainty associated with statistical variation that produces conflict with the determinism of calculating correct numerical answers. It is the uncertainty of planning a probability experiment when you do not know what the outcome will be in relation to the determined theoretical result, that is intimidating for many teachers who like to have worked out all of the answers the night before the lesson.

Historically it was people like John Graunt, Francis Galton, Karl Pearson, and R. A. Fisher[76] who, in seeking to explain observed variation in measurable social and scientific phenomena, developed the foundations of modern statistics. The reason data are collected, graphs drawn, and averages calculated is to manage variation and draw conclusions in relation to questions based on phenomena that vary. What is surprising is that if variation is so fundamental to statistics and statistical thinking, why is more not made of it in curriculum documents and curriculum models such as those of Peter Holmes and the North Carolina project mentioned earlier? One explanation might be that the observation of variation is so obvious it does not require specific comment. If this is so, it is unfortunate because children need explicit connections made in the early years when cognitive processing skills are still developing. Another explanation is that it is difficult to extract variation from the context within which it occurs. Talking about variation in shoe size or the weather immediately conjures up images of variation in a context. Random variation when a die is tossed is easy to imagine. To have a subheading in the curriculum titled "Variation" would require elements from the rest of the curriculum in order to provide examples. A question used as the basis for an investigation assumes some variation will occur or it would not be asked. Data collection caters for variation. Graphs display variation. Averages reduce variation and spreads characterize it. Probability describes random aspects of variation. Conclusions are drawn in the light of variation as described in these many steps. It is hence probably not feasible to adopt a "subheading" approach to variation. What is unfortunate, however, is that so little is explicitly made of the ingredient of variation at each step in the statistical investigation process. It is likely that teachers, particularly those with little formal experience in statistics, would profit from the reminder to make connections with variation whenever they teach a lesson on data or chance.

The need to explore students' understanding of variation in a more specific fashion was recognized during the 1990s[77] and led to the development of some of the tasks used in the later years of the research that was the basis for this book. The work in the area of statistical thinking during that decade[78] also helped raise the awareness of variation as essential in any consideration associated with statistical investigations. Returning to 1990, however, David Moore made a highly significant contribution, increasing the status of variation in his discussion of "uncertainty" in a seminal edited book on new approaches to numeracy.[79] A relatively long extract is given here because of the impact it should have on researchers, teachers, and curriculum designers.

We can summarize the core elements of statistical thinking as follows:

1. The omnipresence of *variation* in processes. Individuals are variable; repeated measurements on the same individual are variable. The domain of a strict determinism in nature and in human affairs is quite circumscribed.

2. The need for *data* about processes. Statistics is steadfastly empirical rather than speculative. Looking at the data has first priority.

3. The design of *data production* with variation in mind. Aware of sources of uncontrolled variation, we avoid self-selected samples and insist on comparison in experimental studies. And we introduce planned variation into data production by use of randomization.

4. The *quantification* of variation. Random variation is described mathematically by *probability*.

5. The *explanation* of variation. Statistical analysis seeks the systematic effects behind the random variability of individuals and measurements.

Statistical thinking is not recondite or removed from everyday experience. But it will not be developed in children if it is not present in the curriculum. Students who begin their education with spelling and multiplication expect the world to be deterministic; they learn quickly to expect one answer to be right and others wrong, at least when the answers take numerical form. Variation is unexpected and uncomfortable. .... The ability to deal intelligently with variation and uncertainty is the goal of instruction about data and chance.[80]

Although Chapters 2 to 6 of this book follow the models provided by curriculum documents, the figures at the beginning of each chapter include a rectangle in the center at the bottom reflecting the foundational importance of variation and its link to the topic under consideration. As well,

Chapter 7 is devoted to students' appreciation of variation and to four case studies that explicitly consider variation in relation to the content of earlier chapters and that indicate how students cope with variation that occurs within the tasks that are presented to them.

1.7 A LAST WORD

Although acknowledging that the school curriculum has a responsibility to provide the foundation needed for students who wish to pursue the study of probability and statistics at higher levels, it also has the responsibility to prepare students to be statistically literate consumers of claims made in wider social contexts. That is what this book is about: the development of statistical literacy through the school curriculum. This is in no way a disadvantage to the high flyers; in fact it may prove an added motivation to encourage students to study statistics at the senior secondary level.[81]

ENDNOTES

1. "Beware the pushy fish-eater" (1991).
2. "Schoolgirls are smokers, drinkers" (1994).
3. Watson (1992).
4. National Council of Teachers of Mathematics (1989).
5. Capel (1885).
6. Moore (1991b); National Council of Teachers of Mathematics (1989); Thompson (1991).
7. Rao (1975, p. 152).
8. Neumann (1966).
9. Holmes (1980, 1986).
10. Holmes (1980, pp. 51–58).
11. Scheaffer, Watkins, & Landwehr (1998); Watson (1998e).
12. Friel & Bright (1998); Friel & Joyner (1997).
13. Wild & Pfannkuch (1999).
14. National Council of Teachers of Mathematics (2000, p. 48).
15. National Council of Teachers of Mathematics (1989).
16. Landwehr, Swift, & Watkins (1987).
17. Newman, Obremski, & Scheaffer (1987).
18. Gnanadeskin, Scheaffer, & Swift (1987).
19. Barbella, Kepner, & Scheaffer (1994).
20. Steen (2001).
21. Stone & Russell (1990).
22. Russell & Corwin (1990).
23. Corwin & Russell (1990).

24. Russell & Corwin (1989).
25. Friel, Mokros, & Russell (1992).
26. Corwin & Friel (1990).
27. Connected Mathematics series, e.g., Lappan, Fey, Fitzgerald, Friel, & Phillips (1997a, 1997b, 1997c, 1997d, 1998a, 1998b, 1998c, 1998d).
28. Burrill & Romberg (1998).
29. Australian Education Council (1991); Ministry of Education (1992); National Council of Teachers of Mathematics (1989).
30. Wallman (1993).
31. Rubin (2005); Wallman (1993).
32. Watson (2000b).
33. National Council of Teachers of Mathematics (1989, 2000).
34. Department of Education Tasmania (2002); Education Queensland (2000).
35. Ministry of Education (1992).
36. Ministry of Education (1992, p. 189).
37. Wallman (1993, p. 1).
38. Gal (2002, pp. 2–3).
39. Dossey (1997); McLennan (1997); Statistics Canada and the OECD (1996).
40. Madison & Steen (2003); Steen (2002).
41. Madison (2002).
42. Rao (1975).
43. Burrill & Romberg (1998); Meletiou-Mavrotheris & Lee (2002).
44. Gal (2002).
45. Steen (1997, 2002).
46. Steen (1997, 2001); Scheaffer (2003).
47. Ministry of Education (1992); National Council of Teachers of Mathematics (1989).
48. Carpenter & Moser (1984).
49. Hart (1981).
50. Truran (1985).
51. Pegg (2002b, p. 255).
52. Case (1988); Pegg (2002b).
53. Biggs (1992); Biggs & Collis (1982, 1991); Pegg (2002a).
54. Watson (1997a).
55. Mokros & Russell (1995).
56. Scott (1997).
57. "Beer gets blame" (1994).
58. Watson & Moritz (2000b), illustrate this interaction based on tasks related to sampling.
59. Pegg (2002a), reports on research involving teachers developing SOLO-based techniques for their assessment tasks, both in terms of setting tasks and devising rubrics for marking schemes.
60. Burrill & Romberg (1998), take this position in presenting new curriculum materials for middle school students.

61. Holmes (1980).
62. Shaughnessy (1997).
63. Watson (1997a).
64. Australian Education Council (1991, 1994a); Ministry of Education (1992); National Council of Teachers of Mathematics (1989, 2000).
65. Watson (1994a).
66. Borovcnik & Bentz (1991); Fischbein & Gazit (1984); Green (1983b); Konold & Garfield (1992); Nisbett, Krantz, Jepson, & Kunda (1983); Pollatsek, Well, Konold, Hardiman, & Cobb (1987); Tversky & Kahneman (1983); Varga (1983).
67. Watson, Kelly, Callingham, & Shaughnessy (2003).
68. The outcomes observed for longitudinal data confirmed observations for cohorts in corresponding different grades surveyed in the same year. The term "development" is hence used in a general sense to describe trends observed across grades. The stratification of the sample across a state education system, the lack of observed change across comparable cohorts after four years, and the non-intervention by the research team from 1993 to 1997, suggests that for the descriptive purposes of this book, the assumptions for a description of development over the school years are reasonable. Reports summarizing outcomes from the survey research with Surveys 1 and 2 include Moritz (1998, 1999); Moritz & Watson (1997a, 2000); Moritz, Watson, & Collis (1996); Moritz, Watson, & Pereira-Mendoza (1996); Watson (1998a, 1998b); Watson, Collis, & Moritz (1994, 1995a, 1997); Watson & Moritz (1999b, 2000b, 2002, 2003a); Watson, Moritz, & Pereira-Mendoza (1998). Reports summarizing outcomes from the Survey 3 research include Watson & Kelly (2002a, 2002c, 2002d, 2002e, 2003b, 2003c, 2003d, 2004c, 2005); Watson, Kelly, Callingham, & Shaughnessy (2003).
69. Falk (1983a, 1983b); Fischbein & Gazit (1984); Fischbein, Nello, & Marino (1991); Gal, Rothschild, & Wagner (1990); Garfield & delMas (1991); Konold & Garfield (1992); Pollatsek, Lima, & Well (1981); Pollatsek, Well, Konold, Hardiman, & Cobb (1987); Tversky & Kahneman (1971, 1980).
70. Reports on these interviews not including longitudinal data include Moritz & Watson (1997b); Watson & Collis (1994); Watson, Collis, & Moritz (1995b); Watson & Kelly (2002b, 2004a); Watson & Moritz (1999a, 1999c, 2000a).
71. Particular aspects of longitudinal understanding are reported in Watson (2001, 2004a); Watson & Caney (2005); Watson & Moritz (2000c, 2001a, 2003b).
72. Particular aspects of cognitive conflict and understanding are reported in Watson (2002a, 2002b, 2004b); Watson & Caney (2005); Watson & Moritz (2001a, 2001b).
73. Reports of these interviews include Kelly & Watson (2002); Watson & Kelly (2003a, 2004a, in press).
74. Watson & Kelly (2002b).
75. Chick & Watson (2001, 2002); Watson & Chick (2001a, 2001b, 2005); Watson, Collis, Callingham, & Moritz (1995).
76. Bernstein (1996); Salsburg (2001).

77. Green (1993); Shaughnessy (1997).
78. Wild & Pfannkuch (1999).
79. Steen (1990).
80. Moore (1990, p. 135).
81. Madison & Steen (2003); Steen (2002).

2

Sampling—A Good Start

The dual notions of sampling and of making inferences about populations, based on samples, are fundamental to prediction and decision making in many aspects of life. Students will need a great many experiences to enable them to understand principles underlying sampling and statistical inference and the important distinctions between a population and a sample, a parameter and an estimate.[1]

2.1 BACKGROUND

This quote from an Australian curriculum document of the early 1990s sets the scene for a consideration of the development of student understanding of sampling. Long before students are involved in inference, however, they are building ideas associated with the concept of sample. In the English language the word *sample* has a colloquial usage with the potential both to assist and to hinder the development of the statistical meaning. The word also has a direct relationship to the part–whole concept that is a feature of many topics in the mathematics curriculum. What sample does not have is an algorithmic foundation that can be memorized and tested in a straightforward manner. The descriptive nature of the concept provides an excuse for some mathematics teachers to skim over it and move on to the more technical and product-oriented aspects of statistics such as drawing graphs and calculating means. Without an appreciation, however, of the part sampling plays in a statistical investigation, the rest of the process can turn out to be totally useless. Students need an appreciation of this contribution, both to carry out their own statistical investigations and to question claims of others if they are not based on adequate methods.

The biggest difference in the use of the term *sample* colloquially and in statistics is related to variation. In the supermarket the purpose of a sample is to show the homogeneous quality of a product being sold. In statistics the purpose of a sample is to show the variation in the population so that it can be characterized and summarized. In the supermarket, if the product is truly homogeneous, then a small sample will serve the purpose of representing the product. In statistics the issue of sample size is important in balancing economy of scale with the necessity to describe the variation in the population as well as possible. Hence students are taught that "larger is better" subject eventually to a law of diminishing returns. Intuitions about these issues take a long time and many experiences to build up.[2] The educational goal for sampling is well expressed by D. B. Orr.

> Sometimes, for theoretical, practical, or efficiency reasons, it is desirable to study (collect data from) less than the entire population. In such cases a subset of the population called a sample is selected. Although data are then collected only from or about the sample, conclusions are drawn (generalized) to the larger population as well ... What is the essential nature of a sample? In a word, a sample should be "representative." This means that, effectively, a sample should be a small-scale replica of the population from which it is selected, in all respects that might affect the study conclusions.[3]

Implicit to this understanding however are many ideas that need to be made explicit to children as they build the foundation for statistical literacy. Probably the greatest difficulty experienced by people in considering samples from populations is to be able to characterize what is necessary to be representative. Early research with adults showed that when presented with contextualized situations involving samples, many difficulties were experienced, including generalizing from a sample that is much too small, focusing on inappropriate features of the information, and combining information in inappropriate ways.[4]

Research associated with school students' understanding of sampling began with the work of Andee Rubin and her colleagues at TERC in Cambridge, Massachusetts and Iddo Gal and his colleagues at the University of Pennsylvania.[5] The TERC group found a tension for senior secondary students between the reality of variability within samples and the need for samples to be representative. Gal's group found for younger children that responses when comparing two groups of data could be distinguished by whether students assumed homogeneity of groups or appreciated natural variation within them. Vicki Jacobs worked with upper elementary students, who often preferred biased sampling methods, such as voluntary participation, due to the fairness of allowing everyone the chance to participate in the sampling process but forcing no one to do so.[6] Similar observations were made by Daniel Schwartz and The Cognition and Technology Group at Vanderbilt.[7] During interviews with elementary students who had been involved in designing their own science experiments, Katy Metz found three attitudes to sample size.[8] Although many supported the power of appropriate sampling, a few put unwarranted faith in very small samples and many others argued against sampling entirely due to the variation in the population and hence the need to measure every element in it. Some of these beliefs are found in the responses to tasks described in this chapter.

The components that contribute to an understanding of sample and sampling are illustrated in Fig. 2.1, along with an indication of how they are linked with each other. The idea of being representative is developed along with the increasing sophistication of describing what a sample is and its purpose. This potentially slow development is seen in Section 2.2. Representativeness is also closely connected to context, which has a large influence on the nature of sampling. This is explored as student understanding develops in Section 2.3. Probably the most familiar of the components in Fig. 2.1 are sample size and method because they appear in formal statistics texts. For school students however there are more fundamental issues associated with their developing understanding. Issues of part–whole relationships generally and the place of the sample–population relationship in this milieu can take time to develop, as can the application of ideas of proportion and percent when beginning to appreciate sample size. These connections are illustrated in Section 2.4, as well as the close link of representativeness to method. Section 2.5 comments on the links between fairness and sampling and how students' beliefs about fairness brought to the classroom from social interactions may interfere with statistical ideas of fairness in sampling. These beliefs may also lead to difficulty in detecting bias in methods sug-

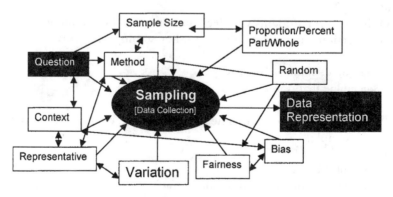

FIG. 2.1.   Links among the ideas and statistical elements associated with sampling.

gested by others. This is particularly true for situations based in social contexts presented in potentially confronting ways in the media. Two newspaper articles are the basis of discussion in Section 2.6 and illustrate the complex nature of the connections required to analyze samples in out-of-school contexts. Finally in Section 2.7 note is made of the link between the terms *sample* and *random* in colloquial and statistical usage. Although it may be considered possible to draw linking arrows between all pairs of ideas in Fig. 2.1, major links as illustrated in the chapter are those highlighted. The part played by variation in sampling may be quite subtle from a child's perspective but an innate appreciation of variation is nearly always present and this will be noted as relevant.

In the following sections examples of students' responses to tasks about sampling are used to highlight the development in understanding taking place during the school years. As well, danger points are pointed out where care must be taken to avoid confounding of misunderstanding. The final section relates the development of understanding to the statistical literacy hierarchy introduced in Chapter 1 and shares some insight into sampling gained from a grade 9 classroom.

2.2   A SAMPLE: WHAT IS IT?

The starting point for exploring the connections suggested in Fig. 2.1 is in the meaning of the word sample itself. What do children throughout the years of schooling conjure up when asked a survey question like, "If you were given a 'sample,' what would you have?" or a series of interview questions such as, "Have you heard of the word 'sample' before? Where? What does it mean?" Answers tend to follow a developmental progression of increasing complexity of description, which also usually reflects increasing grade level.[9]

Of interest for students who have not entered the sampling game, are the connections they make, often to other sound-alike words.

- You put a sample on a letter.
- Something that is too hot.

For those who cannot describe the term as an idea, many can however provide an example.

- A sample of coffee.
- It could be a sample of lipstick or perfume.
- A blood sample.
- A sample of work.

These responses often reflect children's experiences outside the classroom.

The beginnings of ideas based on the concept itself present a single word or phrase reflecting one aspect only.

- A little bit.
- A small portion.
- A test.
- Something the same as something else.

These responses reflect the idea of part without the associated whole or the isolated idea of trying or testing that is the purpose of sampling—to find out what something is like. These responses are followed structurally by those that acknowledge, either explicitly or implicitly, the part–whole relationship innate in the sample and population. The term population, however, rarely appears before the later years of school.

- A little of something, not the whole thing but a little piece of it.
- Only part of the whole thing.
- I'd have, if it was for clothes, a small piece of material.

The presence of the word "of" in descriptions is significant as it usually flags the part–whole understanding present.

Finally the descriptions integrate the part–whole nature of a sample with the purpose of representing the whole. The language of expression varies given students' exposure to formal tuition but it is important to recognize the appreciation shown in simple statements.

- A small portion of something larger to try.
- A thing taken out of a larger group, for you to view as representative of that group.
- A random selection of data from a wider group, meant to represent the entire group.
- You would have a small amount of something, like a new washing-up liquid, to test in your own home.

Again the personal experiences of students are likely to influence their comments and provide the basis for building links to context and other aspects of Fig. 2.1.

The overall progression of responses described here illustrates the developmental hierarchy described in Section 1.4. At the prestructural level students provide idiosyncratic responses not in the domain of the question. At the unistructural level responses employ single elements of the domain relevant to the task, such as an example or a single descriptor. Then follows the multistructural level with responses involving two elements, very often the part–whole relationship but nothing more. The relational level includes responses relating both the part–whole relationship and the purpose of obtaining a sample. In grade 3 about half of students are likely to give prestructural responses, whereas from grades 7 to 11 about half give multistructural descriptions. Only about a quarter of students are likely to volunteer complete descriptions by grade 11.

Awareness of the progression in describing a sample can be useful in building experiences to expand students' appreciation from wherever they display initial understanding. As most students do not begin by offering relational descriptions, it is important for teachers to continue questioning with prompts like, "And so what is the *purpose* of your sample?" or "*How* does a sample do what you claim?" Building on experiences that arise within the classroom can be very useful. A student may have had a blood test or a urine sample and discussion can focus on the purpose of diagnosis. Often students who live in cities have been given samples in supermarkets or pharmacies and these can be used to link to the purpose of manufacturers in providing samples to consumers. In contrast, students who live in rural areas may exhibit detailed understanding in contexts such as sampling the wool from sheep to determine its grade before auctioning. To compare and contrast such descriptions can provide connections that assist students in building a broad understanding of why sampling is important in many aspects of life.

2.3   SAMPLE IN CONTEXT

Direct questions such as those in the previous section are useful in gauging initial understanding, and as shown in some responses, also provide connections to contexts with which students are familiar. For some students, however, providing a context can assist in the recall of meaning. Consider for example the scenario set for the questions in Fig. 2.2.[10] The use of the

(a)	A news person on TV says, "In a research study on the weight of Tasmanian Grade 5 children, some researchers interviewed a *sample* of Grade 5 children in Tasmania." What does the word *sample* mean in this sentence?
(b)	Why do you think the researchers used a *sample* of Grade 5 children, instead of studying all the Grade 5 children in Tasmania?

FIG. 2.2.   Interview questions on sampling in a context.

second question depends to some extent on the response to the first but may provide further evidence of contextual appreciation.

Typical responses show that it is likely to be easier for younger children to identify the term sample in such a context than to construct a description on their own, particularly in terms of the "part" aspect of the part–whole relationship. For Part (a), students without a part concept are likely to relate to ideas of testing or trialing.

- (a) They might take a blood test on them.

Most other responses reflect the part–whole nature of a sample.

- (a) Like, just had *some*.
- (a) Just a few Grade 5 children.

Some students, however, have had experiences that allow them to suggest more complex scenarios for the first question in Fig. 2.2.

- (a) [Say there were] about 10,000 children in Grade 5 in Tasmania and they took about say 50 of them and they found out, because 50 is a small portion of 10,000, they just found out the weights from there.
- (a) They interviewed like a cross-section, all different students from here, there, and everywhere all around Tasmania. They didn't like use every single student, [. . .] just randomly picking them.

Responses to the second question nearly always reflect practicalities indicating that children are aware of the social setting in which sampling takes place, although a few display limited appreciation of the task.

- (b) Because they won't all fit on the scale.
- (b) Because they didn't have enough time.
- (b) They don't really need to study them all . . . it would take up too much time . . . by picking out just a few it's really the same.

Questions such as those in Fig. 2.2 are open-ended, allowing for students to explain as much as they can or feel is necessary. As is seen in the responses to Part (a), the range of response is likely to be quite wide in terms of the elements considered important to include.

2.4 SAMPLE SIZE AND METHOD

Following from the previous section, more questions on the scenario presented there can be used to explore the explicit connections of sample size
and method in the context for those who do not provide such information
on their own initiative.[11] Example questions are shown in Fig. 2.3 and provide starting points for all students. Responses to Part (c) range from agreement to more sophisticated, but generally statistically naïve, suggestions.

Previous experience is likely to be a factor in answers, as shown in the following responses.

- (c) Three to six. . . . Because a sample's just a little bit.
- (c) Could have used 10. . . . It's an even number and I like that number.
- (c) Should use a lot . . . most of the Grade 5 children in Tasmania. [any advantage?] Well you wouldn't know the average, would you, if they only
  sample a few? So probably better off with the whole.
- (c) 100 about . . . usually they have a survey of 100 people in most things.
- (c) It depends on how many Grade 5 children are in the state. I don't
  know, perhaps 10% or 20% of Grade 5 children in the state.

Without considerable experience it is unlikely that students can give statistically appropriate justifications for their choices of sample size but discussion based on a range of reasonable suggestions can lead to the rejection of
sizes that are too small or too large. The developing connection to part–
whole understanding elsewhere in the mathematics curriculum is quite
striking at this point. The increasing sophistication in the previously mentioned responses is associated with increasing appreciation of the need to
quantify the relationship between the sample and the population. At the
lowest levels responses reflect small numbers for a small part without any
reference to the whole. At higher levels, responses recognize the need to
look at the whole population but sometimes go to the other extreme and
reject the sample altogether.[12] Some responses suggest reasonable sample
sizes based on experience but without a statistical justification. At the highest level responses begin to take into account both the sample and popula-

(c)	Do you think they used a sample of about 10 children? Why or why not? How many children should they choose for their sample? Why?
(d)	How should they choose the children for their sample? Why?

FIG. 2.3.   Continued questioning about sampling in context (cf. Fig. 2.2).

tion, and the numerical aspect of the part–whole relationship. The use of whole number comparisons, fractions, and percents provides an opportunity to compare and contrast measures taught elsewhere in the mathematics curriculum.

Methodology provides a challenge but students display increasingly complex understanding of what is involved when sampling takes place. Early suggestions are likely to reflect students' own experiences of selection.

- (d) The teacher might choose people who've been working well.
- (d) Test them.

Understanding the need to measure a particular trait, such as weight, is likely to lead to the introduction of bias in the method of selection.

- (d) There might be some really skinny ones that they choose and some quite fat ones that they choose as well to use, so that they can get really an average of what they are trying to find out.

Some believe that choosing avoids bias.

- (d) They would take all different weights or their roundness or whatever, just differently so they can see the average on everyone . . . not just take all the thin ones and leave all the fat ones out.

The transition toward having a representative sample is likely to occur in stages, with the initial realization of the need for a range but without a specific mechanism to achieve it.

- (d) It doesn't matter . . . they just have to be different people because everybody is not the same.
- (d) Basically as a class because that way then you have got more of a wider range, because you can have your smaller ones and your bigger ones and your 'inbetweens.'

The two ideas associated with random or stratified selection are at first likely to appear separately.

- (d) They should do it by looking at names, not by looking at the actual children, just pick them off a class list or something.
- (d) Get a whole lot of names and just pick them out of a box or something.
- (d) Some that lived in the country and some that lived near the city . . . they live a bit different.
- (d) Pick a few schools . . . 10 out of each Grade 5 so it's just sort of evened out . . . not all from one school.

Increased sophistication of language and justification occurs with more experience.

- (d) Just randomly; you don't want to look at them; you just want to get a computer screen in the office [. . .] If you're going to choose all the fat children, then it's going to put the average up, isn't it? And if you want to be fair [. . .] you'd randomly choose them.

Combining the ideas of random selection and stratification is not easy.

- (d) They could choose . . . firstly choose different people from all different places . . . because the diets would be different in all different places in [the state] . . . and they could do it randomly and just choose anyone. . . or they could try and choose people of a lot of different weights so that they could have a lot of difference because there would be a lot of people different.
- (d) They interviewed like a cross section, all different students from here, there, and everywhere all round [the state]. They didn't like use every single student, [. . .] just randomly picking them.

Another avenue for exploring student understanding of sample size and method is through a scenario where information is required that would come from some kind of survey. The scenario presented in Fig. 2.4 is adapted from the work of Vicki Jacobs and although written in a survey format, is appropriate for group work or discussion in a classroom.[13] Students are asked an open-ended question about how they would conduct a survey and then presented with several alternatives about which to make judgments.

Overall, for students engaging in the tasks in Fig. 2.4 there are likely to be four levels of response reflecting (i) an inability to appreciate the task, (ii) an inappropriate analysis, (iii) an analysis focusing on relevant but noncentral ideas, and (iv) a statistically appropriate response in the context. Examples of these are considered in turn based on the questions asked in Fig. 2.4.[14]

The main source of misinterpretation of the task is related to the belief that the aim is to sell tickets rather than survey students *about* selling tickets. This illustrates a link to literacy for some students and the potential difficulty of reading a multipart narrative. Typical reactions at this level for each part are the following:

- **Survey**: Choose them all because the more raffle tickets they sell the more money they get.
- **Shannon**, 60 from a hat: Bad, too many people.
- **Jake**, 10 from computer club: Good, so you could play it.

MOVIEWORLD

A class wanted to raise money for their school trip to Movieworld on the Gold Coast. They could raise money by selling raffle tickets for a Nintendo Game system. But before they decided to have a raffle they w anted **to estimate how many students in their whole school would buy a ticket.** So they decided to do a **survey** to find out first. The school has 600 students in grades 1-6 with 100 students in each grade.

How many students would you survey and how would you choose them? Why?

Five students in the school conducted surveys.

(a) **Shannon** got the names of all 600 children in the school and put them in a hat, and then pulled out 60 of them. What do you think of Shannon's survey?

☐ GOOD ☐ BAD ☐ NOT SURE Why?_____

(b) **Jake** asked 10 children at an after-school meeting of the computer games club.

What do you think of Jake's survey?

☐ GOOD ☐ BAD ☐ NOT SURE Why?_____

(c) **Adam** asked all of the 100 children in Grade 1. What do you think of Adam's survey?

☐ GOOD ☐ BAD ☐ NOT SURE Why?_____

(d) **Raffi** surveyed 60 of his friends. What do you think of Raffi's survey?

☐ GOOD ☐ BAD ☐ NOT SURE Why? _____

(e) **Claire** set up a booth outside of the tuck shop. Anyone who wanted to stop and fill out a survey could. She stopped collecting surveys when she got 60 kids to complete them. What do you think of Claire's survey?

☐ GOOD ☐ BAD ☐ NOT SURE Why?_____

FIG. 2.4. Questions on sampling in a survey context.

- **Adam**, 100 in Grade 1: Bad, none might not buy any.
- **Raffi**, 60 friends: Good, more money for them.
- **Claire**, 60 volunteers at shop: Good, first in best served.

At the next level students appreciate the task and make understandable suggestions although they are not statistically appropriate.

- **Survey**: 50 students that I meet.
- **Survey**: You would survey them all.
- **Shannon**, 60 from a hat: Bad, he could pick the wrong people.

- **Jake**, 10 from computer club: Good, to give them a hint to buy one.
- **Adam**, 100 in Grade 1: Good, because it is fair.
- **Raffi**, 60 friends: Good, because they are his friends.
- **Claire**, 60 volunteers at shop: Good, it is their own choice.

At the next level suggestions for the survey focus on representative aspects of selection rather than random procedures. As more than one feature is suggested in each of the five alternatives, some students focus on one favorable aspect while ignoring an inappropriate one that should be criticized. Some also display uncertainty about aspects of the alternatives.

- **Survey**: You would survey 60 children, 10 from each grade so you could see an average for each grade.
- **Shannon**, 60 from a hat: Good, there's a lot of people.
- **Jake**, 10 from computer club: Bad, it's not broad enough.
- **Jake**, 10 from computer club: Not sure, because not many different people would go there.
- **Adam**, 100 from Grade 1: Bad, too many people.
- **Adam**, 100 from Grade 1: Not sure, because that's only one class but he surveyed the most people.
- **Raffi**, 60 friends: Good, you get a lot of answers.
- **Raffi**, 60 friends: Not sure, it depends how many of his friends have different opinions.
- **Claire**, 60 volunteers at shop: Good, you just have enough.
- **Claire**, 60 volunteers at shop: Not sure, because people who thought it was a bad idea wouldn't bother.

Inability to resolve conflicting ideas, which nevertheless are recognized, is not unusual for school students at times when they are taking on more complex structural reasoning to deal with more sophisticated tasks.

Finally at the highest level students are able to suggest appropriate methods and recognize bias in others. The consistency of answers across tasks tends to increase as students gain experience across the years of schooling.

- **Survey**: Put all 600 student names in a hat and draw out 65 names.
- **Survey**: 10 from each grade, 5 boys and 5 girls picked at random.
- **Shannon**, 60 from a hat: Good, because it's a good random way to survey.
- **Jake**, 10 from computer club: Bad, not enough people and selectively picked.
- **Adam**, 100 from Grade 1: Bad, not enough different age groups.
- **Raffi**, 60 friends: Bad, they would probably say the same thing.
- **Claire**, 60 volunteers at shop: Bad, some kids might go twice.

Overall there are quite a few different possibilities for discussion in relation to the five alternatives.

The five different suggestions in Parts (a) to (e) of Fig. 2.4 are not equally difficult for students to analyze. Across the middle school years, students are likely to find Jake's suggestion of 10 children at a computer club meeting the easiest to dismiss. This is because there are two difficulties with his idea: the sample size is too small and the group is likely to be biased. The next easiest to criticize is Adam's suggestion of choosing all grade 1 children. The most difficult suggestion for students is Claire's idea of using volunteers, with only about 1 in 20 students likely to see the difficulty. Teachers need to be aware of the subtleties associated with students' conceptions of fairness when considering Claire's alternative.[15]

A less complex scenario for considering the issues linking sample size and methodology is available in the multiple-choice question presented in Fig. 2.5.[16] The context is one that should be familiar to most students and one that presents a dilemma common to adults. Although one response, (B1), is correct, the three alternatives offer a hierarchy of appreciation of the issues.

Mrs. Jones wants to buy a new car, either [Brand 1] or [Brand 2]. She wants whichever car will break down the least.

First she read in <u>Consumer Reports</u> that for 400 cars of each type, [Brand 2] had more break-downs than [Brand 1].

Then she talked to three friends. Two were [Brand 2] owners, who had no major break-downs. The other friend used to own [Brand 1], but it had lots of break-downs, so he sold it. He said he'd never buy another [Brand 1].

Which car should Mrs. Jones buy?

☐(B2) Mrs. Jones should buy [Brand 2], because her friend had so much trouble with his [Brand 1], while her other friends had no trouble with their [Brand 2] cars.

☐(B1) She should buy [Brand 1], because the information about break-downs in <u>Consumer Reports</u> is based on many cases, not just one or two cases.

☐(=) It doesn't matter which car she buys. Whichever type she gets, she could still be unlucky and get stuck with a particular car that would need a lot of repairs.

FIG. 2.5.   Item on buying a new car.

Response (B2), to buy a car based on the experience of three friends, represents the lowest level of response due to the small size and the bias of asking friends. The (=) response, indicating the buyer could be unlucky in buying either car, represents an equivocal view often observed in chance contexts, that "anything can happen," without quantitative appreciation of how likely any of the possibilities may be. This response also acknowledges but does not resolve the dilemma of choosing between the two options. Response (B1), to buy a car based on a report of 800 cases, represents the statistically appropriate response with the benefit of many cases to represent a population reliably.

Well into high school it is likely that only about a quarter of students will choose the statistically appropriate alternative, with most choosing the (=), it does not matter, option. This question is a good one to use as a starter for discussion of sample size, method, and potential bias, as it is likely to generate stories from class members of family experiences of car-buying based on sample-of-size-one information from a friend or relative. It is to be hoped that some of these stories will have negative outcomes to balance the positive ones, in order to make the point about the unreliability of small samples. For some students it will be necessary to point out that asking a friend is in fact taking a sample of size one.

Problems of the type shown in Fig. 2.6 have been used for many years with older students[17] and illustrate the susceptibility to beliefs about variation not being related to sample size when data are collected. It appears clear that school students have little appreciation for the subtleties involved in these problems. The problem shown in Fig. 2.6 is a variation on the classical "hospital" problem that asks about the number of births on each day of the year in two different-sized hospitals.[18] Being based in the context of selecting samples of children from two different schools creates a more complex theoretical model because of the lack of replacement when the sample is selected. This technically, however, does not affect the relative likelihood of the two outcomes and is not likely to be considered by school students who have not been exposed to formal probability at the senior high school level.[19]

Without a distribution to appreciate visually or experiments to perform, it is difficult for students to decipher the information presented in the problem in Fig. 2.6. Often students have difficulty differentiating the information about the schools having half boys and half girls from the task of imagining a sample with 80% boys and cannot provide an answer. The inappropriate use of extraneous information in justifications is frequent even for responses that are technically correct.

- The small sample is more likely to have 80%, because boys like living in the country more.

The researchers went to 2 schools:

1 school in the centre of the city, and 1 school in the country.

Each school had about half girls and half boys.

The researchers took a random sample from each school:

50 children from the city school,
20 children from the country school.

One of these samples was unusual: it had more than 80% boys.

Is it more likely to have come from

☐   the large sample of 50 from the city school, or

☐   the small sample of 20 from the country school, or

☐   are both samples equally likely to have been the unusual sample?

Please explain your answer.

FIG. 2.6.   Choosing samples of different sizes and appreciating variation.

- The large sample is more likely to have 80% boys, because more people live in the city.

In the second response, there is a possibility that the 80% is seen to be more likely to occur in the larger sample because it is a large percent. The choice of equally likely is probably associated with the belief that all samples, regardless of size, reflect the population equally well or the belief that percent is an abstract idea not related to definite numbers.

- Both samples are equally likely, because it is a random process.
- Both samples are equally likely, because a percent isn't a definite number and will be the same for each.

Very unusual are responses that display an appreciation of the relationship of sample size to the potential variation in outcomes.

- I think it [you] would be more likely to get it [the sample of 80% or more boys] from the country school because there are a lot less children, so if you had perhaps a few more, you would bring the percentage up a lot quicker than with this sample [city school].

It is not until simulations are carried out, preferably with the speed allowed by software packages, that intuitions are likely to develop about sampling, sample size, and variation in contexts such as the one in Fig. 2.6.[20]

2.5   SAMPLING AND FAIRNESS

At several places in responses in the previous section the idea of fairness is used either to criticize or to support sampling methods. For some students the statistical idea of fairness, as represented in all people having the same chance of being selected by a random procedure, is acceptable. For others the fact that some people are left out by this process or that some may be chosen who do not wish to participate is seen as unfair. This leads to two types of judgments. In one case students believe that the entire population needs to be canvassed. In the other case students support voluntary polls, such as that proposed by Claire in Fig. 2.4. These are common misunderstandings observed at the middle school level and they need to be worked through carefully to avoid the dual beliefs that one definition of fairness applies in the mathematics class and another outside of school.

The idea of fairness arises periodically throughout this book in different contexts, for example in the consideration of fair dice (Section 5.12). It is important to be aware of opportunities to reinforce old connections to the concept when new ones arise. In collecting repeated small random samples from a class for example, it is likely that one person will be chosen a second time before all people have been selected. This may be considered unfair by some and is an important point for discussion.

2.6   SOURCES OF SAMPLE BIAS

The issue of bias in sampling is crucial to the development of critical statistical literacy and an important component of Fig. 2.1. The possible creation of bias associated with a small sample size or inappropriate sampling methods is dealt with in Section 2.4 and some students are aware of the issue at the time of suggesting sampling methods for a study, and to some degree in judging the alternatives for surveying a school given in Fig. 2.4. The issue of transfer of understanding and questioning bias in sampling to settings where authoritative claims are being made by external "experts" in public settings is exceedingly important. Often school-based treatment of sampling, even if it progresses as far as the types of examples and discussion covered thus far in Chapter 2, does not then proceed to consider authentic socially-based contexts where bias can be questioned. Generally in society there is a lack of willingness to question statements made with the authority backing of a media agency—this is likely to be true for teachers as well as their students. It is at this point that the third tier of the Statistical Literacy Hierarchy introduced in Section 1.4 becomes significant and explicit. Active discussion of such issues needs to take place as a culmination of activities related to sampling in order to encourage transfer into risk-taking environments.[21]

The difficulties that students have in transferring their understanding of bias in sampling to social contexts are illustrated by students' responses to questions about two newspaper articles that report the outcomes of surveys. The articles in Figs. 2.7 and 2.8 can be presented to students in various formats, including surveys and interviews, but they are also appropriate for student group work and class discussion. Illustrations of various levels of engagement with the articles show starting points for student discussion, debate, and cognitive development.[22]

Because the article on guns in Chicago in Fig. 2.7 does not use the words *sample* or *population* but implicitly refers to the population of U.S. high school students in making a claim based on a sample of Chicago high school students, the opportunity is present to ask students if there is anything unusual about the article without specifically referring to any aspect of its content. The fact that there are several numbers and claims in the article makes it a good candidate for student detective work. A general question such as, "Would you make any criticisms of the claims in this article?" is a good place to start. If after some period of struggle there is little or no progress, then a supplementary question such as, "If you were a high school teacher, would this report make you refuse a job somewhere else in the United States?", might help focus attention on the sample versus population issue without being too explicit.

> ABOUT six in 10 United States high school students say they could get a handgun if they wanted one, a third of them within an hour, a survey shows. The poll of 2508 junior and senior high school students in Chicago also found 15 per cent had actually carried a handgun within the past 30 days, with 4 per cent taking one to school.

FIG. 2.7. Newspaper article with population claim based on non-representative sample.

Many students are affected by the emotive nature of the article, do not engage in the statistical issue presented, and are considered prestructural with respect to statistical appropriateness. Such criticisms and comments for the questions in the previous paragraph include the following.

- They shouldn't be carrying guns.
- No criticisms—they do it for their own protection.
- I would take the job because I would carry a gun too if I lived in America.

Becoming involved with the sampling issues, single ideas are often put forward that may be important in the context but are not critical to the claim made. On one hand these reflect the validity of the data.

- How do you know they are not lying?
- They could be telling lies to impress people.

On the other hand, they reflect a belief in the homogeneity of the U.S. population.

- No because the whole of the US would be exactly the same.

The grappling with the sample issue begins with recognition but without resolution.

- If they wanted to get their facts right they should survey *every* school in America.

This opinion reflects the belief expressed in Section 2.4 that all students in a school should be surveyed. Some students struggle with the sample size in relation to the large nation rather than the representativeness of the sample.

- Yes because only 2508 students were surveyed. America's population is very large. More students should have been asked.

Inexperience is likely to be the reason for focusing on sample size but some appear to be appreciating aspects of representing the country as well.

- The claims cannot be correct if only 2508 students are surveyed. The survey should be nationwide to be correct.

There are students, however, who are aware of the necessity of a sample to represent the population it defines.

- Yes. It is generalizing the whole of the USA—when they only surveyed in Chicago.
- The survey has just surveyed one state and related it to the whole USA. It might not happen anywhere else. It is like asking someone a question, and saying that the whole school also answers it in that way.

Although encouraging, these responses are typical of only about one third of students in the mid-high-school years.

The article on the legalization of marijuana in Fig. 2.8[23] is easier for students to analyze than the previous one about Chicago, perhaps because there are many voluntary polls discussed in the media these days and any classroom discussion of surveying would be likely to discuss the topic. The question, "Is the sample reported here a reliable way of finding out public support for the decriminalization of marijuana? Why or why not?", still elicits a wide range of response from high school students.

Again perhaps because the issue is an emotive one, some students focus on the issue of decriminalization itself rather than the issue of the *poll* about decriminalization.

- No, because now scientific evidence shows that the drug should not be used.
- Yes, because most people use it behind the police's back so it should be legalized.

Of those who appreciate the nature of the task some focus on features that, although relevant, are not the major difficulty.

Decriminalise drug use: poll

SOME 96 percent of callers to youth radio station Triple J have said marijuana use should be decriminalised in Australia.
The phone-in listener poll, which closed yesterday, showed 9924 - out of the 10,000-plus callers - favoured decriminalisation, the station said.

Only 389 believed possession of the drug should remain a criminal offence.

Many callers stressed they did not smoke marijuana but still believed in decriminalising its use, a Triple J statement said.

FIG. 2.8. Newspaper article based on voluntary poll.

- Yes it is. It has the right no's + information.
- Yes, because everybody can ring up and have their say.
- Yes, because it was anonymous.

The dilemma of whether a sample size of 10,000 is adequate is still present and for some the only issue that is considered.

- This sample would not be reliable because another 10,000 people surveyed might have a different opinion. The whole population would need to be asked before a decision is made.
- The size is quite large for a survey but not large enough to be extremely accurate.
- Yes, because they used a large enough sample of people to allow both the fors and againsts to show properly.

A misunderstanding of the term *random* is sometimes displayed.

- Yes. It is a random selection of 10,000 people from all around Australia and if 96% of that sample favor decriminalization then maybe someone should do something about it.

Some students recognize a conflict in the information presented, which they find difficult to resolve.

- I think so, because 10,000 plus callers is a huge amount and the percentage of public support for the decriminalization of marijuana is extremely high. I think it could be a bit biased though as mostly teenagers listen to Triple J.

As there are several problems with voluntary polls, students may be satisfied with one reason or may put together an integrated argument.

- No, only the people who care rang up about it.
- No because there are a lot of people who do not listen to Triple J and most of the people that do are teenagers.
- I don't think it's all that reliable because all the people that use marijuana may call more than once just to make sure they will be in favor.
- No, because all the people who smoke it would ring up and say yes to the decriminalization of it, but all the straight people probably wouldn't be listening to a pathetic station like Triple J so they wouldn't ring up to cast their vote. Also someone could ring up for a friend who smokes it.

These two articles deal with issues that are very relevant in students' lives and it is important for them to learn to pull themselves away from the issues for long enough to make judgments about how information has been gathered and reported. Once they can make decisions about the reliability and potential bias of what is presented, then they can debate the issues from an informed perspective—or ask for further data on the issue. These are the types of decisions that citizens are faced with in the media every day. At the grade 8 level about 40% of students are likely to have difficulty engaging with the tasks in these two articles, whereas by grade 11 this drops to about 10%. At the other extreme very few grade 8 students are likely to provide the highest level response for both articles but this rises to about 20% by grade 11.

Teachers may be uncomfortable about using articles such as those in Figs. 2.7 and 2.8 in the classroom. It is precisely in these contexts, however, that students need to develop the critical skills of questioning claims that are inappropriately presented in the media. Authentic instances offer greater potential impact on students' developing critical skills.

2.7 SAMPLE AND RANDOM

Similar to the term *sample*, the term *random* has a colloquial meaning with which school students are familiar, one which is likely to be related to ideas such as haphazard. When asked for a definition of the term many students focus on ideas related to picking, such as picking without knowing or choosing any, or on ideas related loosely to chance. The idea of random as used as an adjective in describing "random sampling," implying that all members of the population (or all samples) have the same chance of being selected, is unknown until explicitly taught. Picking names from a hat without looking is the most sophisticated idea expressed by some students and contains the intuition appropriate for later.[24]

When students are asked to define sample, as discussed in Section 2.2, it is rare but possible (as seen in one example there) for random to be introduced as a descriptor. There are a number of students, however, who have misconceptions about random as used in surveying. The example given in Section 2.6, claiming that the radio poll introduced in Fig. 2.8 was random, appears to indicate the transfer of a haphazard interpretation to the context. Much discussion is needed to reinforce the distinction between haphazard and statistically appropriate interpretations of random in regard to sampling. The term *random* is considered again in Chapter 5 in relation to chance.

2.8 IMPLICATIONS AND RECOMMENDATIONS

Although sampling is just the start of a statistical investigation, the links documented in the previous sections indicate that it is a complex procedure in itself with implications for the rest of the investigation process. To dismiss sampling with a descriptive paragraph or a 15-minute discussion is likely to leave unchallenged many alternative conceptions that students will retain in parallel with the school-based definition. Inappropriate intuitions, for example associated with fairness or random or homogeneity of samples, are likely to interfere later with drawing statistical inferences.

The important part played by an understanding of sampling in the overall context of statistical literacy can be illustrated by considering the three-tiered hierarchy introduced in Chapter 1. Tier 1 covers the definition of terminology. The responses of students in Section 2.2 indicate an increasing structural complexity as more aspects are included and linked together. The importance of the part–whole concept creates links to other components of the mathematics curriculum. The close association in children's minds of the word sample and examples of samples they have experienced leads naturally into connections created in Tier 2 of the hierarchy.

Tier 2 focuses on applying the ideas of samples and sampling in context. The opportunities for providing statistical contexts for building associations are many and varied. As shown in Sections 2.3 and 2.4, students demonstrate increasing appreciation of context, sample size, and method in familiar measurement and surveying contexts. Contexts associated with sampling from repeated trials in chance settings are also important because issues such as variation can be considered without as many outside sources requiring explanation. Context is especially important in providing the opportunity to distinguish different types of data collection that create samples. Measuring and recording the weight of a group of people creates a very different looking data set from surveying people to see if they will buy raffle tickets. These tasks are again different from drawing colored objects from a container with a certain proportion of red or rolling a die repeatedly and recording the successive outcomes. For many students it is difficult to see all of these outcomes as producing samples, and to connect them with the idea of a sample of cheese obtained at the supermarket. It is the building of many associations of different sampling methods for different contexts that provides the foundation for making judgments in critical contexts. It is not necessary however to know everything before being exposed to situations where sampling methods are questionable.

Tier 3 of the hierarchy has the goal of questioning claims made without proper statistical justification. The examples presented in Section 2.6 are blatant in the bias displayed and motivating in the contexts presented. Students' displays of appreciation range from only considering the contextual issue, through various stages of grappling with sample size and method, to sophisticated criticisms. Opportunities for tying Tier 3 critical goals with understanding associated with the aims of Tiers 1 and 2 abound and it is necessary to make explicit connections for many students. It is not always necessary to use emotive and complex contexts such as presented here.

Often causes are supported in media reports with a well-chosen sample of size one: the boy who does not respond to a particular method of teaching reading or the parent who is disadvantaged by a method of determining social welfare entitlements. These should be the topic of classroom discussion. Students should be reminded of the lack of representativeness of a sample of size one, despite the spectacular nature of the observation of that sample.

Explicit discussion of representativeness in samples and its association with variation is exceedingly important and links can be made in relation to each of the three tiers of the Statistical Literacy Hierarchy as appropriate. The part–whole idea leads to the need to define the population carefully in order to know what the part is representing. Discussion of the part that a sample product plays in representing a production-line manufactured product can focus on the assumed homogeneity of the product. Without the "good" sample and the homogeneity, the product will fail to sell. The purpose of sampling in this situation is different from sampling where there is heterogeneity in the population. Introducing another manufacturing context, say the production of shoes, should make students aware of the necessity both to define the population carefully in terms of the consumers' interests and to sample in a representative fashion to gauge the numbers of each size that need to be produced. The issue of sampling in the field of quality control in order to produce the homogeneous product from a production process that contains variation is an important and interesting extension that can be used after students have mastered the basic ideas.

The availability of software that will simulate random sampling either from large data sets such as available from government agencies or from probability distributions, provides the opportunity to consider sample size in a meaningful way faster than by drawing data cards from a large box by hand or throwing dice thousands of times.[25] For most students, however, especially younger ones, it is essential to begin with hands-on activities so that they appreciate the context and how the process of sampling takes place. It is also essential to explain very carefully how the process is being transferred to the computer. Showing sample collection in a "slow" mode at first can help create the connections between individual selections and a growing visual distribution of the outcomes. Students should be constantly questioned about the processes they are observing in order to be sure the appropriate links are being made. Writing summaries afterward in reports or journal entries is important and should include a description of the process as well as conclusions about what happens for example as the sample size increases.

An authentic anecdote from a grade 9 classroom[26] may help reinforce ideas of sample size and method. The setting was a sampling activity[27] prepared by a preservice practicing teacher for a less-than-motivated average-ability mathematics class. Students in the class, working in pairs with paper bags containing 10 bits of colored paper, were asked to take samples of size two without looking, record the results, return the two bits, and repeat the process 10 times. From the results of the 10 samples they were to predict the number of slips of each color in the bag.

The type of recording that occurred is shown in Fig. 2.9. The two boys in question used the first letters of the colors to list their outcomes. Based on the results in Fig. 2.9, they predicted that there were 4 orange, 3 red, 2 yellow, and 1 green slips of paper in the bag. When asked for their method of prediction they said that they made guesses roughly based on the total numbers of each color divided by two. It was not clear that they took into account the fact that some samples contained two slips of the same color, but their prediction was consistent with noticing this information. The boys were not quite correct in their prediction but they were close; the ratio of colors was in fact 3 orange : 3 red : 3 yellow : 1 green.

The class discussed the outcomes and students were asked to speculate about how the number of slips in the sample each time affected the guesses they had made. They were then given another mystery bag with 10 slips of paper and told that they were to use 10 samples of size four in order to make their estimates. The two boys in question, however, were not listening carefully to the teacher's instruction and again proceeded to take 10 samples of size two. Their outcomes are shown in Fig. 2.10 for the colors blue, purple, and gray.

OY
OR
RR
OO
YY
RY
RR
OO
OG
OO

FIG. 2.9.   Recording of samples of size two from a mystery bag.

BB
GP
GB
BG
BG
GB
GB
GB
GG
GB

FIG. 2.10.   Recordings of samples of size two from a second mystery bag.

Just as they were making their prediction, the teacher passed by and asked what they were doing. It was then they found out that they should have been taking samples of size four rather than size two. Not being the most enthusiastic of samplers, or not wanting to waste the data they had already collected, or perhaps feeling it would be cheating to do so, they proceeded to take 10 more samples of size two. The results from these they recorded alongside the previous results as shown in Fig. 2.11. It was at this point that I happened onto the pair and asked what was going on. There was no attempt to disguise the procedure used. They carefully explained what they had done and how they were about to make their prediction based on the total number of each color, this time divided by four. They were asked if they would consider the total number of any color in the lists of four outcomes on their paper. At this point there was disagreement between the boys. One showed surprise as if he had realized something he had missed, pointed to the four Bs, and started to take them into account in the prediction. The other, however, stopped him and said they could not do it because they had taken two at a time rather than four. When asked the implications of the procedure they had used, they realized that they would never get an accurate estimate of the minimum number of each color. {B,B} + {B,B} does not imply {B,B,B,B} and hence a minimum of four blue slips in the bag, because the same blue slips could have been selected each time. Suddenly the advantage of selecting four in the first place was seen and the boys rushed to repeat the 10 samples of size four producing the results shown in Fig. 2.12. From these outcomes they were successful in predicting the contents of the bag, this time 5 blue, 4 gray, and 1 purple.

Although perhaps not gaining assessment points in the "listens carefully to instructions" category from the teacher, I suspect that these two boys had a deeper appreciation for the importance of sample size than did some of the other students who were blindly following instructions without thinking of the ramifications of doing so. In this case the teacher, relatively inexperienced, missed an opportunity to get these two boys to explain their discov-

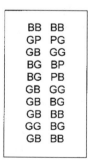

FIG. 2.11.   Appended samples of size two to create samples of size four.

```
BGPB
BBBG
BBBP
PGGG
PBGG
BGPB
GBPG
GBBG
GGBB
BGBB
```

FIG. 2.12.   Samples of size four from the second mystery bag.

ery to the class. This cautionary tale should not be dismissed too lightly as I saw two high school teachers come close to making the same mistake in a professional development session.

ENDNOTES

1. Australian Education Council (1991, p. 164).
2. Moore (1991a).
3. Orr (1995, p. 72).
4. Kahneman & Tversky (1972); Tversky & Kahneman (1971, 1974).
5. Gal & Wagner (1992); Rubin, Bruce, & Tenney (1991); Wagner & Gal (1991).
6. Jacobs (1997, 1999).
7. Schwartz, Goldman, Vye, Barron, & The Cognition and Technology Group at Vanderbilt (1998).
8. Metz (1999).
9. Watson (2004a); Watson, Collis, & Moritz (1995b); Watson & Moritz (2000a, 2000b).
10. Watson (2004a); Watson & Moritz (2000a).
11. Watson (2004a); Watson & Moritz (2000a).
12. Metz (1999), also found this tendency in elementary students who designed their own science experiments.
13. Jacobs (1999).
14. Watson, Kelly, Callingham, & Shaughnessy (2003).
15. Watson & Kelly (2005); Jacobs (1997), also discusses this issue.
16. Fong, Krantz, & Nisbett (1986); Konold & Garfield (1992); Watson & Moritz (2000b). The names of cars have been removed in Fig. 2.5. In the study of Watson & Moritz (2000b), the brand names were familiar to the students.
17. Kahneman & Tversky (1972); Watson (2000a).
18. Kahneman & Tversky (1972).
19. Watson (2004a); Watson & Moritz (2000a).

20. Watson (2000a).
21. Gigerenzer (2002), offers an excellent discussion of issues associated with risk taking and the importance of reporting on the reference set when risks are discussed numerically.
22. Watson, Collis, & Moritz (1995b); Watson & Moritz (2000b); "That's life" (1993).
23. Watson, Collis, & Moritz (1995b); "Decriminalise drug use: poll" (1992).
24. Watson & Moritz (2000a).
25. *Fathom* (2002).
26. Watson (2002d).
27. Lovitt & Lowe (1993, pp. 400–407).

3

Graphs—How Best to Represent the Data

For many people the first word that comes to mind when they think about statistical charts is "lie." No doubt some graphics do distort the underlying data, making it hard for the viewer to learn the truth. But data graphs are no different from words in this regard, for any means of communication can be used to deceive. There is no reason to believe that graphs are especially vulnerable to exploitation by liars; in fact, most of us have pretty good graphical lie detectors that help us see right through frauds.[1]

3.1 BACKGROUND

Edward Tufte's assessment of graphs as similar to words as a means of communication with no more or less potential to deceive is an important issue in considering the place of data representation in the data and chance curriculum. His view that most people have "pretty good graphical lie detectors," however, is not borne out at the school level. It is there that a conscious effort needs to be expended to achieve the skills that will provide the lie detectors required by statistically literate adults.

In contrast to sampling, graphing of data has a firm and explicit place in the data and chance curriculum. Even before the mathematics curriculum was expanded to contain coverage of data handling generally, many textbooks included exercises in graphing, leading for example to histograms. It is interesting that the link to algebraic graphs was often exceedingly tenuous although both types of graphs rely on a coordinate system. Although early in the last century some analytic geometry texts introduced the idea of "empirical curves,"[2] only very recently have curriculum materials again sought to establish meaningful links between graphs of data sets and the graphs of equations that might describe them more formally.[3] As well, only recently have links to other parts of the data handling curriculum been reinforced in curriculum documents. The perception, held by some for many years, that "the graph" was the start and finish of data handling, should be fast disappearing.

The wide range of graphical representations that are available sometimes leads to frustration for teachers when they have a limited time to cover graphing and want to cover just the important types of graphs. There are also occasionally disputes among textbook writers and curriculum developers about details of graph production. When is a bar graph a histogram? When does one leave gaps between bars? When does one connect dots with lines? What are the rules to construct the whiskers on a box-and-whisker plot? These issues are not dealt with here and no attempt is made to provide a comprehensive coverage of all possible graphical representations. Specific curriculum documents provide guidance.[4] What is important, and the emphasis of this chapter, is the story that graphs tell about data: how graphs are created to tell the story and how they are interpreted once created.

One type of graph however deserves special attention because it is used for some of the tasks introduced in later sections. In some curriculum documents and materials it is referred to as a "line plot,"[5] reflecting the scaled base line above which dots or Xs are piled to represent data values. Because of the confusion with the term *line graph*, referring to a graph where straight lines connect data points, the term *stacked dot plot* is used here.[6] It is a more visual phrase that can assist students in distinguishing it from other forms, particularly the line graph.

Because graphing of various sorts has been in the mathematics curriculum for a long time, there has been considerable research on student understanding. Some aspects of the cognitive demands of coordinate graphing are common to the needs of plotting algebraic functions as well as statistical representations, whereas other demands are different for the fields of algebra and statistics. Gaea Leinhardt and her colleagues provided an excellent summary in the general field in 1990,[7] whereas Fran Curcio set the stage for graphing of data[8] and continued updating valuable background information with Susan Friel and George Bright.[9] More specific research on statistical representations has focused very much on the purpose for which graphs are required to be created or interpreted. Sometimes the research has overlapped with the interests of science educators[10] and sometimes more generally with those of psychologists.[11] Lionel Pereira-Mendoza and his colleagues contributed to the understanding of how young children work with pictographs and bar graphs,[12] whereas John Ross and

Bradley Cousins studied high school students struggling with graphing association and correlation.[13] Little research has focused on students' interpretation of graphs in the media but Cliff Konold and his team have considered students' work with stacked dot plots and how these representations assist in the discussion of variation in data sets.[14]

Setting aside distinctions of terminology and details of particular graph types, the important links contributing to an understanding of data representation are shown in Fig. 3.1. Usually several types of representations could be used to illustrate a connection or connections. Keeping in mind the curriculum model suggested in Chapter 1 (cf. Fig. 1.1), data representation is often seen, as it is here, as the link between data collection, often through sampling, and data summary, often through analysis of central tendency and spread. The initial question that led to the data collection, however, may still impinge on the type of data representation selected, and hence the connection is featured. Two major components of Fig. 3.1 are "creation" and "interpretation," reflecting both the demands of the school curriculum that students learn graphing skills and the demands of statistical literacy that people can interpret the graphs produced by others. Both components are linked to the question asked as well as the data representation itself.

The connections associated with the creation of data representations are illustrated in Section 3.2 for a small data set using pictographs, in Section 3.3 for a specific small data set containing several variables, and in Section 3.4 for a claimed relationship without specific data values. Issues raised point to underlying skills that are linked to data representation and may

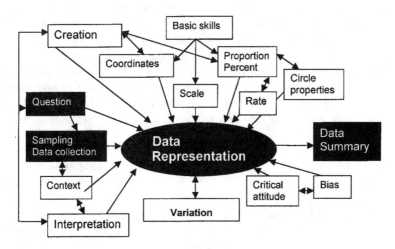

FIG. 3.1.   Links among the ideas and statistical elements associated with data representation.

present difficulties for some students. These include appreciation of scale, proportion and percent, circle properties, and the coordinate system. Noted in Section 3.5, these components may influence graph interpretation but are more likely to affect graph creation. The connections associated with the interpretation of data representations are illustrated in Section 3.2 in the context of pictographs created by students themselves, in Section 3.6 for several types of bar graphs, in Section 3.7 for pie graphs, and in Section 3.8 for stacked dot plots. The examples and responses in these sections demonstrate important links to context, to recognition of bias, to critical skills in error recognition, and to the important influence of variation. Specific comments with respect to bias are made in Section 3.9, whereas the graphing of distributions is discussed in Chapter 7.

In the following sections the examples of students responses to tasks concerning data representation are used to illustrate the development that takes place as the connections are made among the various components in Fig. 3.1. Some asides along the way point to possible classroom interventions. The final section relates the preceding discussion to the Statistical Literacy Hierarchy introduced in Chapter 1 and ends with some ideas for graphing and some typical graphs for discussion from the media.

3.2 GRAPH CREATION AND INTERPRETATION: THE CASE OF PICTOGRAPHS

To gain an impression of what is important to students in telling a numerical story with a graphical representation, asking questions without imposing expectations of convention can be very useful. When given a large piece of blank paper or table top and some small cards with children (named) and books on them, students have a great deal of freedom in telling the story of how many books each child has read. What is important and what could a person who walked into the room and saw the representation tell from it? Children are likely to display one of several levels of appreciation when asked to show that Anne read 4 books, Danny read 1, Lisa read 6, and Terry read 3, using cards depicting children (85mm × 45mm) and books (40mm × 45mm) as shown in Fig. 3.2.[15]

All students who can count associate the appropriate number of books to each child in a many-to-one fashion, indicating an understanding of the task. At what might be considered the beginners' level, typical of younger students, the books are piled next to or on top of the people in such a way that they would have to be picked up again and counted to see how many books had been read. At the unistructural level, students appear to appreciate the need to see each of the books read and the books are scattered around the person who read them in an unsystematic fashion but so they can be counted. System is added to the display at the multistructural level

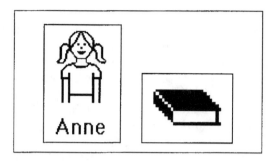

FIG. 3.2. Sample of cards used as materials for representation.

where students provide a baseline made up of the children, making it possible to compare more easily the numbers read by each child. The base line is either a single column to the left of the space provided or a single row at the top or bottom of the space. The order of the base line reflects the order in which the information is read out, without regard to the frequencies involved. At the most sophisticated relational level, with respect to the task, students go to the further step of ordering the children represented along the base line according to the number books they read, with the least and most at the extremes. At each level responses take into account more aspects important in telling a story with a graph, in the end relating the information for the various children. The four levels of increasing complexity of representation are shown in Fig. 3.3.

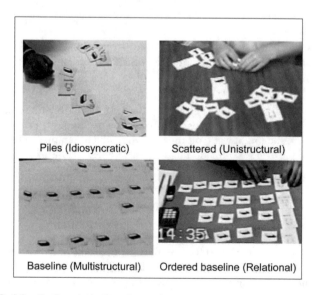

FIG. 3.3. Students' pictograph representations at four levels of response.

Moving from creation to interpretation is natural in a setting such as this because students can be asked what someone just now entering the room could tell by looking at the graph. Drawing away from a graph one has produced to imagine what others would think is useful in planning improvements. Questions such as "Who likes reading the most?" or "Who would most want a book for Christmas?" give an indication of students' appreciation for the context and what they have been told specifically when setting up the graph. Again students are likely to display four levels of increasing complexity in interpreting their own graphs.

For some students, again often younger, personal knowledge and imagination override the information presented to encourage children to make up stories and sometimes change their representations.[16]

[What could a newcomer tell?] They would say Danny has got the less [. . .] it wouldn't be fair to him so I would probably put 2 more in. [. . . after adding a book from the Library] They could tell that now he has read a book and he would probably have a good education [. . .] [Who likes reading the most?] Yes, I would probably say Anne because she has got [. . .] 4 and now she has got 5. She probably loves books and so does Lisa. [. . .]

At the unistructural level students focus directly on the facts, usually considered individually, presented in the graph with no amplification of any sort.

[What can a newcomer tell?] Terry's got 3 books, Danny's got 1 [. . .] [After adding a book] That lots of people read lots of books. [Who likes reading the most?] Lisa, because she has the most books around her.

Students at the multistructural level begin to acknowledge the limitations of the data and include uncertainty in some of their interpretations, often with qualifiers like "probably."

[Who likes reading the most?] Lisa. [. . .] Because she has read 7 books. [Who would want a book for Christmas?] Probably Lisa or Ian. [. . .] Lisa, she reads lots of books, she might want another one to read and Ian maybe because he can't get a lot of books but he might want one.

Then there are students who consistently exercise caution, acknowledging both the relationships among the data and the limitations for interpreting within the context.

[What can a newcomer tell?] They probably think that Anne has something to do with 4 books [. . .] Not necessarily that they had read them. [Who likes reading the most?] You can tell who *reads* the most, which would be Lisa. Not that . . . you'd think . . . you know she has the most books. You won't know if she reads them or likes them the most. [Can you tell who would want a book for Christmas?] Not really—it could be Ian because he doesn't have many books so he would like a book, or it could be Lisa, because she likes reading the most books, she wants another one—but you can't really say.

This response displays the traits of observation and speculation that are hopefully to be developed for applications in social situations when interpreting the graphs of others.

Overall, tasks such as this one are particularly useful for younger children with few preconceived ideas on graphing. Older children, with more experience in formal graphing, may give functional rather than optimal responses because they perceive the task as trivial in nature. Given the number of pictographs that appear in adult media, however, it is important occasionally to reintroduce pictograph tasks throughout the years of schooling. At any grade level, student responses are likely to provide the opportunity for lively debate as different levels of appreciation emerge.

3.3 GRAPH CREATION: THE CASE OF ASSOCIATION (WITH DATA)

Although tasks such as telling a story with a pictograph allow students considerable freedom in developing representations, they are restricted by the materials provided. Suggesting students produce their own representations to support hypotheses formed based on a given data set adds another degree of freedom. Using the same data set for individuals or groups in a class makes it possible to compare and contrast the output. Such tasks obviously depend on the previous experiences that students have had with graphing. Students, however, can be quite creative in their representations and it should be the success in telling the story of the data rather than the reflection of convention that is assessed. Such an activity also provides the opportunity for students to exhibit some of the connections they have made or are making among the ideas in Fig. 3.1.

Although for some time it was accepted that upper elementary or middle school students should not be set tasks involving association of variables[17] when they had not been taught to draw scattergrams or calculate correlations, associations among variables can be based in contexts that are understandable and motivating to students in these grades. This is now accepted in most curriculum documents.[18] Providing open-ended activities allows students to display the complexity of their understanding of the issues involved in showing associations. This can then be built upon with class discussion and further less open tasks can be pitched at the appropriate level.

Consider a task appropriate for students from grade 5 upward based on 16 data cards. Each data card contains the name, age, favorite activity, eye color, weight (in kg), and number of fast food meals eaten per week, for a person, with an age range of 8 to 18 years.[19] The associations presented in the data are suggestive of a relationship between weight and age, between weight and fast food consumption, between age and fast food consumption, and between favorite activity and fast food consumption. All associations contain variation and none are unrealistically extreme (the data set is in an appendix to Chapter 3). The connection of data representation and context is an important motivator in tasks such as this.

In this context and with the open-ended nature of the task to provide graphical evidence for relationships believed to exist in the data set, students, often working in groups, are likely to display considerable difference in their ability to transform hypothesized associations into a graphical form, particularly when several variables are involved. The spread of outcomes in a single class is potentially very wide, providing information on processing capacity as well as surprises at the sophistication shown with some naïve graphical intuitions.

Although it is likely that all students who engage in the task understand about fast foods and can speculate about "causes," typically there are a few students who cannot represent a single variable in a numerical fashion. A prestructural representation by one such student is shown in the first "graph" in Fig. 3.4(a) and it does not appear to show an appreciation of the contextual nature of the task. At the unistructural level students are able to appreciate the need to depict individual aspects of the data set or a meaningful subset. This is usually done in a table as there appears to be no felt need to display a trend or relationship. One such table is the representation in Fig. 3.4(b). Moving into the realms of graphing the first stage is the production of graphs of frequencies for a single variable. These graphs are most likely to be bar graphs, due to students' previous experiences, but occasionally pie charts or line graphs are presented. It is significant that for students entering a realistic context with several variables for the first time, they are likely to rely on previously learned forms rather than inventing something new or taking on a suggestion from a teacher. Two multistructural graphs showing the number of students for each favorite activity and the number with each eye color are shown in Fig. 3.4(c) and (d).

The most sophisticated, relational representations are those that attempt to show the relationship of two or more variables. Many students appreciate the fact that there may be an association of several variables, for example weight, age, and fast food, or gender, age, and fast food. Drawing a representation of this, however, is difficult even for those with graphing skills taught at higher levels. Figure 3.5 contains several attempts by stu-

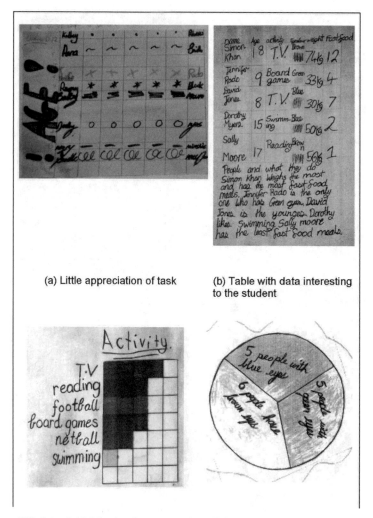

FIG. 3.4. Initial levels of representation of data settings with associations.

dents in grades 5 or 6, the first of which, (a), tries to tell the story of favorite activity (indoor or outdoor sports), age, and fast foods. With some hints on what a scattergram is and motivation to tell a story, many students produce graphs like in Fig. 3.5(b), which is a quite conventional form to show an association of weight and fast food consumption. The transition from a bar graph, with which most students are familiar, to a scattergram sometimes leads to a retention of bars as is seen in the graph in Fig. 3.5(c), which uses the heights of bars to show both the association between age and weight and differences between boys and girls.

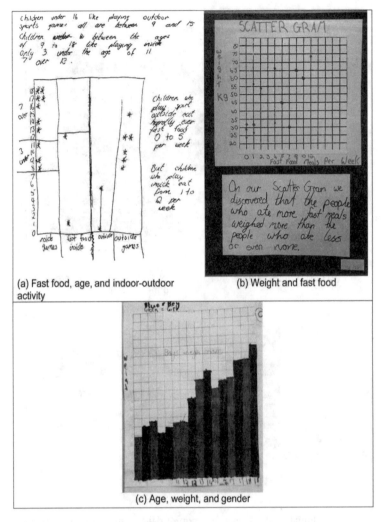

(a) Fast food, age, and indoor-outdoor activity

(b) Weight and fast food

(c) Age, weight, and gender

FIG. 3.5.   Representations showing associations in a small data set.

What is fascinating with tasks such as this one based on data cards is the creativity shown by many students in trying to tell a story. Sometimes the attempts are quite sophisticated given the background of students and although they would not satisfy a statistician, they show excellent intuitions. A few students who are familiar with the arithmetic mean are likely to use it to summarize information as they create a representation. An example is shown later in Section 4.6. For the data cards task this might involve averaging the number of fast foods for each age group so that there is only one value to plot for each age on a graph.[20]

3.4 GRAPH CREATION: THE CASE OF ASSOCIATION (WITHOUT DATA)

Most tasks involving graphing that are set for students in school are based on actual data sets such as those described in the previous two sections or on tasks where students collect their own data as part of an investigation. Outside of the school context, however, people are rarely presented with data sets. Instead they hear or read about differences, trends, or associations in data sets stated verbally. Part of the task in interpreting the claim made is to imagine what the suggested relationship is like. Hence one of the skills required for statistical literacy is to translate a statement of association, for example, into a representational form to interpret and perhaps to question. To give students practice in this skill while still at school is important as it is not an easy task. Being dependent on having an actual set of data when creating a graph can make it difficult to imagine what to do with a verbal claim: the appropriate form of graph to use, the scale appropriate for reasonable values in the context, and the actual shape that should be associated with the claim.

The newspaper article shown in Fig. 3.6 presents an excellent opportunity to practice drawing a graph based on a claimed association, in this case "an almost perfect relationship between the increase in heart deaths and the increase in use of motor vehicles."[21] Adding to the complexity of interpreting the extract is the further mention of four other variables. The reader needs to focus on what is most important in characterizing the claim made in the headline. The two possibilities that arise for using this article in the classroom are to gain practice in expressing the claimed relationship in a graphical form and then to question the basis on which the claim is made. The second possibility is considered in Chapter 6.

Given the task "To draw and label a sketch of what one of Mr. Robinson's graphs might look like," the initial reactions of some students reflect their lack of experience with this type of task.

Family car is killing us, says Tasmanian researcher

Twenty years of research has convinced Mr Robinson that motoring is a health hazard. Mr Robinson has graphs which show quite dramatically an almost perfect relationship between the increase in heart deaths and the increase in use of motor vehicles. Similar relationships are shown to exist between lung cancer, leukaemia, stroke and diabetes.

FIG. 3.6. Newspaper article claiming association.

- I can't draw a graph because there are no numbers.

The belief that without numbers there can be no graphs needs to be undermined as early as possible and examples from the media are a good starting point. Other students who may have similar beliefs but do not express them, are likely instead to draw pictures such as those shown in Fig. 3.7. Whether these students do not know how to draw a graph at all, or an appropriate one, is unknown but they appear to be able to read and comprehend aspects of the context. Other students show that they know that the task is to draw a graph by providing some kind of framework like in Fig. 3.8. The students, however, show no appreciation of the context as do those who draw the representations in Fig. 3.7. In terms of the Statistical Literacy Hierarchy suggested in Chapter 1, these students do not appear yet to have achieved a first tier ability to deal with graphs in a basic fashion.

Quite a few students from the middle school level are willing to attempt the task and demonstrate the types of graphs to which they have been exposed, mainly line graphs, bar graphs, and pie graphs. Figure 3.9 contains rudimentary graphs with no suggestion of context or appropriate trend. These graphs are an indication of the difficulty of moving from the first tier of statistical literacy understanding to the second.

As students' attempts demonstrate greater sophistication there is increased recognition of context (e.g., in labeling of graphs) and of the need to show some kind of relationship (e.g., increasing to the right). The students drawing the graphs in Fig. 3.10 appear to struggle with sorting out the importance of the many variables mentioned in the article. This single ap-

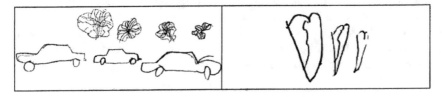

FIG. 3.7.   Representations related to context only.

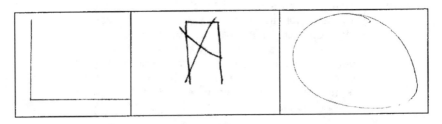

FIG. 3.8.   Graphical outlines with no content.

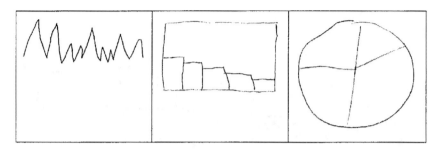

FIG. 3.9. Rudimentary graphs with no context or trend.

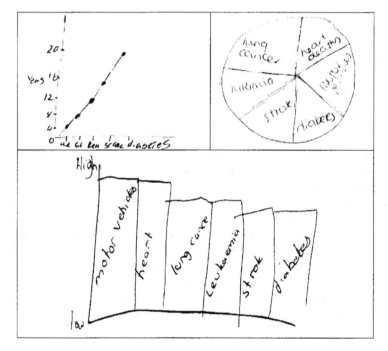

FIG. 3.10. Line, pie, and bar graphs with all variables but no relationship to claim.

preciation of the need for variables overrides the showing of a meaningful relationship; although one graph does include a line of increasing slope, it is not meaningful in terms of the labeling.

At the multistructural level are responses of students who appreciate the need to show an increasing relationship but who can only cope with one variable and time. Students who produce graphs such as those in Fig. 3.11 are nearly there in understanding and representing the context as expressed in the article.

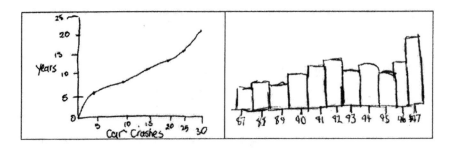

FIG. 3.11. Line and bar graphs with time and one other variable.

At the relational level, responses appreciate that time is significant in this task because it is what ties together the two variables, heart deaths and motor vehicle usage. For the students who realize this, there are several ways of drawing the required graph. Statisticians would be likely to suggest a scattergram with heart deaths and vehicle usage plotted on the two axes for a successive number of years. Some students also take this approach, and as is shown in Fig. 3.12, with more or less concern for detail of scale, and little regard for variation. Very few students indicate points lying along a trend line. Because these graphs do not mention time it has to be inferred that these students appreciate the part it plays. There are, however, other ways that students represent the relationship where time is explicitly shown. One way, as shown in Fig. 3.13, is to draw two graphs, one for each of heart deaths and vehicle usage, plotted against time, usually with time on the horizontal axis. Given the limited exposure to scattergrams for some students, this is a creative use of their resources if the time scales are the same. Previous experience is also shown in the use of bar graphs, as well as line graphs for the task. A variation on this approach is shown in Fig. 3.14, where students draw side-by-side bars for the two variables or two lines for the two variables showing a similar trend. Although many of the graphs could be

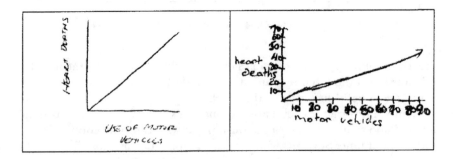

FIG. 3.12. Graphs showing a positive relationship as claimed in article.

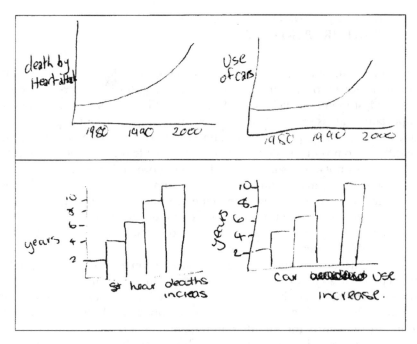

FIG. 3.13.   Side-by-side graphs based on time to show an association.

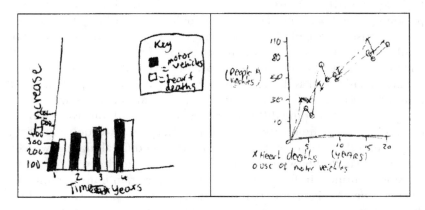

FIG. 3.14.   Side-by-side bars or "parallel" lines to show an association.

criticized for missing or unrealistic detail, as "sketches of graphs" they show quite sophisticated understanding of the relationship claimed in the context, as would be expected as a goal of the second tier of the Statistical Literacy Hierarchy. It is likely that about 1 in 10 of grade 6 students, up to 4 in 10 of grade 9 students, can produce graphs of these types.

3.5   SCALE, COORDINATES, PERCENT,
CIRCLE PROPERTIES, AXES

Issues linked to creating representations including scale in graphs are seen
in the previous two sections. When creating a graph with data provided or
collected, students virtually never forget to put in the scale. As accuracy is
important, scale is essential. When creating a graph without explicit data,
labeling and scale appear to be less important to students. Not only may it
be difficult to invent a scale for a nebulous variable but also there is nearly
an excuse for not doing so. In a situation like shown in Fig. 3.14, the realization that the scale may be different for two variables portrayed on the same
axis may not be obvious. Even remembering to label an axis with the variable recorded is an issue for some and reminders need to be made similar
to the cues used in Section 3.2: what would someone who just came into the
room be able to glean from your graph?

The connection of understanding of proportion and percent to graphing depends to some extent on the context of the task. Although some students in dealing with tasks like presented in Section 3.3, show class data, for
example eye color, in a bar chart, others attempt a pie chart. Creating and
adjusting pie charts for slightly different numbers of data values can be
challenging in working out the part–whole relationship to percent and the
slices of a pie. If, for example, a group of three wished to add their own data
to those on the 16 data cards in Section 3.3, questions like "What would one
person's percent be?" and "How many people [out of 16] fit into 31%?" are
likely to arise but are often not easily answered by those who have only recently learned about percent. Changing a "whole" pie from 16 people to 19,
and the consequent change of percent values, may not be intuitive at first.[22]
Practice at tasks such as these, however, helps create "aha" experiences that
consolidate wider understanding in the mathematics curriculum.

Significant among the difficulties students have with the association of
two variables and the creation of a scattergram is the relationship of the
single point that occurs on the graph to the two points along the two axes
that created it. Points, wherever found, are often considered as representing single entities. In fact this is true in a scattergram but the entity has
two defining characteristics that determine its location in a setting where
the trend over many entities is important. Following on from work with
"people graphs" for very young children to report frequency by having
them line up behind the characteristic with which they are associated,
people graphs also can be very helpful with older students to help distinguish two variables and their relationship to the point represented.[23]
Laying out the perpendicular axes, with the origin, on the floor or play-
ground, students can stand on a point, facing the origin, and extend their
arms at right angles to indicate the measurements on each axis that deter-

mine where they are standing on the scattergram. Anecdotally this has been found to be a very useful technique.

3.6 GRAPH INTERPRETATION: THE CASE OF BAR CHARTS

Bar charts, perhaps as derivatives of pictographs, are the graphs met most frequently by students in the elementary school years. As such they provide links to other basic aspects of the mathematics curriculum, particularly for younger children. One-to-one correspondence, addition, and subtraction, for example, are involved in the basic interpretation of bar charts, and judicious questioning can also focus discussion on issues related to the building of proto-statistical intuitions. Consider, for example, the bar graph in Fig. 3.15 that records how children in class arrive at school. This particular version of the bar graph, which is often a basis for this theme, has moveable bars that disappear in a slit at the base line.[24]

Asking students what they can tell from the graph allows for a display of the natural starting points for graph interpretation. Some students, often

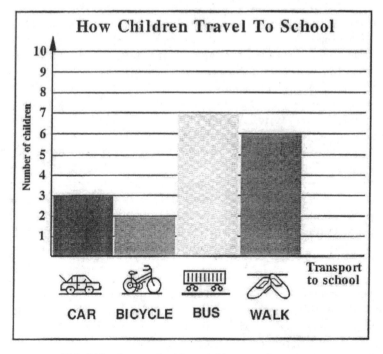

FIG. 3.15. Bar graph of how children travel to school.

younger, use their personal experience and imagination associated with the topic, rather than information in the graph to tell a story.

- That the car takes a long time, bicycle takes even a longer time, bus takes about not as long as you think, and walk probably takes a long time too.

Sometimes even a prompt to read from the graph, for example how many come to school by car, is not successful in focusing attention.

- Yes, I suppose so, I think, well I probably think that four people would fit in the car to go to school and one on the bicycle and ten on the bus and one person walking.

Other students glean relative information from the appearance of the graph without paying particular attention to the scale provided on the left side.

- Most children are taking the bus to school and that most children don't really ride to school that much. Most children take the bus instead of the other things. If the bus is full they would walk and if that is too tiring then they would take the car and the bikes. Not many children ride the bikes.

When asked specific questions about how many come by car, how many more walk than ride bicycles, and how many children are in the class, the use of scale becomes essential. As well, it is necessary to know the basic mathematical skills to apply in context. Most students by grade 3 can cope with these questions, appreciating that addition is appropriate for finding the total in the class and subtraction is appropriate for "how many more" questions. Accuracy varies, however, and should be judged separately from the conceptualization of the problems. Some students interpret a question like "how many in the class" as an opportunity to use their own experience and suggest numbers like 36 "as a bit of a guess," probably based on the size of their own classes. These are important points at which to distinguish between external contextual knowledge and information explicitly provided in a graph, reinforcing the importance of the context connection in Fig. 3.1. Graphs with the potential to change, as the one shown in Fig. 3.15, can also be used for prediction and beginning inference, and this is discussed in Chapter 6.

Beginning tasks to interpret bar graphs with young children lead to tasks with older students that are based on presentations in the media and the goal of critical interpretation that may detect errors. Classical examples in this regard are associated with cutting off the vertical scale in order to accentuate small differences. Other types of errors also occur and can be used to assist students in developing critical skills of graph interpretation. The

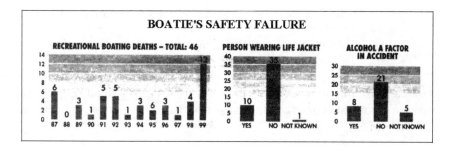

FIG. 3.16. Graphs part of a newspaper story reporting on boating deaths.
Used with permission of *The Mercury* newspaper, Hobart, Tasmania.

graph shown in Fig. 3.16, derived from local data on boating deaths, provides such an opportunity.[25] The challenge is to set a question for the task
that is not overly leading, such as "Can you find any errors in this graph?"
Particularly when students are beginning to appreciate the consideration of
the context as well as the representation, it is important to ask open-ended
questions. Quite a few students do not think to be suspicious of a media
presentation and focus on other issues that can form the foundation of productive class discussion. The trap for some teachers is to believe there is a
right answer to criticizing a graph (e.g., "the sum of the numbers in the
graph is 50, not 46 as reported in the header") and after finding it one
moves on to the next task. This misses the point in that there are many aspects of the graph to interpret and discussion should be broadly based. The
range of student responses to a task such as, "comment on any unusual features of the graph," illustrates how rich the experience can be.
    Some students find nothing unusual in the graphs.

• They all look okay to me.

Others make comments that are difficult to interpret.

• They are all bar.

The second statement could be a belief in an unusual feature or just an observation of the presentation. Some students take up the context but appear to believe that the task is to interpret the message for people in boats.

• They need to wear a life jacket.

Further, it is possible to make direct interpretations of the graphs without
mentioning anything unusual, at least not unusual by general knowledge
standards.

- Boating deaths happen because someone is not wearing a life jacket or drinking alcohol.
- People not wearing life jackets have a higher chance of drowning.

The graphs in Fig. 3.16 contain a great deal of information and for some students it is difficult to sort out salient features, leading to picking aspects that are not unusual from a graphing perspective or that are misrepresentations.

- That wearing a life jacket is the highest. Recreational boating deaths has the least.

Students may take the task as one to look for unusual aspects of specific graphing features.

- There are gaps between the yes, no, not known.

Some of these types of comments appear to reflect classroom experiences and norms.

- They have numbers on top of the bars. The Y and X axes are not labeled.
- The numbers on top of the bars make it easier. The way the numbers on the side go up in 2s and 5s.

This also extends to repeating high values on the graph.

- 12 people died in '99. 35 people weren't wearing life jackets.

The attempt to interpret high values in context, however, can lead to confusion, for example about the relationship of the information presented in the different graphs.

- The biggest failure has been the recreational boating deaths. The second was not wearing life jackets.

Many students are able to perceive the messages in the graphs appropriately and pick out at least one contextual feature that might be considered unusual.

- There are a lot of unknown deaths. It has increased through the year 99.
- The amount of deaths is the highest amount in the last 12 years. The majority were not wearing life jackets.
- That no one died in 1988 and in '99 12 people died. That alcohol does not cause many deaths.

Combining of context and graphing comments is also common for those who take the task seriously but are not searching for potential errors.

- No one died in 1988. There is no years under the horizontal axis in graph 2 and 3.
- All the numbers are confusing. And the fact that certain things were not known.

Of those who consider the context and the graphical features, some contrast features based on the variation shown in columns in the graphs. There is increasing complexity shown in how many elements of the graphs are used to make comments. Some focus on only one column at a time.

- I think 35 is a bit too high for no life jackets. The alcohol should be higher.
- Only 8 people in accidents were drinking alcohol. Only 10 were wearing life jackets.

Others compare two columns at a time.

- Suddenly you have 6 deaths in 1987, then none in 88.
- Alcohol factor "yes" are lower than "no." Person wearing life jackets "no" are bigger than "yes."

Some comments implicitly recognize all columns by making comments on the most frequently occurring columns.

- There were more deaths in '99 than in any others. Most of them weren't wearing life jackets.

Appreciation of variation is also shown in comments related to trends in the data.

- It shows that people don't like to wear life jackets. More deaths in boats have happened lately than in the older days.

A few students explicitly mention variational aspects of the graphs, showing an appreciation of the message conveyed and potentially unusual trends or changes.

- In some years there were heaps and they dropped to none. Most of them weren't wearing life jackets.
- In a range of just 11 years (88–99) there were a lot more deaths.
- I think it is strange how much the first graph varies. It is strange how the second 2 graphs weren't combined.

The scarcity of such responses, reflecting a consideration of all data presented, suggests a starting point for class discussion, apart from just finding mistakes.

Finally of interest are those few students who detect the errors as a part of their analyses.

- In 99 it doubled the next highest deaths. In 95 it says 6 but the bar graph only goes up to 2.
- The axes aren't labeled. The first 2 graphs both have 46 pieces of information (people). The 3rd graph has only 34.
- The first one says total: 46, but the graph shows 50 people.

Although these students find and discuss the features that were the reason for choosing the graph to show them, the other responses illustrate the increasingly sophisticated understanding of graph interpretation, and in particular the nature of the variation that is displayed in the graph. Much classroom discussion could be based on the actual issue of what seems important to one student not being considered important by another. A class debate could be a useful exercise.

A graph that links data representation more formally to other parts of the mathematics curriculum is shown in Fig. 3.17.[26] It is a very complex picto-bar graph containing information on discounts obtained for telephone calls for different lengths of time for a call. There are several unusual and potentially misleading aspects to the graph including the uneven vertical and horizontal scales, the truncated vertical axis, values appearing to decrease with height, and the decrease in linear height of the final phone (on the right) being four times as great as the actual percent discount. To calculate the actual price of calls of various lengths requires repeated interpretation of the graph and careful use of number skills, particularly related to percent. Just explaining the representation, however, is a complex task itself. As a test of statistical literacy the interpretation of this graph is one of the most complex that students could be expected to face when they leave school.

Two types of tasks can be used to explore student interpretation of the graph in Fig. 3.17. One focuses on its meaning in context and whether there is anything unusual about it, Parts (a) and (b). The second asks for calculation of the cost of calls of different lengths. This can be scaffolded in two stages to assist students and document levels of understanding. For example, if the standard rate is $1.00 per minute and one has already talked for 30 minutes, Part (c) asks, "How much would the next 10 minutes cost?" Then Part (d) asks, "How much did the first 30 minutes cost?"

For the general interpreting tasks, reading the meaning from the headline does not necessarily reflect understanding of its implications. A common attempt to paraphrase falls short of what actually happens.

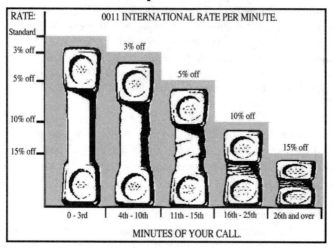

The longer your overseas call, the cheaper the rate.

RATE:
Standard
3% off
5% off
10% off
15% off

0011 INTERNATIONAL RATE PER MINUTE.

3% off
5% off
10% off
15% off

| 0 - 3rd | 4th - 10th | 11th - 15th | 16th - 25th | 26th and over |

MINUTES OF YOUR CALL.

(a) Explain the meaning of this graph.
(b) Is there anything unusual about it?
Suppose the standard rate is $1.00 for 1 minute.
You have already talked for 30 minutes.
(c) How much would the next 10 minutes cost?
(d) How much did the first 30 minutes of the phone call cost?

FIG. 3.17. Picto-bar graph on the cost of telephone calls of differing length. Used with permission of *The Mercury* newspaper, Hobart, Tasmania.

- The longer you are on the phone, the less you pay.

Students are often unaware of the impact of dropping a couple of words like "per minute." Other interpretations show varying degrees of awareness of what the graph is about.

- It tells you how many calls you make.
- It shows you when to ring; for example, ring 4–10 October and it's 3% off your normal phone call.

Lack of concentration on the axis labels is a common error and it is interesting that the "th" and coincidence of numbers suggests reading the scale as days of the month.

The next level of confusion of interpretation of the graph itself arises in deciding whether the discounts apply to the final length of the call or to different time intervals that make up the call.

- The longer you spend talking on the phone to an overseas person the cheaper your call becomes; for example, if you spend 26 minutes on the phone you get 15% off the cost of your call.
- Standard rate gets cheaper as the minutes pass, while talking on the phone; that is, first 3 mins. costs standard rate, next 1–6 mins costs 3% less than standard, next 1–5 mins costs 5% less than standard, next 1–10 mins costs 10% less than standard.

Moving from the appreciation of the context of the graph to critical analysis of its presentation, although there are several possibilities for criticizing the graph in Fig. 3.17, some students are taken with the unusual appearance of the graph.

- They used phone instead of a line graph.
- There's no way you can do that to a phone. In the last phone, the ear part of the phone wouldn't reach when you're talking in it.

For some students the conflict of decreasing bars seen in the graph, and an increasing cost expected over time, is too much to resolve. The concept of rate is not fully appreciated and instead associated with total cost.

- Yes, the longer you call it costs extra for lines etc. Why does it get cheaper?
- It should cost more the longer you talk but it doesn't. And if you talk for a great amount of time it might end up being a 100% off.

Other students, however, understand the use of rates and suggest the graph's potentially misleading appearance.

- Yes, at first glance you'd think you could stay on there all day and not pay anything, but you can't.
- The presentation is a bit silly (the phones). The untrained eye might think their call actually got cheaper!

The scale on the vertical axis attracts the attention of some students who are familiar with different graphing conventions.

- The highest rate of discount is at the bottom—the start is higher and it declines when graphs usually incline.
- It's not drawn to scale. It's kind of back to front. You'd think the big phone would represent big saving.

A step further is the recognition of the visual appearance of the graph in terms of the percent discount claimed and the proportion of the bar represented.

- On the graph, the 15% mark is around 1/4 of the original price. Once you reach 26 minutes the charge stays fixed.
- The size of the phone handle is not representative of what percent you get off.
- The prices only go down a fraction, and not a lot, like most people would think it was.

Finally, few students recognize the unusual and uneven use of scale for the width of bars on the horizontal axis. Overall this graph provides many opportunities for connections to be made with other parts of the mathematics curriculum, including rates, percent, proportion, and fractions. At this point the links can also concentrate on language and concept reinforcement.

To go further and calculate the price of a long international call becomes a structurally complex task requiring several numeracy skills. Asking a two-part question allows students to demonstrate partial understanding of the graph's meaning even if they cannot keep track of the overall task. This scaffolding, however, does not assist all students. Some appear to ignore the information in the graph altogether and answer $10 (or $40 with careless reading) to the question about the "next 10 minutes" and $30 to the question about the "first 30 minutes."

For the "next 10 minutes" question, Part (c), many students offer incomplete responses, such as 3% (based on misreading the graph), 15%, 85¢ (price for one minute) or $1.50 (the discount not the cost). The steps required for an appropriate response, either working with 85% at the start or subtracting $1.50 from $10.00 to obtain $8.50 at the end, illustrate basic calculations expected with percent in the middle school. There is no doubt that finding the required information in the graph adds to the complexity of the task, but this is what is required for statistically literate adults who wish to understand their telephone charges.

Calculating the cost of a call of 30 minutes duration, Part (d), based on a standard rate of $1.00 per minute, is a task requiring repeated steps of the above type, an awareness of the different time intervals for which the rates apply, and accurate addition of the intermediate answers. Even for students who understand the requirements of the task, computational errors are common. One difficulty is the systematic misreading of interval lengths by subtraction yielding all time intervals one minute less than the correct value. This results in a cost of $23.12 for the 30-minute call, rather than the correct cost of $27.79. By the end of high school around 10% of students without specific instruction can be expected to solve a task like this, including those with small technical errors. As an authentic task from the media it provides an excellent challenge to the critical literacy skills of students without expecting numerical skills beyond the mathematics curriculum. It illustrates many of the connections in Fig. 3.1.

3.7 GRAPH INTERPRETATION:
THE CASE OF PIE CHARTS

The pie chart is a commonly used graph in the media because it gives a ready view of parts of the whole and their relative sizes. The connection of pie chart understanding to that of part–whole in fractions and percents elsewhere in the mathematics curriculum was noted in Section 3.5. Although in some quarters recommendations for creating pie charts have diminished due to the complex requirements related to ratio, proportion, and calculations based on 360° in a circle, the continual presentation of pie charts in the public media means that interpreting them is a must, even if the technical skills for creating them are missing. This requires the fundamental link to part–whole and percent understanding.

The pie chart shown in Fig. 3.18 provides an excellent opportunity for students to show their part–whole understanding of percent and how it applies to the interpretation of pie charts in context.[27] In terms of the Statistical Literacy Hierarchy described in Chapter 1, the first task is to gain an appreciation for the context of the message in the graph. The second task is to question the make-up of the graph, which in fact purports to represent 128.5% of the grocery market shares.

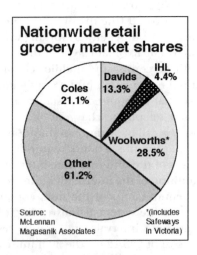

FIG. 3.18. Authentic pie chart from a media source.

Levels of interpretation of what the pie graph is about range in their structural complexity reflecting increasing appreciation of the context. Some students cannot begin to engage with the item when asked for its meaning.

- Don't know.
- I was absent when we learned pie graphs.

A few students appreciate that the heading for the representation reflects what it is about.

- It shows Nation wide retail grocery market shares.

Without further discussion, however, it is difficult to know if students can further integrate the heading with the rest of the information provided. Many students offer a single facet of the graph in explaining its meaning.

- I think it is about all of the people who have taken out shares.
- It means how many people go there.
- How much money is being made.

These responses illustrate how important the first links to context can be in interpreting a graph. The first misunderstands the use of the word *share*. The second equates market share with number of shoppers and appears to translate percent to a number ("how many"). The third appreciates the overall context but again emphasizes quantity rather than percent and does not go on to consider relative information about different groups. Other responses indicate more appreciation without detail.

- It says how well those shops are selling.
- It tells us what % they have sold.

Detail may be provided in a step-wise fashion, such as,

- That Coles got 21.1%, Davids 13.3%, . . .

or in an integrated way, such as,

- It shows who out of 5 markets has the most share of the grocery market.

In noting unusual features of the graph, again several levels of appreciation are revealed in student responses. Some students do not focus on the statistical nature of the message but on details that reveal what they notice and hence things to discuss in the classroom in the context of deciding what is important.

- It's cut into all different shapes.
- It doesn't say what "Other" shops are.
- They are all decimal like 21.2, 13.3, 28.5, 61.2.
- The black part.
- I can't figure out why Woolworths have a star and the rest don't.

The variety in these responses not only indicates the necessity to develop skills in separating important from irrelevant issues, but also shows students how their own constructions of graphs should avoid misleading trivia. At a higher level are responses that focus on the statistical message but miss the main point.

- Coles is one of the smallest market shares.
- The heading doesn't fit in.
- Other is bigger than the rest.

The final response is the most frequently made suggestion of this type. The statistically inappropriate, and hence unusual feature of the graph is noted by students in two ways.

- Where it has Other, it says 61.2% and the percentage of that section on the pie is less than 50%.
- The percentages add up to 128.5. They should equal 100!!

The first answer shows good connections with the part–whole nature of percent and the visual appearance of the pie chart, whereas the second focuses directly on the issue of the whole as 100%. Although the error in this graph is striking to most mathematics teachers it is important that, as a task, the interpretation of the overall graph is more than an addition problem to be given a "right–wrong" assessment. As illustrated here, many issues arise that warrant classroom discussion.

Although most media errors in pie charts occur on the "high" side, occasionally examples appear that add to less than 100%, such as the graph shown in Fig. 3.19 representing causes of deaths that adds to 72.51%.[28] Even for students who have been recently taught how to create their own pie charts and who can explain the process, it is likely that only about a third will pick up the error in this graph without first having experience in media contexts.[29] It appears essential to begin linking pie charts to social contexts and media examples, even good ones, as soon as they are introduced as a technique for representing data in the classroom.

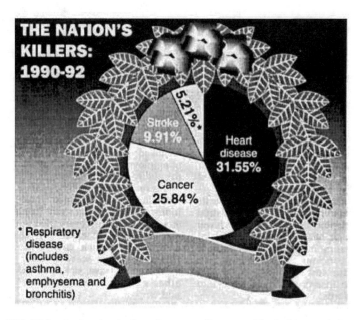

THE NATION'S KILLERS: 1990-92

Stroke 9.91%

5.21%*

Heart disease 31.55%

Cancer 25.84%

* Respiratory disease (includes asthma, emphysema and bronchitis)

FIG. 3.19. Authentic pie chart from a media source. Used with permission of *The Age* newspaper, Melbourne.

3.8 GRAPH INTERPRETATION: THE CASE OF STACKED DOT PLOTS

If the critical interpretation of graphs that appear in the media is a goal of statistical literacy when students leave school, what are some starting points to make them aware of the issues involved? One approach is to begin with graphs that are relatively easy to understand and create for oneself. An example is the stacked dot plot, which in recent years has been introduced in many curriculum materials and documents.[30] A transition between the pictograph and the bar graph or histogram, the stacking of dots or Xs, one for each observed value on the horizontal scale, eliminates the need for a vertical scale. Students can hence concentrate on the horizontal scale with a visual impression of the frequency distribution associated with a data set.

Tasks designed to engage students in interpretation of stacked dot plots can not only consider the standard form of the plot but also foster students' emerging critical skills in judging appropriate representations. The stacked dot plot in Fig. 3.20 reports on the number of years that the families of students in a class had lived in their town.[31] There are various levels of complexity that are observed in student interpretation of graphs such as this: from misunderstanding, to reading specific values, to contrasting values, to observing overall relationships among the data. The stacked dot plot in Fig.

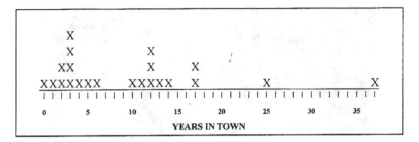

FIG. 3.20.   Scaled stacked dot plot of how many years families in a class have lived in their town.

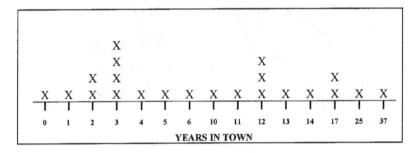

FIG. 3.21.   Unscaled stacked dot plot of how many years families in a class have lived in their town.

3.21 is a variation on the one in Fig. 3.20, in which the horizontal scale only contains values that actually occur in the data set. Although including all of the values the visual appearance of the distribution is quite different. Asking students to compare and contrast the two plots can provide a foundation for critical thinking that can later be applied to graphs with more subtle forms of bias.[32]

When asked what they can tell by looking at the two graphs, there is not very much difference in the comments made by students for the two representations. There are some who misinterpret the message, either because the frequencies portrayed by the Xs are confused with the numbers on the horizontal scale, or because the label is ignored.

- 3 is the biggest family. [Fig. 3.21]
- The families were big but as time went on they went down. [Fig. 3.20]
- Most people have lived here for 1 year. [Fig. 3.21]

At the next level many students are able to report accurately on at least one aspect of the data represented in the individual stacks of Xs.

- One person has not lived in the town for a year. [Fig. 3.21]
- Someone stayed there for 10 years. And someone stayed there for 1 year. [Fig. 3.20]
- 12 years has one less than 3 years. [Fig. 3.21]

The last comment, although an accurate reading of the Xs and label, does not connect the information to the context of families living in the town. This is an important point for discussion when interpreting a graph.

Summarizing the information from more than one stack of Xs may focus on the highest frequency or most extreme values.

- A lot of people were here 3 years. [Fig. 3.21]
- Not many people lived here long. [Fig. 3.20]

Summarizing may also take into account many values and the shape of the distribution.

- More families lived in their town around the 5/4 year mark. But 10 to 15 years is quite popular. [Fig. 3.20]
- Most of the population has lived in the town for 0–6 years. [Fig. 3.20]
- Lots of people have moved in over the last few years. [Fig. 3.20]
- Most people have resided there for less than 13 years. [Fig. 3.21]

The summary statements that consider clumps or trends are also more likely to include speculation related to the context.

- They came in 2 groups. Maybe when someone said it was a great town to live in. [Fig. 3.20]
- Probably a "boom" of population. Populations increase dramatically in a short period of time, then a drought. [Fig. 3.20]
- I can tell it is a fairly new town for most people especially since only two people have been there for over 20 years. [Fig. 3.20]

Although interpretations for the two plots are similar, there is a tendency for more students to comment on clusters when describing the appropriately scaled plot. Given the visual appearance of the plot, this is not a surprising outcome, but should be a feature of classroom discussion. If students want to tell a story about clusters of data then appropriate scaling is necessary.

When students are asked to describe differences between the two plots, many do not realize that the same data are represented in each.

- Less people live in their town in [Fig. 3.20] than [Fig. 3.21].

- [Fig. 3.21] shows you more into the future by 2 years.

Quite a few students focus on the general aesthetic appearance or personal preference with little justification.

- [Fig. 3.20] is a lot harder to read than [Fig. 3.21].
- [Fig. 3.20] is in groups. [Fig. 3.21] is spread out.

Some students also focus more explicitly on the layout.

- [Fig. 3.20] went up in 5s. [Fig. 3.21] missed out numbers in between.
- [Fig. 3.20] was easier to tell how long the majority had lived in the town which was 0–5 because it counted in 5s.

A few students acknowledge that the data are the same only the scales are different.

- There is no difference . . . except that [Fig. 3.20] shows the spaces whereas [Fig. 3.21] doesn't.
- [Fig. 3.21] skips the years out that aren't being used. Both graphs show the same information (not a difference).

When further asked which plot tells the story better, students usually display one of four levels of appreciation. Many cannot make up their minds or give idiosyncratic reasons. Roughly equal proportions of students choose each plot as better saying it is "easier" to read or giving a reason based on misreading the graph. In these transitional cases, choosing Fig. 3.21 is considered less statistically appropriate than choosing Fig. 3.20. Fewer students choose Fig. 3.20 accompanied by statistically appropriate reasoning.

- [Fig. 3.20] because [it] is more visual and you can notice the time difference in how long each family has been there more precisely.

In class discussion students may be reluctant to concede that the plot in Fig. 3.21 is "wrong." Being "right" or "wrong" is not the issue here and certainly Fig. 3.21 conveys exactly the same information. The issue about "how well it tells the story" is what statistics is about and helping students to appreciate that the plot in Fig. 3.20 is statistically appropriate because it tells the story better is the goal of considering tasks like this one. It is likely that general experience with graphs over the middle school years assists students in appreciating the scaled graph *if* they are presented with it first for consideration.[33]

3.9   DATA REPRESENTATION AND BIAS

Bias in graphs has been mentioned throughout the sections on graph interpretation. This is natural in that the aim of the school curriculum is for students not only to create their own representations in an unbiased fashion
but also to be sufficiently critical thinkers able to detect bias in the graphs
of others. Opportunities sometimes arise in the classroom, however, to discuss bias if it occurs as part of student activities. Particularly when students
with limited previous experience are asked to create representations, bias
may inadvertently creep in. Such a situation is likely to arise when tasks like
the activity based on 16 data cards introduced in Section 3.3 are used.

In attempting to represent associations found or believed to exist among
several variables, it may be expedient to simplify a data set, say by representing it by its largest value. This is the procedure followed in the bar graph in
Fig. 3.22, where the largest number of fast food meals per week is plotted

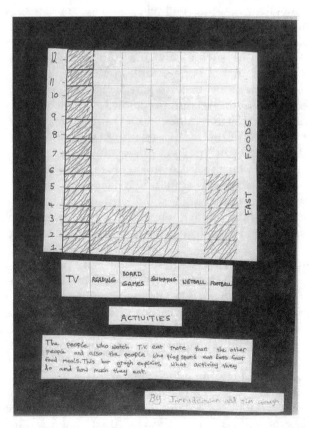

FIG. 3.22.   Biased bar graph created for fast food consumption and favorite
activity.

for each of the favorite activities of the 16 students in the data set (cf. Appendix to Chapter 3).[34] The statement accompanying the graph, however, does not indicate how the representative values were selected for each group and instead makes the claim, "The people who watch TV eat more than the other people and also the people who play sport eat less fast food meals." Even at the upper elementary level, students should be able to discuss the difficulties inherent in such representations and suggest alternatives. Such events also provide the opportunity and motivation to move to media examples to raise student awareness that inaccurate representations, whether inadvertent or on purpose, are common in daily social settings.

3.10   IMPLICATIONS AND RECOMMENDATIONS

Data representation is one of the essential components of statistical investigations. It is not the beginning but builds upon appropriate data collection and sampling. It then leads to a data reduction phase of investigations. Movement in this direction takes place when summary statements begin to be made about graphs, such as noticing clumps and spread. The many other connections shown in Fig. 3.1 indicate that graphing both uses and reinforces many other skills that are part of the mathematics curriculum. The dual roles of creation and interpretation are essential and again can be developed in such a way to reinforce both. To have created graphs should make students aware of the components to observe in graphs they interpret. To judge critically the graphs of others should provide students with a background against which to create their own meaningful representations. Keeping in mind the context within which data representation takes place and where bias can occur naturally should influence the quality of the output obtained. Returning to the quote at the beginning of this chapter, the development of "good graphical lie detectors" is a goal of the statistics curriculum.[35]

The contribution that data representation makes to the overall goal of building statistical literacy can be seen with reference to the three-tiered hierarchy introduced in Chapter 1. The initial building of first tier skills related to creating graphs takes place over many years of schooling and as noted in earlier sections of this chapter employs many other topics in the mathematics curriculum. The increasing structural complexity, in moving from pictographs, to stacked dot plots, to bar graphs and histograms, to time series graphs and pie graphs, to scattergrams of two variables, requires much planning on the part of teachers and much discussion in the classroom. In pictographs or stacked dot plots the frequencies are "countable." In histograms the scale is required to read the frequencies. In pie graphs parts of the whole tell the story, usually in percent or fraction form. Time series graphs provide a transition from one-variable to two-variable representations. In many ways scattergrams are the most difficult as students need to make the connection of one point with two coordinates, the two coordinates representing two variables measured on the single entity that is represented by the point. It is quite clear that mastering all aspects of graphing is not possible before introducing the second and third tier of the statistical literacy hierarchy. What is needed is an appreciation of the type of graph that is going to be placed in context.

Another important feature in developing graphing skills is giving students opportunities to create their own graphs, without rigid rules. Often using starting points that do not involve paper-and-pencil, for example involving linking blocks or people graphs, can create more meaningful connections for students than filling in boxes on a grid of a worksheet. Graphs such as those in Figs. 3.5(a) and (c) and 3.13 indicate that students can make meaningful representations without following exactly the conventions that statisticians would use. Even the occasional creation of bias, as shown in Fig. 3.22, can be useful both for the creator and for other members of the class, in highlighting the meaning of bias and how to avoid it. The pride of ownership of graphs that students create for themselves is usually obvious in the summaries they write or present orally, and this motivational issue is likely to be very important as students are encouraged to progress to the higher tiers of statistical literacy.

Graphs without context cease to be interesting very quickly. That is one of the great features of pictographs—they are bound to context by their very nature. Their introduction in early childhood to document stories in the classroom, such as favorite fruit or number of siblings, is excellent for building an expectation for the purpose of graphing throughout school. It is unfortunate when sometimes techniques of graphing are divorced too long from context. Being involved in classroom investigations that require all components of the data handling curriculum again creates connections with context and motivation for learning particular graphing techniques when they are necessary. Including activities that are based on media reports where both context and graphical representations must be understood to make sense of the message is an essential part of building second tier skills. In many cases these activities may end up being cross-curricular involving scientific or social understanding.

Again as for sampling, moving into the third tier of the hierarchy requires enough understanding of context and representational forms to be able to start questioning claims made, either by classmates or in the media. A detective mentality, which questions or looks critically at every graph until it is fathomed, is the goal. Working with a software package that creates whatever the user tells it may assist learners in sorting out the useful representations from the rubbish. This must be done with some critical skills, however, as graphics packages are notorious for producing beautiful graphs that are meaningless.

In an era when software packages are becoming ever more user friendly and adapted for use by younger and younger children, a cautionary note must be sounded. Students still need experience creating graphs of their own. There are two main reasons for this. Throughout the elementary and middle school years students should be encouraged to create their own representations to tell the stories of their data. Some of these will be unconventional but will do a good job. Links can usually be made from these early attempts to more conventional forms and the experience can be very motivating. Only being exposed to forms on a computer screen can be limiting. The second reason is that students need practice at linking meaning to the symbols used in graphing and practice at labeling and deciding on scale (where appropriate). This is more quickly and thoroughly reinforced by doing it, by making graphs. This is not to say students should always be forced to draw their own graphs. Balance is the important ingredient and this is probably best judged by a teacher who observes the class carefully to judge readiness.

Two other types of graph deserve mention because of their growing popularity. First is the stem-and-leaf plot. This plot is a transition between a table and a graph, presenting numbers visually to tell a story. It is closely linked to an understanding of the place value number system and effective use of the plot depends on judgments about how the distribution of the data is reflected in the "places" of the numbers in the data set. The stem of the plot reflects the places for the overall range of the data and the leaves reflect the detailed variation in the place or places to the right. Elementary examples are often based on data sets with values between 0 and 100 where the stem is the tens digit and the leaf is the units digit. Authentic data sets however do not often fit this model and it is necessary to plan carefully how to define the stem to obtain a reasonable presentation of the distribution. For introductory work teachers should make the decisions and gradually students develop this skill. The reinforcement of place value understanding from elsewhere in the mathematics curriculum is an important bonus and the stem-and-leaf plot can be introduced to young children as soon as they are working with place value.[36]

The link between stem-and-leaf plots and stacked dot plots is close, with the former based on separation of data into discrete bundles whereas the latter uses a continuous number line scale. Turning a vertical stem-and-leaf plot 90° so that its stems are on the horizontal axis makes it possible to compare and contrast the two representations. This is a good exercise to explore student understanding of the purposes of the two representations.

The other type of representation gaining popularity is in fact a transition from a graph as the most complete detailed depiction of the data set to a statistic that summarizes or reduces the data to a single value. The box-and-whisker plot is based on five significant values in an ordered data set: the lowest, the highest, the middle, the middle of the lower half, and the middle of the upper half. These five markers divide the data sets into four equal parts by frequency.[37] The interesting feature of a box-and-whisker plot is the "shape" of these parts in relation to the overall scale and limits of the data sets. The box surrounds the middle half of the data with the center marked and the whiskers extend from either end of the box to the extremes values in the set (details of the definition of whiskers vary but are not of concern here). The "smaller" the box, or half of a box, in relation to other parts of the plot, the greater the density of the data points within it. This inverse relationship is another important link to other areas of difficulty for students in the mathematics curriculum. Many experiences and much discussion are necessary to reinforce understanding. As box-and-whisker plots represent a transition from a graphical representation to a summary statistic, the five numbers tell much, but not all, about the distribution of values in a data set. The middle number is the median, which is one of the averages discussed in the next chapter, whereas the other four numbers document the spread.

Although stem-and-leaf and box-and-whisker plots are becoming more common in schools, and particularly the latter in reporting testing outcomes to students, they are not yet popular in the public media. Their links to statistical literacy are hence more tenuous to this point. Over time however they will undoubtedly become popular and students will need to be aware of the usual pitfalls of using them: exaggerating scale or choosing "places" for stems and leaves to make the data appear to conform to a bias of the presenter.

Working among various graphical forms with students provides links among skills and mathematical concepts related to graphing. It also helps to develop appreciation for which types of graph assist in displaying the message to be told. Anecdotal evidence of working with teachers who have little experience with stacked dot plots or box-and-whisker plots suggests that they appreciate the ease of getting data directly and quickly into a visual form with the stacked dot plot without having to worry about many graphing skills. Then using this representation as a way of concretely introducing the box-and-whisker plot helps to reinforce ideas of middle without having to use a complex formula for finding the median. The middle of the data can be found by counting Xs on the stacked dot plot and similarly the middles of the lower and upper halves can be found by counting. This is also a concrete link to quartiles.

The values in the data set in Fig. 3.23 are the right foot lengths in centimeters of 20 people. Counting 10 values from either end shows that the middle of the data set is between 25 and 26 cm, or 25.5 cm. In either the

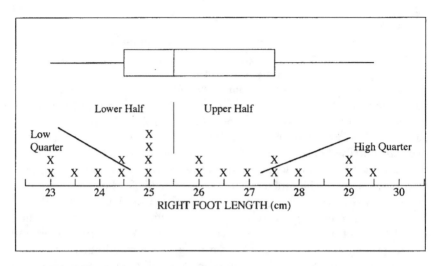

FIG. 3.23. Stacked dot plot and the creation of an associated box-and-whisker plot.

upper or lower half of the data set, the fifth value from either side is the same, due to repeated data points. Hence the lower quartile of the data set is 24.5 and the upper quartile is 27.5. In the case of this data set there are an even number of values overall and in each half, presenting the opportunity to discuss how to determine the middle when it is not a single value in the data set. Marking these values as shown in Fig. 3.23 dramatically displays the four quarters of the data set and the middle half can be pointed out and drawn in as a rectangle, either above the writing as shown or by erasing the words first. Having the box-and-whisker plot drawing exactly above the stacked dot plot reinforces the five values used in creating it and shows the features of the original data set that are still available in the box plot. A major advantage of this double representation is the opportunity to discuss the density of values in the stacked dot plot corresponding to the areas in the box and the length of the whiskers. The idea of the *middle half* of the data set is also important since the box is created by first considering the upper and lower halves of the data set. This type of representation is relatively easy for teachers to create on a white board and also for students to reproduce if desired.

While waiting for the newer representations to appear in the media, there are still many opportunities to develop critical statistical literacy skills using bar graphs that appear in newspapers.[38] Although probably the most common misleading feature of graphs in newspapers is the cutting off of the vertical scale in order to make variation in height appear as large as possible,[39] the two graphs in Fig. 3.24 are good to use with students from the

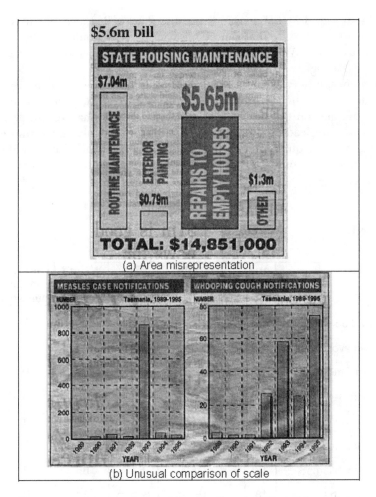

FIG. 3.24.   Graphs from the newspaper for discussion. Used with permission
of *The Mercury* newspaper, Hobart, Tasmania.

upper elementary level. Questions such as the first two asked for the telephone graph in Fig. 3.17 could be used, focusing on meaning and unusual
features. In the graph in Fig. 3.24(a),[40] besides noting informally the visual
appearance of the double-width bar, links can be made to ratio, proportion, and part–whole relationships by working out the areas of the rectan-
gles, summing them, and comparing the fraction of the area represented in
each bar with the fraction of the money involved. This issue of graphical in-
tegrity is dealt with in considerable detail and with many examples by Edward Tufte;[41] it is difficult to go beyond his fascinating account. The two

graphs in Fig. 3.24(b)[42] are individually quite well drawn but it is their placement side-by-side that can be misleading. Why would they have been placed like this? What message is the article stressing about measles and whooping cough?

Students get very excited in discussing graphs such as those in Fig. 3.24, and can be motivated to look for examples of their own, in newspapers, on television, and on the internet. When a student, of whatever grade level, brings me a misleading or erroneous graph from the media, I know we are making progress on the third tier objective of the Statistical Literacy Hierarchy, critical questioning. Edward Tufte would say that the lie detectors are in place.

APPENDIX

Name	Age	Favorite Activity	Eye Color	Weight (kg)	Fast food meals per week
David Jones	8	TV	Blue	30	7
Brian Wong	9	Football	Green	26	1
John Smith	10	Football	Green	29	0
Adam Henderson	12	Football	Blue	45	5
Andrew Williams	14	TV	Blue	60	10
Peter Cooper	16	Board games	Green	54	2
Scott Williams	17	TV	Blue	65	8
Simon Khan	18	TV	Brown	74	12
Rosemary Black	8	Netball	Brown	24	0
Jennifer Rado	9	Board games	Green	33	4
Anna Smith	11	Board games	Brown	32	1
Kathy Roberts	12	Netball	Brown	32	0
Mary Minski	13	Reading	Green	55	3
Dorothy Myers	15	Swimming	Blue	50	2
Sally Moore	17	Reading	Brown	56	1
Janelle MacDonald	18	Reading	Blue	66	4

ENDNOTES

1. Tufte (1983, p. 53).
2. Palmer & Krathwohl (1921, Chapter X).
3. National Council of Teachers of Mathematics (2000, p. 163).
4. Australian Education Council (1991, 1994a); Department for Education (England and Wales) (1995); Ministry of Education (1992); National Council of Teachers of Mathematics (1989, 2000).
5. Bereska, Bolster, Bolster, & Scheaffer (1998, 1999); National Council of Teachers of Mathematics (2000).
6. Konold & Higgins (2002); Konold, Robinson, Khalil, Pollatsek, Well, Wing, & Mayr (2002).
7. Leinhardt, Zaslavsky, & Stein (1990).
8. Curcio (1987, 1989).
9. Bright & Friel (1998); Friel, Bright, & Curcio (1997); Friel, Curcio, & Bright (2001).
10. Beichner (1994); Brasell & Rowe (1993); Roth & McGinn (1997).
11. Bryant & Somerville (1986); Wainer & Velleman (2001).
12. Pereira-Mendoza (1995); Pereira-Mendoza & Mellor (1991).
13. Ross & Cousins (1993a, 1993b).
14. Konold & Higgins (2002, 2003); Konold, Robinson, Khalil, Pollatsek, Well, Wing, & Mayr (2002).
15. Watson & Moritz (2001a).
16. Square brackets surround questions from the interviewer or additional nonverbal information; [. . .] indicates omitted comments and . . . indicates a pause by the student.
17. National Council of Teachers of Mathematics, *Standards* (1989).
18. Australian Education Council (1991); National Council of Teachers of Mathematics, *Principles and Standards* (2000).
19. Chick & Watson (2001); Watson & Callingham (1997); Watson, Collis, Callingham, & Moritz (1995).
20. Chick & Watson (2002).
21. Crawford (1991); Watson (2000b).
22. Chick & Watson (2002).
23. O'Keefe (1997).
24. Watson & Moritz (1999c).
25. Haley (2000); Watson & Chick (2004).
26. "The longer your overseas call" (1993); Moritz & Watson (1997a).
27. Watson (1997a); Webb, O'Meara, & Brown (1993).
28. Farouque (1994).
29. Watson (1999).
30. Bereska, Bolster, Bolster, & Scheaffer (1998, 1999); National Council of Teachers of Mathematics (2000).
31. Konold & Higgins (2002).

32. Watson & Kelly (2002d).
33. Watson & Kelly (2002d).
34. Watson & Callingham (1997).
35. Tufte (1983).
36. Dunkels (1988).
37. Dossey, Giordano, McCrone, & Weir (2002); Landwehr, Swift, & Watkins (1987).
38. *Mercury* Web site—Numeracy in the News: ink.news.com.au/mercury/mathguys/mercindx.htm
39. Rosato (2002).
40. De Cesare (1996).
41. Tufte (1983, Chapter 2).
42. Rose (1994).

4

Average—What Does It Tell Us?

It is difficult to understand why statisticians commonly limit their inquiries to Averages, and do not revel in more comprehensive views. Their souls seem as dull to the charm of variety as that of the native of one of our flat English counties, whose retrospect of Switzerland was that, if its mountains could be thrown into its lakes, two nuisances would be got rid of at once.[1]

4.1 BACKGROUND

Francis Galton made this observation at the turn of the 20th century and his criticism continued to be appropriate in many mathematics classrooms throughout the century. What he could not foresee, however, was the appropriation of the term *average* by the general populace in a wide range of social contexts to describe a variety of conditions related to typicality.

In the English language the word *average* has many connotations, from the colloquial "mediocre" to the mean algorithms taught in mathematics classrooms, both arithmetic and geometric. The association of average with the arithmetic mean by most high school mathematics teachers probably reflects their backgrounds and the history of the mean in the curriculum, but it is unlikely to reflect the everyday connections made by their students. The arithmetic mean has had a checkered history that has left it by default as the major summary statistic employed at the school level. For that reason, average is the focus of attention in the chapter on the data reduction phase of the statistical investigation process. This does not mean that other ideas for reducing the complexity of data are not relevant and some of these are considered.

Historically the arithmetic mean has probably been associated with the mathematics curriculum longer than any other idea or tool used by statisticians. In the late 19th century, problems were being set for students that involved weighted means and working the standard algorithm backward.[2] These were typically artificial word problems based on a few values and contexts such as the price of eggs or daily school attendance. All through the 20th century the arithmetic mean was a topic covered in arithmetic and algebra books for school students.[3] It was not until the end of the 20th century that the mode and median were introduced into the school mathematics curriculum in conjunction with the data handling curriculum.[4] This history probably explains why the mean is still the focus of many teachers in the classroom—it is the measure with which they are most familiar. Despite moves to non-parametric statistics, the mean is also still the most commonly used statistic overall in science and society. The mode is the most controversial of the three measures with some statisticians claiming it is not a measure of central tendency.[5] David Moore and George McCabe for example, do not mention the mode in their well known *Introduction to the Practice of Statistics*.[6]

There has been more research on understanding of the arithmetic mean than other topics in the data handling curriculum, except perhaps for understanding of graphical representations. It began at the college level with interest in the difficulty of students in solving weighted mean problems.[7] Various researchers then began to look more broadly at student understanding at the high school level, considering representativeness, location, expectation, mathematical properties (e.g., the sum of deviations from the mean is zero), and abstract statistical properties (e.g., the average may have no counterpart in physical reality).[8] Others have found that whereas students from the elementary level upward have increasing facility with the algorithm for the arithmetic mean, they cannot use it to solve an open-ended task or do not consider it as a tool in a situation such as comparing two groups.[9] Very little research has specifically considered ideas associated with the median or mode but Jan Mokros and Susan Jo Russell for example found "middle" and "most" ideas suggested by students in their study when asking more generally about average,[10] as is seen in some of the responses in this chapter.

As the mathematics curriculum expands to include data handling and all aspects of statistical investigations, the concept of average needs to be broadened and linked to other relevant components of the investigation process, as shown in Fig. 4.1. The focus on the algorithm for the arithmetic mean to produce a correct answer for every "average" problem needs to be replaced with a focus on context to make meaningful summary comments

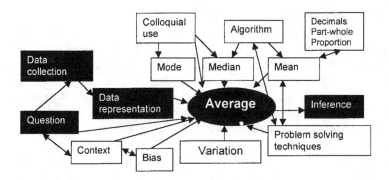

FIG. 4.1. Links among the ideas and statistical elements associated with average.

about data sets using appropriate measures of middle. In particular, average, in whichever guise, as a reflection of central tendency needs to be related to spread and variation within data. In terms of the contribution made to statistical literacy by the idea of average, the three measures of mean, median, and mode are all important. The term *average*, however, is sometimes presented in the media in a way that makes it difficult to tell which statistic is being used as a measure. On one hand the arithmetic mean may be assumed to be the "average" when it is not. Its susceptibility to extreme values may make it inappropriate but being hidden behind the term "average" makes it difficult to tell whether the mean has been used or not. On the other hand the presentation of an average to two decimal places is usually a clue to the average being the mean.[11] Whether the two decimal places are meaningful in the context may be another matter entirely. Although the poor relation in some ways, the mode, often defined and then forgotten in the middle school years, is frequently used in the media to describe typical behavior when percents are involved. A claim that golf is the most popular sport in the country is definitely based on the mode.[12] The median is very likely to be the average reported when government figures are produced about human populations.[13] These contexts provide good examples for discussion of the shape of distributions and outliers, and hence why the median is often the appropriate statistic to use.

The following sections of this chapter use examples of students' responses to tasks involving averages to highlight the development taking place during the school years and the connections that assist in broadening the data reduction phase of statistical investigations. Because *average* is a term like *sample* that has uses outside of statistics, it is important for teachers to know what students are thinking at the beginning of any classroom discussion on the topic. The issue of colloquial usage in relation to all three measures of central tendency is the focus of Section 4.2 and again many ideas that teachers take for granted may not be obvious to their students. This is even true as averages begin to be used in the contexts appropriate to statistical investigations, as is seen in Section 4.3, for example with links to decimal number understanding. Section 4.4 focuses on the particular difficulty of bias. The traditional link of the arithmetic mean to problem solving based on working the algorithm backward and working with weighted means is the focus of Section 4.5, with note taken of the connection to proportional reasoning more generally. As inference is usually the next stage in a statistical investigation following data reduction using averages, this link is explored in Section 4.6. The final section relates the development of understanding to the Statistical Literacy Hierarchy introduced in Chapter 1 and suggests media-based activities for linking context to conceptual understanding.

4.2   AVERAGE: WHAT DOES IT MEAN?

The starting point for considering the development of understanding associated with the connections in Fig. 4.1 is in the meaning of the word average itself. There are two ways of exploring the meaning with students. One is to ask directly what the word means.[14] Another is to relate a question more personally to the child, asking for example, "If someone said you were 'average', what would it mean?"[15] The second approach allows students more freedom to explain the colloquial contexts within which they are familiar with the term. It may not, however, encourage optimal responses from some students in terms of their overall understanding in a variety of contexts. For younger students it is less intimidating. The links among many of the elements in Fig. 4.1 are seen in the responses of students.

There are likely to be three levels of response to a personalized form of the question about average. At the prestructural level there is no clear indication of a meaning for the term. Some students are unfamiliar with the term and say so.

- I have heard of it but I don't know what it means.

Some have the term confused with another meaning.

- You are not the best friend for me.

Others recall a context where the word is used but cannot explain its meaning any further.

- You are average height or average age.

At the unistructural level responses reflect a single idea or synonym for the term average. These colloquial phrases are descriptive in nature not suggesting any type of measurement.

- That you were okay.
- I am a normal, everyday person.
- Common.
- The same as everyone else.

Although the last description suggests a relationship with a larger group, the idea of sameness with *everyone* reflects homogeneity rather than variation in representation.

More complex responses elaborate beyond a single general idea to describe how the average relates to a data set of which the students are a part or sometimes to a method for obtaining the average from the data set. These multistructural characterizations can be associated with ideas related to any of the three measures—mode, median, or mean—although the words themselves are not used. With respect to the idea of mode, the following responses differ from the last one in the previous paragraph by referring to *most people* rather than *everyone*. These responses recognize variability, or at least a lack of total uniformity in the population or group being considered.

- You were the same as most people.
- That in some way you are in a most common result in some sort of test or exam.

More common than focusing on the modal aspects of average, is reference to the idea of middle; this is a precursor to the median.

- Not really good and not really bad. In between.
- That I was halfway between a set of something—for example 3 and 5, so I would be 4.

Some students combine ideas associated with the mode and median in their descriptions.

- It means that you are not really smart or not very well in studies etc., but in the middle as most people are.

Very few students, when asked about themselves identify being average with the arithmetic mean but some responses may reflect recent classroom experiences.

- It is if you have some numbers, you add them together and then divide by how many numbers.

It is very rare for students to use words like *representative* to describe average when asked about being average themselves, an ingredient likely to produce a relational level response.

For many students, asking a more formal question about the meaning of "average" does not change the type of personalized or colloquial response. The following two responses are similar to those in the previous paragraph.

- It would mean that you weren't really bad at spelling but you weren't really good at it either. You were half and half.
- Average is like . . . the middle standard. It's not very, very good but it's not very, very bad. It's like the middle. So if you said the television program was average, it means that it wasn't very good and it wasn't very bad.

When asked for the meaning, however, more students attempt a definition associated with the mean.

- Find out if you added all the people's scores together, what was the score that was . . . That's not necessarily the most common, is it? . . . The score that is like, don't know how to say it. [. . .] You add the number of people up and you divide it by the score that they got and that gives you the average score. [. . .]

That these attempts are not always completely successful suggests that more time needs to be spent on the contexts within which the algorithm is applied: "adding and dividing" is not sufficient.

What is striking about students' responses to basic questions about average is that most and middle are natural descriptors; the mean is not. Of those students who give multistructural responses, by far the most common type reflects the median concept of middle, with about a fifth as many reflecting the mode, and exceedingly few the mean.[16] Building initial discussion of central tendency and representativeness in terms of these two ideas, leading to median and mode, would appear to be a way of providing meaningful links for students.

4.3 AVERAGE: WHAT DOES IT MEAN IN CONTEXT?

Considering context more explicitly further reinforces the importance of the connections in Fig. 4.1. Building on students' initial responses to the meaning of average, an understanding of average in context can be explored with questions like those in Fig. 4.2.[17] Some students, especially

> A research study found that "Australian primary school
> students watch an <u>average</u> of 3 hours of TV per day."
>
> (a)   What does the word "average" mean in this
>   sentence?
>
> (b)   How do you think they got this average (3 hours
>   of TV per day)?

FIG. 4.2.   Questions about average in context.

younger ones with little experience of average, have difficulty, particularly
with Part (b). Of interest are the levels of response leading to an appreciation of the average in the role of reducing the complexity of the data while
representing them in some fashion.

On a basic level, the context provides for colloquial interpretations of
the questions about meaning and method. Beyond that, the ideas expressed may not move past storytelling or proto-statistical intuitions.

- (a) Around 3 hours.
- (b) By watching someone in their daily life. [One person or lots of people?] Yes, one person.

The second response is an excellent starter for discussion of collecting data
to find an average and can be compared with reports based on single-
person samples sometimes found in the media. Other younger children focus concretely on the "how" of Part (b), again stepping back to the necessary data collection.

- (b) Probably somehow got a little powerful little camera and disguised it
  on one student and then another student to see how long they have
  been watching the TV instead of probably getting on with their homework after school.
- (b) Well, maybe they might have something to eat and get changed when
  they come home and in the middle of that they watch TV and then
  have tea and might watch a bit more and then probably go to bed.
  [. . .]

Again as in the case of the word "sample," adding context can assist some
students to give "average" a meaning at the next level of sophistication. The
following responses are not uncommon after an inability to define the term
in an earlier question.

- (a) About, sort of around, 3 hours, near.

(b) They probably add up all the children's hours of TV they watched and they sort of compared them and they like, all of them were around, sort of near 3 hours.

The idea of "adding up" is a common intuitive idea, although the implications are ignored.

- (b) [What might some say?] Maybe that they didn't watch any or that they watched a lot more than 3 hours and they might have all added up that the average was 3 hours. [What then?] They would probably add them all up and see which is more likely than the others.

The modal idea also appears at this level as a meaningful straightforward summary for some.

- (b) Well probably the most would be 3, so they have got 3 in there.

Similarly the mean is sometimes suggested without any further discussion of why it would be appropriate.

- (b) By working out the average like. Oh, I've forgotten how to do it, add it up and divide by the number of whatever.

The most sophisticated responses to this task often link two (or more) ideas of central tendency and at least implicitly include a need to represent a group of children.

- (a) It means most of the children watched TV for 3 hours a day.
- (b) First they asked lots of people what they watched and wrote them all down and then add them together and divide them by the number that you had, the people that you had counted. [. . .]
- (a) Well, average means, say, there's 100,000 kids in primary school and something like, about 40% watch 4 hours and the other 60% watch . . . another 40% watch 2 hours and some watch 3 and a half and they just found out the middle number between all of the people.

Although problems that ask for the calculation of the arithmetic mean from a data set do not encourage consideration of the variation displayed in the values, the presentation of ten identical numbers with a request to find the mean, would surely draw questions. In fact such an exercise is a good "catch" question to see if students appreciate why they would want to find a mean. Many students who have a colloquial understanding of average, however, infer a background against which being "normal" is judged. As seen in the examples in this section, those who can begin to describe the average of 3 hours watching television per day, put these accounts against a background of varied data points.[18] This is true for some quite young students.

- Well, the average, that means not everyone would, but just like primary school students . . . some could have watched 5, but that's not the average . . . But they would say that is the average because the more people would watch 3 hours. I mean if you draw up a graph of how many people watch 3 hours per day and how many watch 5 and 2 or 1 . . . I mean it could be like, say there's 20 in the class or something, 10 people watch 3 hours per day and 6 could watch 2 hours per day and 4 could watch 4, or something like that.

This modal appreciation is well expressed in an environment displaying variation. Older students are likely to be more succinct in describing the mean.

- Well some watch more, some watch less, but when you add them together and divide it by whatever, how many watch it, then it is an average of 3 hours.

The idea of the range sometimes arises when middles are considered.

- People think that children at primary school mostly, most of them watch 3 hours, at least 3 hours of television a day. [How do they decide?] Because it would probably be like some kids might watch like 8 hours and some kids might watch like 10 minutes and it would be an in-between number.

An open-ended question based on the word *average* is more likely to draw out ideas of middle or most than mean, which is not surprising because the idea of balancing all values in a data set with the mean is a more complex representation than the mode or median. Presenting students with a decimal number to represent an average, however, can help explore whether an idea of arithmetic mean has developed to the point that a link with decimals is natural. Although of course it is not impossible for a median or mode to appear in a decimal form, often the main clue in media stories that an average is a mean is its numerical form in relation to the numbers in the associated data set. Questions like the ones in Fig. 4.3 are useful to see what sense students can make of a decimal average.[19] The responses can reveal whether students have an appreciation yet for decimal numbers as representing parts and wholes, as well as whether they can make links to the arithmetic mean.

Across the middle years of school a wide range of responses is likely to occur for the questions in Fig. 4.3. For students without an appreciation of either decimal numbers or averages, the context is all they have to rely upon.

Let's say you are watching TV, and you hear:

"On average, Australian families have 2.3 children."

> (a)   What can you tell from this?
>
> (b)   How can the average be 2.3, and not a
>   counting number like 1, 2, 3, or 4?

FIG. 4.3.   Questions related to understanding the arithmetic mean.

- (a) Well, it might be because they might just want that many children or something like that.

Some students have an appreciation of the part–whole nature of decimals but not an understanding of how the arithmetic mean operates within that structure. This may result in two quite different interpretations of 2.3 children.

- (a) Well, that they have got 2 full grown kids, and one's not full grown yet.
- (a) Well, someone might have 2 children, a mum might have 2 children or something, and she might be pregnant.

These suggestions warrant discussion in the classroom because of the opportunity to make meaningful connections with the part–whole concept and how it is represented with decimal numbers. Extending this appreciation to adding and dividing in order to even a distribution, resulting in decimal parts that are not realistic in terms of the number of children in a family, is a challenge for many students well into the middle school. The following responses illustrate the lengths some can reach in rationalizing a decimal-part scenario.

- (a) It says that most Australian families have two older children and say one infant or child under the age of 5 or whatever. [. . .]
- (b) Well, because the average is of like the older children, which they could say is fully grown or my age or whatever. And the .3 is a child that is growing up to be an older child. So that, like, say the kid is 3 now, once it turns to be 10, it will get to be 1, so they will have 3 children sort of thing.

For some students there is an appreciation of the fact that 2.3 somehow represents the size of families but it is not clear that they understand the part played by the decimal point in the number.

- (b) Well, some have 2 children and others have 3. More likely to have 2 though.

- (a) That out of a certain amount of Australian families, the most common amount of children is 2.3.
- (b) When looking at Australian families they usually have between 2 and 3 children, because you can't get .3 of a person, so they would have to have between 2 and 3 children.

The last response at first appears to acknowledge the impossibility of .3 of a person but then contradicts this with the word "between." Even for those who understand that decimals can arise when the arithmetic mean is calculated, it is not an easy phenomenon to explain.

- (b) Because they added all the kids up and got a bit left over.
- (b) With the average, it wasn't an even average. So, they had to go down to points.
- (b) Most families would have around 2.3 children, and it's not like there's a child who's so small that it's a .3, but it's all divided . . . like you add up the number of children and then you divide it by the number of families and it came out at 2.3.
- (b) That people, evened out, have 2.3 children. You can't have .3 of a child but that is just how it worked out. I know because my aunty has 4 children and I'm an only child. That's five for two families. That's 2 and a half people.

The final response would provide an excellent contribution coming from a class member when this issue is discussed.

An appreciation of the algorithm for the mean is not a prerequisite before students can begin discussing variation in data sets, even when they do not have tables or graphs in front of them. Students who do not have appropriate appreciation of the average of 2.3 children, nevertheless know that families vary in size. This is seen in the use of language such as "most Australian families have . . . ," "some would have 2 and others 3," "they usually have between . . . ," and, "that people, evened out, have 2.3 children."

A less open-ended way of quickly assessing student understanding of the arithmetic mean is to provide a multiple-choice task such as shown in Fig. 4.4.[20] There are no tricks and the algorithm is introduced in the "forward" direction to support students. The algorithm must be sufficiently well understood, however, to recognize the significance of the total at its heart.

Assuming that an alternative is selected by agreement with its content, rather than by guessing, it is possible to suggest levels of understanding associated with the choices. At the lowest level are the responses (a) and (b), exhibiting a single idea about average that appears influenced by the average measure of 2.2, but which does not *account* for how the average of 2.2 is a central measure. The first part of each response shows a hint of a modal idea but the inconsistency of the rest of the statement is not recog-

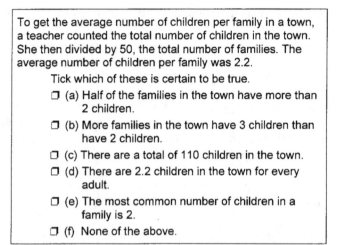

FIG. 4.4.   Questions to unravel understanding of the arithmetic mean.

nized in relation to the stated average of 2.2 in the core of the question. Alternatives judged to be at the next level are potentially more complex in recognizing the average as a central or typical measure of the data, either a rate (d) or a modal value (e). Responses that select (f) possibly reject the other responses as they do not satisfy the student's functional definition (e.g., a student using a definition of average as "middle value" might be expected to respond (f)), yet fail to consider option (c) by testing 110/ 50, which indeed yields an average of 2.2.[21] Responses selecting (c) either test the algorithm to verify $110/50 = 2.2$, or else reverse the algorithm by multiplying $2.2 \times 50 = 110$, indicating the student can relate the algorithm to the concrete situation.

The lowest level alternatives, (a) and (b), are chosen less often across the middle school years, but into high school it is still likely that only around a third of students are able to select the appropriate alternative. Slightly changing the context for the presentation of the algorithm appears to cause considerable difficulty for many students and using an item like the one in Fig. 4.4 in the classroom may assist teachers in evaluating whether classroom work has succeeded in getting across the appropriate message.

Providing authentic reports from the media gives an opportunity to make judgments that are potentially meaningful, while at the same time realizing how difficult interpretations can be. Consider for example the article and accompanying questions shown in Fig. 4.5.[22] In one sense Part (b) of the question is easier to answer than Part (a) if the term *median* is known, because the term *average* in Part (a) used with "average wage-earner" is nebulous.

> ## Hobart defies homes trend
>
> AGAINST a national trend, Hobart's median house price rose to $88,200 in the March quarter - but, Australia-wide, the average wage-earner finally can afford to buy the average home after almost two years of mortgage pain.

   (a)   What does "average" mean in this article?
   (b)   What does "median" mean in this article?
   (c)   Why would the median have been used?

FIG. 4.5. Media article and questions on "average" and "median."

As in the case of the other examples, some students lack the foundation to get started in the context, and perhaps the most they can do is repeat the phrase where a term occurs.

- (a) Average: The average wage earner in Australia.
- (a) An Average means that it is small and good for little families.
- (b) Median is when something rises.

Single ideas are also common, as is the unistructural over generalization to the entire population.

- (b) Median means normal.
- (a) Average means about the same as everyone or anything.

At the multistructural level, responses are structurally more complex in describing central tendency for a data set or the method for obtaining the average from a data set. For the average in Part (a), all three interpretations are suggested although again the specific terms are not used.

- (a) To obtain the average wage earner, all the amounts are worked out and the average wage is the wage that most workers get. The average home is similar.
- (a) Average means not a mansion but not a bomb shelter. But a house that's in between.
- (a) Average = a lot of numbers added up and divided by how many numbers there were at the start.

Descriptions of the median in the context appreciate its meaning but often lack completeness; for example the numerical example in the second response also could fit the mean.

- (b) The median means that the middle of the range house is around $88,200.
- (b) Median—middle score in size order; for example, 3 houses cost 50,000 + 100,000 + 150,000, median = 100,000.

The relational level responses not only often distinguish between average and median, but also sometimes appreciate the nebulous nature of the use of the word *average* in contrast to *median.*

- (a) The earner of a middle sort of wage. In this article I do not believe they are using average in the normal way, but as a sort of colloquial word.
- (b) The middle priced house. Not an average which would include all of the extremes, the $100,000 and $23,000 houses. Out of 100 it would have 49 1/2 above it and 49 1/2 below it.
- (a) Middle range. In this case it is not specific, just not high, not low.
- (b) It means the middle price; that is, if all scores were put in order, the one in the middle would be $88,200.

To be able to appreciate the nuances of the usage of statistical terms in authentic contexts is an important aspect of the second tier of the Statistical Literacy Hierarchy. To go on to use them to question potential bias moves into the third tier of the hierarchy. This is explored with the house price example in the next section.

4.4 AVERAGE AND BIAS

A growing familiarity with the meaning of average and of variation leading to extreme, outlying values, can be used as a basis for discussing which of the three measures of average is least likely to be biased by these extreme values, another important link in Fig. 4.1. This is a particularly important issue in terms of statistical literacy in social contexts where it is essential to report accurately the measure of average used in order for the reader to judge its likelihood of representing what is intended.

Continuing with the example presented in Fig. 4.5, it is essential to understand the distinguishing features of the arithmetic mean and median in order to appreciate why it may be important to use one or the other.[23] In responding to Part (c) about why the median would have been used to characterize house prices, some students indicate an awareness that the median is somehow better without specific evidence as to why.

- (c) It is more accurate than the mean.

Some appreciate the goal but again lack a justification as to why.

- (c) Because it is most representative of the type of house the average Australian family can afford.

A few students realize the potential bias of using the mean and describe well why the median should be used.

- (c) To find the middle price without overbalancing it with a big number or two in an average.
- (c) Because it shows a fair representation of the prices. If the average was [sic] used, a particularly cheap or expensive house would muck up the fair representation.
- (c) It allows an average which is not "thrown out" by very large or very small numbers—e.g. a mansion. In this case, a median gives a better indication of the price of an "average" house.

By the time students reach high school, specific experiences in various contexts are needed to build the intuitions that help students question whether the appropriate measure is being employed. Without the intuitions, only about 10% of students are likely to make the connections for themselves.

Activities to build awareness of the advantages and disadvantages of the three measures of central tendency can be quite straightforward. Consider for example the following data set of measurements of the mass (in grams) of a small object weighed on the same scale separately by nine students in a science class:

6.3   6.0   6.0   15.3   6.1   6.3   6.2   6.15   6.3.

Many questions can be based on this data set, from asking for a calculation of the mean, median, and/or mode, to asking what is the "best" way to determine the mass of the object from the data collected.[24] Because the task involves a list of numbers, students are apt to see it as a calculation problem and neglect to explain their answers. Given the likelihood of numerical errors, students should be encouraged to justify their answers with words.

The technical difficulties experienced with tasks based on the data set in the previous paragraph illustrate further the links from average to other components of the mathematics curriculum. In ordering the numbers from smallest to largest many small errors of carelessness occur but the most common error is to place 6.15 after 6.3 rather than between 6.1 and 6.2. Doing this changes the value of the median and hence provides a clue as to what has happened, even if the numbers are not explicitly listed. The problem of representing place value appropriately in decimal numbers is well known[25] and here is a good place to pick it up and have a discussion in a measurement context that may assist students in making meaningful connections. Even with the assistance of calculators, errors abound when calculating the arithmetic mean of the data set. Forgetting to divide by 9 is also common. Presenting a number in the 60s as an average for the data set indicates a lack of understanding of what an average is meant to do. Discussion of estimating what a reasonable average, of whichever type, ought to look like before doing a calculation, is essential to avoiding some careless errors.

The big issue with this data set in terms of bias, however, is the presence of the outlier measurement of 15.3 and how students deal with it. Unfortunately when it is not brought to their attention most students ignore it. In the context of determining the mass of the small object in a science class, if used in calculating the mean, it creates tremendous bias producing a value greater than 7. The straightforward context and small data set provide the opportunity to explore bias and how the three measures of central tendency deal with it.

If given freedom to choose a method to find the "average" mass, the overwhelming majority of students use the mean. If all three options are offered, students are more likely to attempt other measures than the mean but with mixed success. The levels of response reflect increasing appreciation of the purpose of the task and increasing facility with the numerical skills required to calculate a measure. These are reflected in more complex structures of responses. Contradictions are prominent at the lowest level.

- Choose most common but produce a value other than 6.3.
- Choose median but give a value other than 6.1, 6.2, or 6.3.
- Choose mean but calculate values outside of the interval 6 to 8.

These students appear to recognize terminology but cannot apply it in context. At the next level some recognition of appropriate values or procedures is shown.

- Choose most common and give a value of 6.3 but no further justification.
- Choose median and give a value of 6.1, the middle of the unordered data set.
- Choose mean and produce an inaccurate value in the interval 6 to 8.

Students at the next level appear to have the procedures correct but miss subtleties or make numerical errors.

- Present mode correctly and justify by saying if most students agree, it is the most accurate.
- Choose median and evaluate as other than 6.2, due to an incorrect ordering of the data set.
- Choose mean and evaluate as 7.18 (or similar number between 6 and 8) ignoring the presence of the outlier.

The infrequent highest level responses appreciate the nature of the bias introduced by the outlier.

- Choose median and order correctly, obtaining 6.2.
- Choose mean but reject outlier as measurement error and obtain value of 6.17.

Some would suggest that responses to tasks like this are "right" or "wrong." Analyzing the progress made in some responses using a scheme such as suggested here, however, can assist teachers to scaffold the understandings of students at the appropriate places in their development.

4.5 AVERAGE: THE CASE OF PROBLEM SOLVING

This section considers the link to problem solving involving the arithmetic mean that historically was the first point of contact between statistics and the school mathematics curriculum. At that time, however, the use of the mean provided a context for the presentation of algebra word problems in conjunction with practicing algorithms. Except for the mean being a numeric algorithm-based summary of a set of numbers, its representational attributes were largely ignored. In fact if algorithms were memorized and applied appropriately, there was little need to understand what information might be contained, or interesting, within the sets of numbers. Happily this situation has changed with the introduction of other statistical concepts into the school curriculum. The deconstructing of a mean can lead to a consideration of variation in the data set it represents. The representative nature of the mean can be considered in making sense of why one would want to combine data sets to obtain a weighted mean. Although it is still necessary to know algorithms, it is also important to understand their connections with the purposes of using summary statistics.

Examples of two types of problems are presented in order to explore the development of student ability to combine the algorithmic numerical skills with the appreciation of the contexts within which they are used. Although the problems are structurally more complex than earlier examples, the development shown in responses offers indicators for teachers and those

planning instruction. These are among the more technical and sophisticated goals of statistical literacy that not all students are likely to attain.

Consider the problem in Fig. 4.6,[26] which is a variation on the closed al-
gebra-type problem that specifies a mean and all but one contributing
value, with the goal to find the missing value. This is an extension of the
task to explain the meaning of an average of 2.3 children per family introduced in Section 4.3. Although there are constraints imposed by the mean
and the number of families, it is an open-ended task in the sense there are
many possible responses, many statistically sensible (in terms of distribution) responses, but no uniquely correct response. This type of task often
upsets students who are expecting mathematics problems to have one answer so they can know when they are correct.

The cognitive demands of the task, besides its open-endedness, include
thorough knowledge of applying the algorithm for the arithmetic mean in
both the "forward" and "backward" directions. Because the algorithm is initially taught in the forward direction to find the mean, this facility appears
first, and it is the ability to turn the process around that many students find
difficult, as is seen in Section 4.3 with the task in Fig. 4.4. Starting with the
mean, some students do not realize that multiplying it by the number of values (n) produces the sum of all values that contribute to the mean. The development of understanding necessary to be successful at the task is likely to
be observed in stages as students master the structuring of their understanding of the mean, the context for the task, and its openness.

At the prestructural level of response students appreciate the nature of
the task only to the extent of realizing that they must make up sizes for families. This may be accompanied by storytelling.

- Well, I would say they would have between 1 and 4 children but I do know a
  family that has about 6 children.
- I don't know really. Just what the parents want, they only want, you know,
  that much children, it really depends.

Generally the first mathematical step toward a solution is to apply the mean
algorithm in a forward direction in its entirety to made-up data. The process is greatly assisted if students understand what 2.3 means and make rea-

---

> Let's say the average for 10 families is
> 2.3 children.
>
> If the Grants have 4 children, and the Coopers
> have 1 child, show how many children the
> other 8 families might have.

FIG. 4.6. Problem requiring the mean algorithm to be deconstructed.

sonable starting estimates. Some make an attempt but cannot put all of the pieces together.

- You've got 8 families there and you've already got 5 children and so the average is 2.3 children. So you could average it 2.3, 2.3, and 2.3, or times it, and then add on 5 and sort of then get—because it's the average and you don't know how many people—that's how they average it out.

The following responses, although the first includes an adding error, display an appreciation of the algorithm and decimals, and satisfaction with an estimate for the answer.

- Eight times 2 for these families, 8 times 2 is 16, and 5 more for the other families is 20, divided by 10 families is about 2.3, is 2.
- They might have 2 to 3 because if you add it all up . . . Say another 4 families have 2 and other 3 families have, oh . . . another 4 families have 3. Four times 3 is 12 and 2 times 4 is 8. Eight plus 12 plus 5 should be 25. Ten goes into 25, 2.3 or something like that.

Other responses show a greater skill at adapting values to make the decimal value exact, while still working in a forward direction.

- If the other 8 families had 2 [children], 2 8s are 16, plus 4 is 20, plus 1 is 21, then divide by 10 . . . would be 2.1, so 2.3, so some of them had to have 3 [children] to make it higher . . . 2 would have to have 3 [children] and 6 of them would have to have 2 [children] . . . I figured out that 2.1, you'd need .2 more, so just say 2 of the families had to have 3 [children].

At the next stage students use the mean and the 10 families to calculate the total of 23 children, and then work backward to provide values for all 8 families.

- (Writes 2, 4, 1, 2, 3, 3, 2, 1) [How did you decide on what numbers? You have been changing them?] Well, you would have to have 23 children to get the average of 2.3 for 10 families and I took . . . There's 5 here, so I had to get them to add up to 18, so I just wrote down the numbers.

Some students appreciate that there is no need for closure on an exact answer.

- If there were 10 families and 2.3 that would be 23 children altogether and so if there's 4, and 1 would be 5, take 5, it would be 18. So each of them could have any amount of children, as long as they altogether added up to 18.

Others suggest a distribution.

- ... that's 18. So I reckon the rest of it would be fairly evenly divided.

A few students do not appear to consider the possibility of individual families but are comfortable with means.

- Okay, so 23 children, so there is 18 amongst the other 8 families, so the other 8 families would have 2.25 children each.

Even among students who complete the task successfully there is scope for considerable discussion of the strategies used. It is also possible to consider variation by listing some of the solutions and discussing which are the most reasonable in the light of the mean of 2.3 children per family. There also may be debate about whether the final answer of "2.25 children per family" is an appropriate answer to the question.

The second type of problem is the classical weighted mean problem. Consider a form of the problem shown in Fig. 4.7 and stated in the context of the average number of hours of television watched per day as investigated in the task introduced in Section 4.3.[27] As a ratio and proportion problem, this one again provides links with the numeracy skills and reasoning in the mathematics curriculum. It is also, as in the previous example, associated with appreciating the relationship of the mean and the total number of hours of television watched for the two groups of people. For those who have learned the algorithm for solving the problem, it can be a mechanical exercise. Of particular interest however are the reasoning employed by those who have not yet met the algorithm and the extended reasoning used by those with the algorithm in order to make sense of the answer in the context and in terms of proportions.

As might be expected from the presence of four numbers in the statement of the problem in Fig. 4.7, students with little experience sometimes attempt what appear to be random combinations of operations to use the numbers and often ignore some of the information. Although appreciating

---

Another study found that:

25 country students watched an average of 8 hours of TV per weekend;

75 city students watched an average of 4 hours of TV per weekend.

Show how to get the average TV viewing time for the total 100 students.

FIG. 4.7.   A weighted average problem set in the context of students' television watching time.

the general context, some students appear to neglect to take into account the reasonableness of their answers.

- (Writes down "4 ÷ 3 = 1.3 then I added 1.3 to the 8 = 9.3.") I divided that [4 hours] by 3 because that's 3 times that and added it on to the 8 hours. I don't know why but . . .

Others can appreciate the need to have an answer between 4 and 8 hours per weekend.

- Add the amount of kids together and you get 100 and divide it by the 12 hours of TV. [. . .] [So you would expect it to be around 8 hours 20 minutes?] No. [What might you expect it to be around?] I would expect it to be less than 8 hours because there's more city children watching 4 hours than there is country children watching 8 hours.

Those who can apply the mean algorithm in the forward direction can sometimes see the need to combine the two data sets but cannot do it.

- Add them all together, all the hours and then divide it by 100 this time because there's a lot of them. [Could you use the information provided to find the average overall?] I don't know.

Some students in this situation claim it is impossible to solve the problem because the individual numbers of hours that each of the children watched are not given. These students have not made the connection between the total number of hours watched by a group and the average multiplied by the number of people, at least not in this more complex setting.

As would be expected, many students average the two means, ignoring the number of students in each group. Sometimes there is no justification other than "you add and divide" but other times there is an appreciation for the need of a "middle" answer.

- You add up the 8 and the 4 which is 12 and then you divide it by 2 so the average is 6 hours. . . . Or else you could just say what's in the middle and that's a 6 anyway. So the average would be 6 hours per student.

Although incorrect, such a response provides a starting point for discussion of the meaning of the number used for division to find an average and how a group is represented by that average.

There are students, usually older, who parrot off the algorithm producing an immediate answer of 5 hours per weekend with no additional indication of what this number means to them. Of interest, however, are those who struggle at first and then work their way through the problem, with understanding of the context, the proportional setting, and the meaning of the algorithm.

- You would add them so that's 100 and the hours would be 12, so you divided 100 by 12. So the average would be . . . according to this it would be 8.33, but that can't be right. [Why can't that be right?] Because it would have to be somewhere between 4 and 5. I reckon it would be more towards 4 because more of them [city] are doing it, more of them are watching. [. . .] It would be about 5. [. . .] 25 times 8 is 200, so that's their total viewing time. 25 times 4 is 300, so that's their total viewing time. So the total viewing time is 500, divided by 5 is 100, or 500 divided by 100 is 5. So the average time would be 5.

Others have a strong sense of the ratios involved based on the two sets of students, and with an appreciation of what the arithmetic mean represents, do not need to use the algorithm itself.

- I would expect the average would be somewhere around 4.3 or something [. . .] because there's a lot more people with 4 rather than 8. [. . .] Because there is not many of a lot, not much of a lot rather than a lot of not much. It would be probably closer to a lot of not much, which would be about 4 point something.
- If you divide these [25 and 75] by 25, so that's 1 and that's 3, so that's 8 plus 4 plus 4 plus 4 equals 20, and divide that by the 4 because there's 4 samples there, so it is 5 hours average.

The responses of students demonstrate that there is much more to weighted mean problems than an "algebra word problem." The creation of meaning for average in a slightly more complex context and the opportunity to make links with the understanding of ratio and proportion make these problems good extension activities when data reduction is the topic of interest.

4.6 AVERAGE AND INFERENCE

As can be seen in Fig. 4.1, average as a way of reducing data perhaps to a single value, leads to the inference stage of a statistical investigation. How averages may be used depends on what questions are asked and of course in many school-based problems, as in the previous section, have the finding of an average as their main objective. One of the goals of the overall data handling curriculum and of statistical literacy, however, is to have a range of tools, of which average is a significant one, that are available when a range of questions is posed. The test comes when students are asked to make comparisons or judgments about data sets at other times and places without specifically being told to use averages. What is the natural tendency in terms of choosing a method and a statistic for making a decision?

Although the major discussion of inference takes place in Chapter 6, it is of interest to observe whether students suggest an average in contexts where it has not been mentioned recently, when asked to make predictions or support hypotheses. In straightforward contexts the observation of students' suggestions for data reduction or summary often show good intuitions.

Consider again the task in Section 3.2 to create and interpret a pictograph, and then to make predictions based on it.[28] Of interest here are the questions about two children, Paul and Mary, not in the original data set, who are introduced into the scenario near the end of the protocol. Students are asked to predict how many books each has read. For the youngest students this is an impossible task as they consider there is no information available. For elementary students the context and their own experiences provide stories for how many books Paul or Mary have read.

- [Paul?] Maybe 2 [. . .] Because he might not like reading so he might think reading is a bit boring.

Some are prepared to guess.

- [Paul?] Four. [Why?] I don't know. [Just anything?] Yes, just any number.

For students who use the information displayed in the pictograph there is sometimes an interesting tactic, opposite to what would be expected statistically.

- [Paul?] He could have read 2 or 5. [Why?] Because we are missing a number all the way along.

This filling in of gaps in the data may reflect an unwanted link between data handling and pattern recognition in the mathematics curriculum. These responses do not show any recognition of the possibility of using the available data to predict a missing value, except perhaps in the last example to fill in gaps.

There are students from the middle school grades and higher who realize the possibility of making predictions based on the available information and some type of central tendency.

- [Paul?] Three. [Why?] Because everybody has read 1 to 6 and 3 is in the middle.

- [Paul?] [. . .] It would probably be between 0 and 7. [Mary?] Well, all the girls seem to read more than the boys but it might be different for the 2 new people. [How would you predict?] [. . .] Anne and Jane have both got 5 and Lisa has got 7. Then Mary would probably have between 5 and 10. Boys are between 1 and 4 so probably between 0 and 5 for Paul.

For a few students the arithmetic mean does occur as a way of making a prediction.

- [Paul?] Just the average of these. [How?] You just add them all up, then divide it by the total number of people.
- With Paul you could take an average . . . because boys don't seem to read as many as girls. So I reckon Mary would probably read more than Paul. [How for Paul?] You'd add 1 and 5 . . . [up to] 12 and then divide by 4, which is about 3.

It may be surprising to some teachers that so few students think of the mean or the "middle" in a context such as this. It is probably due to the emphasis on the algorithm in the classroom and the lack of accompanying applications when the averages are introduced. Not that the goal is for students *always* to think of the mean or median when summarizing data sets—the goal is eventually to have a repertoire of tools to use.

In the case of upper elementary students analyzing data presented in Section 3.3 including several variables accounting for age, weight, and fast food consumption, the mean is rarely considered as a tool for summarizing data to support a hypothesis.[29] This is likely to be because there are so many variables involved that the load for decision making is too great. A few students use the mean to average two or three values of another variable, say weight or number of fast food meals, for each age in order to simplify the drawing of a graph with age along the horizontal axis. Others may find the means for two variables for boys and girls to provide a way of comparing them. This is shown in Fig. 4.8 where sports, average age, average weight, and fast foods are compared for boys and girls. Although criticisms can be made of the choice of data and the presentation with the conclusion in the middle, this poster provides an excellent starting point for class discussion of the choice of statistics appropriate to summarize data and lead to conclusions.

One of the main examples considered in Chapter 6 is based on a scenario where students are asked to compare the performance of two classes based on data presented in graphs.[30] For some comparisons the classes are of equal size but for one they are not. In this case it would be natural to consider using the arithmetic mean to balance the two sets in making a comparison. Of interest is the observation that very few older students, who have been exposed to the mean, think of using it.

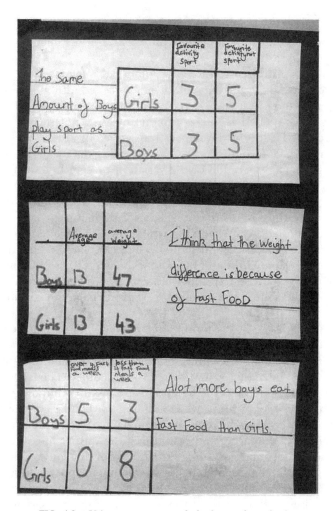

FIG. 4.8. Using an average to help form a hypothesis.

4.7 IMPLICATIONS AND RECOMMENDATIONS

The concept of average occupies a significant and yet controversial place in the data handling curriculum. As the arithmetic mean it is historically and statistically prominent as the statistic whose algorithm is accessible at the upper elementary level. At times this leads to overexposure because it can be used to "illustrate statistics" and marked right or wrong on a test, without the use of many words. The median and the mode are often portrayed as the poor relations of the mean. For the median this is a great injustice, as is the presentation of complex formulas involving odd and even ns for finding the median. Using words like *middle*, graphs such as stacked dot plots, and counting strategies can build intuitions for the median in a very straightforward fashion.

What must be stressed is the representational role played by an average in terms of the data in the data set. Ideas associated with middle and most are very familiar to students in describing "average." The idea of balance in the sense incorporated in the arithmetic mean is not second nature to many students. It must be developed from judicious work with data—viewing graphs of data in conjunction with calculating the mean can be helpful in this regard. Consideration of the variation present in a data set represented by a mean or median is very important because of the implications of leaving part of the story untold. Incorporating discussion of the range, peaks, and skewness of distributions lays a foundation for later work with the standard deviation and helps to counter the belief that one is "finished" with summarizing a data set once the mean is calculated. The introduction of five-number-summaries and box-and-whisker plots, as noted in Section 3.11, not only provides a transition between graphs and summary statistics, but also broadens the scope of summary statistics from just considering the arithmetic mean.

Because the usage of the term *average* is so common in society, understanding of its many facets is an essential part of statistical literacy. Like the term *sample* it has many meanings, in this case both colloquial and statistical, which must be mastered and linked to each other. The first tier of the Statistical Literacy Hierarchy—the understanding of terminology—reflects both of these types of meaning while building a structural complexity, both in terms of appreciating the representational purpose of finding an average and in terms of comparing and contrasting the various measures. As with the case of sample, understanding develops from single ideas, drawn from social usage, building to sequential ideas relating to appreciation of how to find a median or mean. These procedural aspects, often the focus of classroom exercises, are only part of the understanding necessary for the first tier of statistical literacy. The goal is to appreciate how a particular measure represents the data set and that representation is indeed its purpose.

The second tier of the Statistical Literacy Hierarchy focuses on applying the understanding of average in various contexts, mainly social but also scientific. The social foundation for many colloquial uses of the word *average* is likely to create links between the first and second tiers from the beginning. This can provide motivation for sorting out relevant definitions for use in different contexts. Learning to interpret what is intended, or asking questions when the intent is not clear, is an important trait to develop. The use of cross-curricular activities and projects is a natural way to build intuitions for proper application of different measures. Across the school curriculum appropriate measures should be modeled along with justifications. It is also important to introduce reports from outside the school environment, particularly good media reports that are explicit in the use of appropriate averages. This can build students' confidence and experience for the time when they have to make decisions outside of a supportive teacher-led environment.

With respect to the third tier of statistical literacy, the scope for consideration of data reduction is wider than just average, but it is most likely to start with average. The goal is for students to question the nebulous use of the word without explanation, to assess the appropriate usage when meaning is clear, and to question those usages that are inappropriate. As well, students need to be aware that the reporting of an average may not be enough to tell the story of a data set. They need to have a battery of questions concerning range, outliers, spread, and shape. These relate not only to the sensitivity of the average used but also to other data reduction measures such as the standard deviation. For those who go on to study this statistic, it will make more sense if intuitions about the shapes of distributions have been established throughout the middle school years.

Most media outlets, through hardcopy newspapers or on-line sites, provide a large number of reports based on averages. Searches of sites for the word turn up many possibilities and the main difficulty is having time to pick out the most appropriate. Although as noted earlier the mode attracts the least attention of the average trio in terms of exercises in the classroom, students need to be exposed to its frequent use in reporting survey results. The claim that "The average shopper is likely to be a woman aged about 40, employed, married or living with a partner, and likely to have no children living at home"[31] is based on the following data:

76 percent of main grocery shoppers are female,

52 percent of respondents had no children living at home,

the largest group (29 percent) were in the 35–45 age range,

66 percent were married or living with a partner.

Although the use of the general term average may mask which of the three measures is being used, sometimes a clue in the decimal representation signals the arithmetic mean. "The survey found cats caught 4.67 prey per year, of which 1.57 were native and 3.10 introduced species"[32] is certainly employing the arithmetic mean. Extracts such as these not only illustrate the use of the mean but also provide the opportunity to question which is the most appropriate of the three statistics to use. The reporting of means to two decimal places can be linked to decimal representation generally and understanding can be tested by discussing the meaning of .67 of a prey and the necessity (or otherwise) to report this level of accuracy.

The discussion of a media report can lead to some quite concrete work with representations, especially with sense-making of the decimal form of a mean that cannot exist in the data set, as illustrated in the previous paragraph. Consider a report on traffic crossing a bridge in a city where many commuters cross per day and congestion is bad.

> Recent surveys showed the 60,000 cars that cross the bridge each day carried an average of only 1.2 people . . . If the average [were] lifted to 1.5 or 1.6, the number of cars crossing the [river] could be reduced by 15,000 a day.[33]

Besides checking the numerical claim in the extract, and perhaps discussing the psychology of using the arithmetic mean as the average, it is possible to draw pictures of a bridge with cars and people to represent the three averages and see if the differences among them are noticeable. Depending on the age of students it may be most beneficial to concentrate on the desired mean of 1.5 people per car, reinforcing links to .5 and a half. Figure 4.9 shows three possible configurations of 10 cars on the bridge.[34] The first, although statistically meaningful, has no meaning in the real world and needs to be dismissed as a method of providing scenarios that could link an

FIG. 4.9. Scenarios for an average of 1.5 people per car on a bridge.

actual situation with a mean. For children completing this task there are often many issues: how many cars to use, what about buses, is it possible to have a car with 0 occupants? As much freedom and creativity as possible should be allowed within the ability range of class members.

The software available today allows for tasks like the one just described to be carried out in pictorial or graphical form.[35] For consolidating the link between graphs and averages, it is a good exercise to use a drag-and-drop facility to move individual data values and observe what happens to the mean (and median) in the process. This is an excellent way to observe the effect of an outlier and the visual appearance may be a better reinforcement than repeating a tedious calculation by hand.

Given that measures of central tendency are going to remain at the heart of data reduction in the school mathematics curriculum, it is essential to reinforce continually the connections illustrated in Fig. 4.1. Ideas of average must be broadly based, particularly with reference to sources of variation, to graphical representation, and to the data set itself. This is reinforced in the words of Jan Mokros and Susan Jo Russell.

> Until a data set can be thought of as a unit, not simply as a series of values, it cannot be described and summarized as something that is more than the sum of its parts. An average is a measure of the center of the data, a value that represents aspects of the data set as a whole. An average makes no sense until data sets make sense as real entities.[36]

ENDNOTES

1. Galton quoted in Bernstein (1996, p. 171).
2. Capel (1885).
3. Hart (1953).
4. Australian Education Council (1991, 1994a); Department for Education (1995); Ministry of Education (1992); National Council of Teachers of Mathematics (1989, 2000).
5. Utts (1999), displays some skepticism in saying "Another measure of 'center,' called the mode, is occasionally useful" (p. 107).
6. Moore & McCabe (1993). In Moore (1991a), the mode is defined in a text for liberal arts students but dismissed as "little used, because it records only the most frequent value, and this may be far from the center of the distribution of values," p. 207.
7. Hardiman, Well, & Pollatsek (1984); Mevarech (1983); Pollatsek, Lima, & Well (1981); Reed (1984).
8. Goodchild (1988); Leon & Zawojewski (1991); Strauss & Bichler (1988).
9. Cai (1995, 1998); Gal, Rothschild, & Wagner (1989, 1990); Mokros & Russell (1995); Watson & Moritz (1999a).

10. Mokros & Russell (1995).
11. "Australia hotting up" (1997).
12. "Golf most popular sport" (1995).
13. "Aussies living for longer, ABS says" (1994).
14. Watson & Moritz (2000c).
15. Watson & Moritz (1999b).
16. Watson & Moritz (1999b).
17. Watson & Moritz (2000c).
18. Watson & Moritz (2000c).
19. Watson & Moritz (2000c).
20. Konold & Garfield (1992); Watson & Moritz (1999b).
21. It would be possible to interpret response (f) as correct, if one assumed the average of 2.2 were the result of rounding to one decimal place. Under this assumption of rounding, the total number of children would be certain to be in the range 108–112, though not certain to be 110 as response (c) asserts. There is however, no evidence found in students' responses from research that this interpretation is considered.
22. Megalogenis (1990); Watson & Moritz (1999b).
23. Watson & Moritz (1999b).
24. Watson, Kelly, Callingham, & Shaughnessy (2003); Watson & Moritz (1999b).
25. Steinle, Stacey, & Chambers (2002), discuss these issues in a section called, "Summary of misconceptions about decimal numbers."
26. Watson & Moritz (2000c).
27. Watson & Moritz (2000c).
28. Watson & Moritz (2001a).
29. Chick & Watson (2001); Watson & Callingham (1997).
30. Watson & Moritz (1999a).
31. "Spending a penny in supermarkets" (1996).
32. "Cats get bad press: survey" (1994).
33. "Let someone else drive, bridge commuters told" (1994).
34. Watson (1999); Figure 4.9 drawn by Helen Chick.
35. For example, *Tinkerplots* developed by Konold & Miller (2005).
36. Mokros & Russell (1995, p. 35).

5

Chance—Precursor to Probability

Phenomena having uncertain individual outcomes but a regular pattern of outcomes in many repetitions are called random. *"Random" is not a synonym for "haphazard" but a description of a kind of order different from the deterministic one that is popularly associated with science and mathematics. Probability is the branch of mathematics that describes randomness.*[1]

5.1 BACKGROUND

In many places in the world, probability preceded statistics into the senior school mathematics curriculum. It was seen as part of pure mathematics, a theoretical study based on sample spaces. Theorems were learned and probabilities calculated for events, often requiring formulas for permutations and combinations. It was not necessary to toss a coin or roll a die; in fact, it would have been seen by some as muddying the waters by producing outcomes slightly at variance from the theory. The curriculum reform that brought data handling into the mathematics curriculum also had to address the precursor to theoretical probability and its relationship to data handling.

The considered opinion after much debate was that in order to address the important issues relevant to teaching data-based statistics today, the curriculum should have much less emphasis on formal probability.[2] This is reflected in recommendations to change the scope of probability at the school level to reflect the study of random events, the development of appropriate probabilistic intuitions, a basic understanding of language and simple events, an appreciation of distribution and the addressing of mis-conceptions.[3] The aim is to support data handling through an empirical frequency-based approach to probability that is also an important founda-tion for later work in theoretical probability. Random activities, such as roll-ing dice, can also provide data for data handling topics in the curriculum. Many curriculum documents adopt the approach of using the term *chance* to distinguish the more intuitive and experimental aspects of the topic from the study of theoretical probability based on sample spaces.[4]

Whereas the word *probability* has a mathematical connotation to most people, even if they have not studied the subject, the word *chance* is one with many colloquial meanings, some apparently at odds with more theoretical aspects of probability. Similar to the words *sample* and *average*, there are many intuitions brought to school associated with ideas of chance. In a classroom it is possible to find children from families who bet on horses and buy lottery tickets, and from families who believe the events of the world are completely determined by a supernatural being and who would forbid any sort of gambling. Intuitions and subjective beliefs are the starting points for a chance curriculum and these are usually expressed through language rather than through numbers. The beginning of the chance curriculum is hence similar to that of the sampling curriculum, being based on descrip-tive activities. In building an appreciation of a frequency approach to chance there is the necessity to perform trials, comparing favorable out-comes to total outcomes. This comparison is linked to other part–whole ideas in the mathematics curriculum and parallels the development of the part–whole concept in the sampling component of the curriculum. The number of connections to fundamental concepts across the mathematics curriculum, as well as links across the school curriculum and outside of school where uncertainties abound, make chance an important part of the curriculum. The necessity to appreciate the nature of chance for decision making in many contexts outside of school makes it an important contribu-tor to statistical literacy.

The first major research into people's understanding of probability was done in the field of psychology and focused on misunderstandings that oc-cur when decisions are made in complex contexts. Amos Tversky and Dan-iel Kahneman found that people misjudged likelihood due to the influence of their own available understanding of context and biases, due to misjudg-ing the representative nature of information provided, and due to overcon-fidence in small samples.[5] This type of research is far removed from the cal-culation of probabilities based on sample spaces or frequency counts but it is an indicator of the dilemmas faced by people in relation to statistical liter-acy outside of school. The question of how much and what sort of work should be done at the school level to help alleviate these misconceptions is a vexing one. Recently Gerd Gigerenzer has challenged the earlier research and suggested that considering frequencies rather than probabilities can alleviate some of the difficulties people encounter in this area.[6]

The initial research of the psychologists was carried out with college students. The next generation of research moved to the school level and had two perspectives. The work of educational psychologist Ephraim Fischbein and his colleagues continued to consider student understanding in contexts reflecting earlier concerns, while at the same time asking questions of a more conventional nature based on random devises and potential outcomes.[7] David Green followed this latter approach and went further to consider the association of probabilistic judgments in relation to proportional reasoning and the nature of random behavior in judging runs of particular outcomes and in judging two-dimensional representations of potentially random outcomes.[8] This research revealed many types of misunderstanding, suggesting that appropriate intuitions are not inbuilt and that many experiences need to be planned and carried out in order to reconstruct concepts that will lead to correct judgments in conditions of uncertainty.

Recent research into students' understanding of chance and probability has become more broadly based, including all ages in schooling and considering more diverse aspects of chance, as well as those considered earlier.[9] Particular issues addressed for example include cultural influences on students' thinking and beliefs,[10] the effect of context on reasoning,[11] the use of chance language to express uncertainty,[12] belief in an "outcome approach" that leads to deterministic rather than probabilistic reasoning,[13] beliefs in luck and fairness,[14] the dilemma of dealing with variation in chance settings,[15] and the "equiprobability bias" that considers all possibilities equally likely.[16] As well, specific event-related topics of research interest have included compound events,[17] conditional events,[18] and conjunction events.[19]

Three major aspects of chance understanding are considered in this chapter based on tasks completed by students across the years of schooling. The first is associated with students' appreciation of the language of chance and its relation to context. The second relates to the traditional ideas that are considered important in relation to the measurement of chance. Links to other parts of the mathematics curriculum are evident here. The third theme involves more general links, for example, of chance to fairness and risk. Figure 5.1 shows the connections among the topics related to the themes that are covered in the following sections. The terms *subjective, frequency,* and *theoretical,* as adjectives to describe chance or probability, are mentioned earlier in this section and might be thought by some to be missing elements in Fig. 5.1. They are, however, potentially descriptors in relation to various interpretations of most of the ideas in the figure and as such would be associated with a large web of duplicate arrows. Although not in Fig. 5.1, they are used as descriptors as appropriate throughout the chapter.

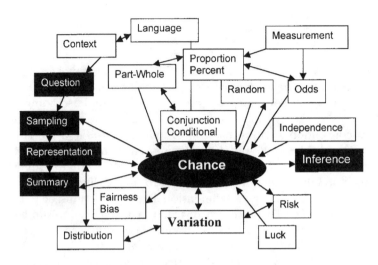

FIG. 5.1.   Links among the ideas and statistical elements related to chance
understanding.

The link to distribution, shown in Fig. 5.1, is explored briefly in this chapter
and considered again in Chapter 7, where the focus is on variation.

The first four sections of the chapter deal with links associated with
chance language, starting with the description of the term *random* in Section 5.2. This is followed by examples of links to context involving students'
choices in describing certain, impossible, and possible events in Section
5.3. Authentic contexts are introduced involving the evaluation of newspaper headlines in Section 5.4 and the interpretation of a risk factor in Section 5.5. Links to part–whole and percent understanding are important in
these sections. The measurement of chance is addressed in the next five
sections, with Section 5.6 considering single events with connections to
part–whole understanding. Section 5.7 then introduces repeated occurrences of single events. Section 5.8 looks at independent events with extended links to mathematical skills. Conjunction and conditional events are
considered in a qualitative fashion in Section 5.9, and odds in a media context return to focusing on links to ratio and proportion in Section 5.10. The
next three sections consider general issues connected to chance, including
luck in Section 5.11, fairness and bias in Section 5.12, and risk from a different perspective in Section 5.13. Throughout these sections links to sampling and data representation recur and context continues to be important.

These sections provide examples of student responses to tasks illustrating the development of chance understanding and the many connections
in Fig. 5.1. Comments for the classroom are included occasionally. The final section summarizes the implications of the development of student understanding in relation to chance and associates them with the Statistical

Literacy Hierarchy introduced in Chapter 1. It closes with an anecdote in relation to the non-equivalence of two six-sided and one twelve-side dice.

5.2   CHANCE LANGUAGE: DEFINITION OF RANDOM

One of the most difficult words to define related to the chance and data curriculum is *random.* Even senior students and teachers find it difficult. The description provided by David Moore at the beginning of this chapter is not easy to paraphrase in a shorter form. The idea of "haphazard," rejected by Moore, is nevertheless commonly used from childhood to adulthood to describe the uncertainty of random occurrences. This phrase ignores the pattern aspect of random events occurring in chance and data distributional contexts. The complexity of the concept makes it important to begin discussions with students early and continue them, hopefully with increased sophistication, throughout the school years. Exploring contexts where students believe random happenings take place is an important foundation for later work.

One way to gain an initial impression of children's understanding of random processes is to ask a question like, "What things happen in a random way?"[20] Confusion with the term *ransom* is not uncommon, even at higher grade levels.

- People hold you for money.

There are also cases where it is very difficult to appreciate whether there is a haphazard connotation intended.

- Fighting.
- Girlfriends.

Some students appear to have heard the word in the expression "random order," and so respond with a statement that reflects being "ordered," which may be a precursor to views of random as "unordered" or "mixed." It is difficult to discern if these responses have any connection to David Moore's description at the beginning of this chapter. They express an idea about random that is strongly linked to experience without clearly establishing links between the term and exactly what it refers to.

- Things happen one after another, sort of in order.

Other responses include examples from natural, unpredictable phenomena.

- It will rain.

- Accidents happen in a random way.
- Leaves falling off a tree.
- Birth of a newborn child, or death of an old man/woman.

Some students identify random with a specific, humanly-constructed event or process.

- Surveys are done randomly.
- In sports you are randomly drug tested.
- Random breathtesting by police.
- On the CD when you press RANDOM PLAY it plays the tracks at random.

Other responses provide an example of random happenings in the context of games or competitions, often with a defining characteristic of selection or choice. These models embody the meanings commonly associated with random, such as unpredictability and equal likelihood.

- Picking a name out of a hat.
- Competitions and tattslotto and Keno and that kind of stuff.
- Getting picked for a prize. "You're randomly selected."

In contrast to the earlier type of response that implies order, others describe situations without order or with "any order." This idea is often included with responses that attempt to define random related to chance, unpredictability, and lack of a pattern. Again, students refer to either random processes or random outcomes.

- When you get things mixed.
- Quickly, roughly, any old way, etc.
- They happen in no pattern or order.
- Things that happen with no system involved.

These responses focus on a single characteristic and for students who can engage with the task are the most common across grades.

Some students, however, can suggest more than one context, showing a multifaceted appreciation of random. Generally these are given in a list with no generalizing characteristic across them mentioned.

- Wind direction; computer number choice; coin tossing.
- The rolling of a dice; when rain comes from the sky; what the weather is like.
- Tattslotto numbers; numbers of birds flying in groups; wind gusts.

Other responses include an example and a simple defining characteristic.

- Death because you never know if you're going to be next, you just have to wait and see.
- Rain. Thunder. As weather is unpredictable.
- Random is anonymous, people are checked at random for their blood/alcohol level.

There are also some responses that describe aspects of a random process without a specific example. These responses often involve an idea about selection or being picked, with the added specification that the selection is being made without a system or reason.

- If something happens in a random way it just comes about by chance. It means it wasn't particularly meant one way or another.
- Something is chosen without thinking; that is, a number is picked out of 10.
- Someone or something is picked without looking for your name or things like that (picked out of a hat).

A few students link a description with more than one aspect to an example. These are the most sophisticated responses to be expected before a formal definition is introduced.

- Random things happen out of the ordinary, it is unpredictable like the lotto and weather.
- Anything that does not "occur" on a regular basis or in a pattern (i.e., lotto numbers).
- Picking jellybeans from a packet. You choose the colors randomly and don't know which one you'll get. Nothing influences your choice.

Asking specifically for the meaning of the word *random*, as well as for "an example of something that happens in a random way," increases the percent of multiple-aspect responses but there are still few at the level of the previous three.[21] It is often possible however to distinguish increasing sophistication in the meanings offered. Single aspects often focus on "picking" but no further qualification.

- Choose something. Random breath test.

Slightly more sophisticated are responses that include a method.

- Picking in any order. The songs on the CD came out randomly.

Again the most sophisticated intuitive ideas are similar to those volunteered earlier when only asked for examples.

- Like chosen anonymously. Choosing anyone. Picking teams by pulling names out of a hat.
- Something unpredictable and you don't know what will happen. Drawing names out of a hat.

5.3   CHANCE LANGUAGE AND LIKELIHOOD OF EVENTS IN CONTEXT

Curriculum documents suggest a focus on the language aspects of chance from early childhood before the time when assignment of numerical values to events is a reasonable expectation.

Use, with clarity, everyday language associated with chance events.
Possible activities:

- Clarify and use common expressions such as 'being lucky', 'that's not fair', 'always', 'it might happen', 'tomorrow it will probably rain'.
- Use the vocabulary 'certain', 'uncertain', 'possible' and 'impossible' appropriately, recognizing that, while there is an element of uncertainty about some events, others are either certain or impossible (e.g. I think it is certain that our teacher would be over seventeen because you usually only finish high school then).
- Use language such as 'very likely', 'unlikely', 'more likely', 'less likely' and 'equally likely' to describe events which relate to the experience of the child (e.g. how likely are the events 'we will do some maths in school today', 'the egg will crack if I drop it'? is it more likely that it will rain in July or that it will rain in January?).[22]

Asking students to describe the likelihood of suggested events, as noted here is one way to discuss chance language. Another is to ask students to think up their own events that are certain, impossible, or possible to occur.[23] This provides the teacher with information on the contexts that are available to students in imagining chance happenings and on the appropriateness of initial understanding. It can also provide starting points for class discussion and debate. Figure 5.2 illustrates one way of initiating such a discussion by having students *first* fill in three open-ended statements.[24]

Almost all of the responses of students to these questions reflect one or more of the following contexts: personal reference to self, the immediate environment of the school, or the wider world outside the school. It is important to consider and discuss the meaning of each term as described by students. There may be disputes concerning the colloquial use of the words

> (a) One thing that will certainly happen today is _____
>
> (b) One thing that is impossible today is _____
>
> (c) One thing that might possibly happen today is _____

FIG. 5.2.   Open-ended statements about chance.

"impossible" and "certain" to mean "for all practical purposes impossible" or "certain as far as I know." The following illustrate responses to the three questions from a personal perspective.

- (a) I'll play basketball.
- (b) I will grow 7 feel tall.
- (c) I might get hurt.

The next set of responses refers to the school environment, classes scheduled, lunch, or going home, and often includes "we" referring to the class.

- (a) I'll have Science.
- (b) Getting out of school work.
- (c) The teachers might go on strike.

The world outside of school features in the following set where the weather and world events attract attention.

- (a) The world will turn.
- (b) Snow.
- (c) That it will rain.

A combination of these contexts is shown in about a quarter of responses across grades.

- (a) I will have maths class.
- (b) The school to fall down on just me.
- (b) For me to fly to the moon.
- (c) The school fire alarm could go off.
- (c) That I'll go to athletics training.

For younger students, it is more likely that they will focus on the school environment for certain events and world contexts for impossible and possible events. Older students are more likely to focus on world or mixed contexts for all three types of events. Personal contexts are the least common of the three contexts for all three questions but still more common than no discernable context.[25] Student willingness and ability to answer these questions makes them a good starting point for class discussion where it can be expected that all, or nearly all, students can take part.

5.4   CHANCE LANGUAGE IN CONTEXT: EVALUATING NEWSPAPER HEADLINES

Although the tasks discussed in the previous two sections explore students' appreciation of chance language in contexts with which they are familiar and offer the opportunity to widen the scope of that appreciation, skills in statistical literacy are enhanced when students are asked to engage with specific social contexts that potentially involve decision making. One nontrivial aspect of this literacy goal is to be able to evaluate, perhaps as a percent, fraction or decimal, a likelihood expressed in language. This challenge is often encountered in media reports with headlines trumpeting strong or weak chance.

Some of the early suggestions for creating connections between chance language and numerical representations of chance are based on the number line.[26] A line labeled "impossible" at the left end, "certain" at the right end and "even chance" in the middle can be used to place other chance words in their appropriate locations. This type of exercise is often accompanied by much debate from students. Relabeling the line 0 to 1 with 1/2 or .5 in the middle, or 0% to 100% with 50% in the middle, can help in the transition to numerical forms. Introducing other fractions, decimals, or percents along the line reinforces the part–whole nature of the representation of probabilities in relation to certainty (with "probability 1"). The connections among words expressing chance, numbers expressing chance, and the part–whole relationship expressed in fractions and decimals between zero and one and in percents between 0% and 100%, are essential in building an early appreciation of what chance is all about. Using the number line to reinforce this understanding assists many students in making the concrete, visual links clear.

These connections across mathematical topics can be extended to have a direct link to statistical literacy by choosing extracts from the media to be placed along the number line. Consider for example the task based on the newspaper headlines shown in Fig. 5.3. Here students are asked to place seven statements of likelihood on the 0–1 number line and are assisted by the labeling of a "50–50 chance" in the middle and the placing of appropriate descriptors at either end.[27]

The goal of the task in Fig. 5.3 is chance language evaluation, both absolutely for each of the seven phrases and relatively in relation to each other. Many arguments are likely to occur if it is claimed that there are unique cor-

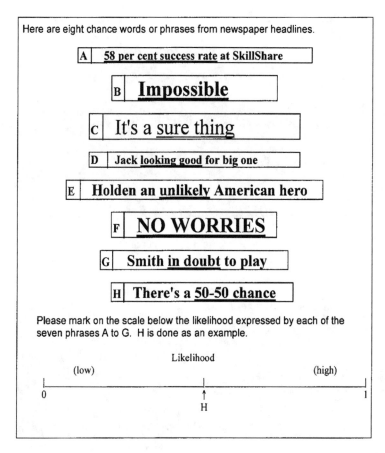

Here are eight chance words or phrases from newspaper headlines.

| A | **58 per cent success rate at SkillShare** |

| B | **Impossible** |

| C | It's a <u>sure thing</u> |

| D | **Jack <u>looking good</u> for big one** |

| E | **Holden an <u>unlikely</u> American hero** |

| F | **<u>NO WORRIES</u>** |

| G | **Smith <u>in doubt</u> to play** |

| H | **There's a <u>50-50 chance</u>** |

Please mark on the scale below the likelihood expressed by each of the seven phrases A to G. H is done as an example.

Likelihood

(low)   (high)

0   H   1

FIG. 5.3.   Task to assign likelihood to chance phrases in newspaper headlines.

rect solutions to the task. Discussion among alternatives, however, is useful in helping students realize that statistical literacy is often more likely to be about qualitative skills of evaluation and interpretation than about quantitative calculations. Two aspects are then of interest: where students place the phrases in relation to the whole length of the line and the ordering of all seven phrases.

Some translation of the marks made as responses is needed for a detailed analysis of the placement of the phrases along the number line. Given the possibility of different line lengths in centimeters or inches, percent is likely to be the best way of measuring along the line and reinforcing the part–whole nature of the likelihood being evaluated. Producing a distribution of these percents is a good way of helping students appreciate the variation likely to occur when they are discussing likelihood with others in colloquial

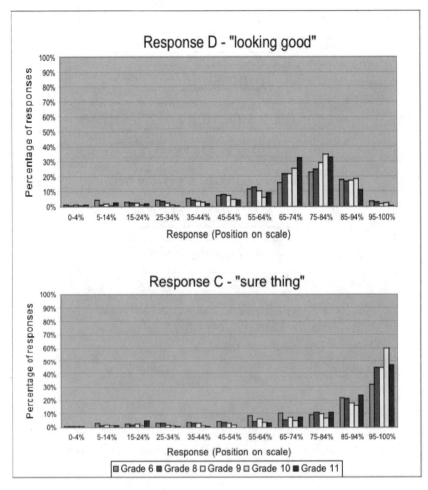

FIG. 5.4. Percents of grades 6 to 11 placing two chance phrases along the number line.

terms. A comparison of the two graphs in Fig. 5.4 for example, shows how the percent evaluation varies for the phrases "looking good" and "sure thing," there being closer agreement among students on the latter than the former.

The most common ordering of the headlines from least to most likely is the following: Impossible, Unlikely, In doubt, 50–50 chance, 58 percent success rate, Looking good, No worries, and Sure thing.[28] "Unlikely" and "In doubt," as well as "No worries" and "Sure thing," are most often the ones interchanged and this is not surprising. Students improve in their ability to rank the headlines according to likelihood with grade level, but in high school only about half would satisfy these criteria, including the two possible swaps of phrases. This kind of result indicates the need to see literacy and numeracy as requiring integrated attention at the high school level. In terms of statistical literacy this might be considered a low level skill but it is an important part of interpreting messages in wider social contexts.

5.5   CHANCE LANGUAGE IN CONTEXT: INTERPRETING RISK

There is considerable concern about school students' participation in risky behaviors, such as smoking, alcohol consumption, drug use, fast driving, or unprotected sexual activity. Those who work in this area, however, seldom study students' ability to connect risk statements to numerical forms that can give insight into relative frequency of occurrence. Without some appreciation of the likelihood of occurrence of some threat, perhaps in percent terms, there are two possibilities: students may ignore the threat altogether, or in some cases students may actually be misled by propaganda or erroneous claims.

The question shown in Fig. 5.5 is a good starting point for assessing student interpretation of a risk statement and beginning discussion on quantitative versus qualitative interpretations.[29] Although presenting this task as an open-ended question might be favored by some teachers and it certainly is an option, the multiple-choice alternatives provide the opportunity to dis-

---

A bottle of medicine has printed on it:

> **WARNING: For applications to skin areas there is a 15% chance of getting a rash. If you get a rash, consult your doctor.**

What does this mean?

- ☐   (a)   Don't use the medicine on your skin – there's a good chance of getting a rash.

- ☐   (b)   For application to the skin, apply only 15% of the recommended dose.

- ☐   (c)   If you get a rash, it will probably involve only 15% of the skin.

- ☐   (d)   About 15 out of every 100 people who use this medicine get a rash.

- ☐   (e)   There is hardly any chance of getting a rash using this medicine.

FIG. 5.5.   Interpretation of a percent chance in a social context.

cover the difficulties of some students who may have reading problems and focus only on 15% as a cue in choosing a response (alternatives (b) and (c)). As well there is the opportunity to discuss the interpretation of 15% as "a good chance" (a) versus "hardly any chance" (e). This translation of a number to a verbal statement, the opposite issue to that discussed in the previous section, highlights the psychological influence of the type of risk involved. If there were a 15% chance of death, the interpretation might be entirely different.

It is encouraging to note that although in the upper elementary grades, many students are persuaded by the distracters involving percent notation ((b) and (c)), toward the end of high school this drops considerably with about 90% of students focusing on the appropriate interpretation and the remainder choosing option (e). In terms of a hierarchy of choices to inform teachers about student thinking the following may be useful.

- Options (b) and (c) indicate inappropriate interpretation.
- Option (a) indicates a vague colloquial interpretation that is not meaningful in the context presented.
- Option (e) indicates an informed colloquial interpretation.
- Option (d) indicates a numerical interpretation that reflects the message.

The interpretation in option (d) also reinforces the connection of likelihood to part–whole percent understanding. Again this is an important foundation stone in building statistical literacy.

5.6   MEASURING CHANCE: SINGLE EVENTS

The connections of measurement to chance in various forms begin with the simplest case of a single event. Traditionally random devices have been used to create contexts for measuring chance. These are useful because the unpredictability of the random process is usually self-evident. This means that it is possible to concentrate on the "pattern" aspect of the random process without many extraneous factors. Except for discussions of "how you instigate the action" that produces the outcome (e.g., roll the die or spin the spinner) the process is considered, at least by teachers and statisticians, to be straightforward. Whether children see the process in the same light is a matter of debate and certainly should be a feature of classroom discussion. Subjective beliefs are common in chance contexts for people of all ages. It is the transition from subjective probability (e.g., "I always lose") to frequency-based probability to theoretical probability, which is the goal of the school curriculum in terms of chance.

> Consider rolling one six-sided die. Is it easier to throw
>
> (1) a one, or
>
> (6) a six, or
>
> (=) are both a one and a six equally easy to throw?
>
> Please explain your answer.

FIG. 5.6.   Basic single event chance question involving a die.

Starting points for discussion are likely to link subjective beliefs with intuitive theoretical understanding of the random generator being used. Conventional questions like the one in Fig. 5.6 can provide much information on children's thinking *if* they are required to explain their answers.[30] As a multiple-choice type question it is the justification that determines successively higher levels of understanding. Choosing the "correct" answer of "equal" does not necessarily imply a sophisticated understanding of the likelihood.

Responses are likely to encompass four levels of justification. At the prestructural level are responses that do not address the nature of the die appropriately or are based on personal belief or experience.

- (=) Because 2 is easier to throw than 1.
- (6) Because it is highest.
- (1) Because you usually want a six but it hardly ever happens.

At the unistructural level are responses that acknowledge the single aspect of uncertainty associated with the die without any physical or theoretical explanation. This is sometimes called the "anything can happen" view of chance and the phrase is often heard in many social contexts where uncertainty is present.

- (=) It might land on anything.
- (=) Because you never know what you'll throw.

More complex responses that make qualitative statements based on the physical structure of the die or the associated chance, are considered multistructural.

- (=) As it is a cube, it is equally easy to throw any number.
- (=) Because there is only one six and one one.
- (=) They both have the same chance.

Some responses go further to quantify the measurement of chance associated with the outcomes.

- (=) There's a 1/6 chance of getting any number.

The expectation for students to give the highest level response increases with grade and exposure to classroom experiences. Once hearing the "correct" answer, however, teachers should not neglect discussion of the less sophisticated reasoning and should create connections from a general belief in chance to the relationship with the physical device to the theoretical probability.

There are various forms of tasks that introduce more complexity in the interpretation of the random generation of outcomes. One such task, presented in Fig. 5.7, presents two categories of outcome but within them different numbers of possibilities.[31] It is possible to be confused as to which is important, boys and girls, or the 29 names. Again it is the explanations given by students, not the multiple-choice response, which determine the increasingly sophisticated levels of response.

Imaginative responses to the question in Fig. 5.7 reflect student beliefs other than related to the chance context.

- (g) It's more likely to be a girl because the teacher is a girl.
- (b) Boys have lucky things in the stars.

Of those who interact with the context, the "anything can happen" view may also be expressed in the method of choosing.

- (=) You could get both.
- (=) Because she had her eyes closed.

A mathematics class has 13 boys and 16 girls in it. Each pupil's name is written on a piece of paper. All the names are put in a hat. The teacher picks out one name without looking. Is it more likely that

(b) the name is a boy, or

(g) the name is a girl, or

(=) are both a girl and a boy equally likely?

Please explain your answer.

FIG. 5.7. Single event chance question with different numbers of possibilities for two categories of outcome.

A consideration of the two possible categories of outcomes, boy or girl, is likely to be the explanation for the following response.

- (=) The chance is the same.

Conflict at this point is sometimes acknowledged but not resolved completely.

- (= g) Equal. But girls have a bit of an advantage.
- (=) It might be a boy, or girls probably have a bit more of a chance, but it depends how well they are mixed.

Of the responses that appreciate the necessity to consider all of the names in the hat, some are qualitative in nature.

- (g) There are more girls.

Others explicitly mention the numbers important in making a qualitative decision.

- (g) Because there are 16 girls and 13 boys and girls would have more of a chance.

Without prompting only a few go further to quantify the probabilities involved.

- (g) Because girls have 16/29 chances, while boys have only 13/29 chances.

Problems such as this one are important because they provide the opportunity for so many levels of development of understanding to be displayed. Particularly for elementary students the distinction between this task and the previous one is important as students are exposed to different sample spaces where random processes occur. Although it is unlikely that the phrase "sample space" would be introduced, there is the opportunity to produce lists of all possible outcomes from tossing the die $(1, 2, 3, 4, 5, 6)$ or drawing a name from the hat (boy$_1$, boy$_2$, . . . , boy$_{16}$, girl$_1$, . . . , girl$_{19}$) and discuss their similarities and differences and the probabilities for events that can be defined.

While still considering outcomes of single events, it is possible to add another complicating feature, that of comparing two such events. Traditionally such events have been based on drawing objects, like marbles, from containers with fixed ratios of two colors. Although there are many possibilities, consider for example the problem in Fig. 5.8.[32] This is a more complex

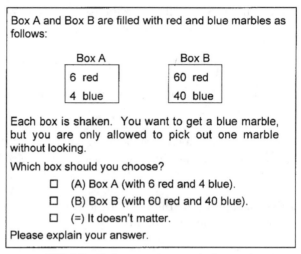

FIG. 5.8.   Task comparing two single events.

problem than the previous two, with four pieces of relevant information rather than two, and allows many more possibilities for students to display their understanding. It is interesting to observe the types of comparisons made in coming to a decision: between boxes, between differences within boxes, and finally between proportions in boxes. Multiple appropriate and inappropriate links to the idea of proportion in the mathematics curriculum are found in the responses of students to questions such as these.

Many levels of response are likely to be observed in the explanations given for the task in Fig. 5.8. There are some students who do not make comparisons but rely on imagination.

- (=) Red and blue are both my best colors.
- (B) Because it's my cross country group.

The first response illustrates why multiple-choice questions without explanations are virtually useless. At the next level are responses that express a single idea of the "anything can happen" type in justifying the choice of equal. One suspects that similar reasoning might be employed if the ratios of marbles in the two boxes were different.

- (=) Because you could get red or blue.
- (=) Because there's blue in each.
- (=) You can't really tell if it is red or blue.

There is then a jump in sophistication of responses when students recognize that frequency plays some part in the decision process. The simplest comparison is based on the total number of marbles in the boxes, ignoring the two colors of marble.

- (B) You would have more marbles to pick from.
- (A) So there aren't so many to choose from.

Other students go a bit further and qualitatively consider a comparison of the boxes in relation to the colors across boxes.

- (A) Less red.
- (B) Because there are more blue in Box B than Box A.

These students appear to appreciate that the task is one that has to do with frequency *and* color but can only focus on one color across boxes. Some students expand on this with a primitive quantification.

- (B) You have more of a chance with 40 than 4.

The next jump in sophistication appears when students employ all of the information gleaned from the two boxes to make comparisons based on differences within rather than between boxes.

- (=) Because there are more reds in both boxes.
- (A) Because there are only 2 more reds in A and 20 more in B.

The first response justifies equality in a qualitative fashion that requires more accuracy to be completely appropriate.

Although some responses partially justify a correct choice using differences, proportional reasoning is required for a full justification. Some students appear to recognize this but make single statements without further amplification.

- (=) They both have the same chance.
- (=) Because they are filled alike.

Others state a property that is the same for each box without quantifying it.

- (=) It doesn't matter because they both have the same average.
- (=) It doesn't matter . . . it's hard to explain. Both boxes have the same fraction of blue marbles.

More sophisticated mathematization occurs when the association is made of the same ratio in each box with a multiplicative factor accounting for the apparent "difference" in the boxes but a difference not affecting the chance of obtaining a blue marble.

- (=) There are just ten times the same amount of each in box B.
- (=) The chances are the same, it's 1:10 scale, there are still the same amount of chances for either boxes of getting a blue one as there are a red one.

Finally within-box mathematization occurs and a comparison shows equal ratios, fractions, or percents across boxes.

- (=) It doesn't matter, for the factor of both boxes are blue over red, which is equal to Box A = 4/6 = 2/3 and Box B = 40/60 = 4/6 = 2/3.
- (=) Because there are 40% blue in each box.

The range of responses to this task is great and all levels are likely to be represented in a classroom. It may be difficult, however, for those suggesting the lower level responses to appreciate the proportional reasoning used in the higher level responses. The connection to ratio, proportion, and percent is crucial to success and reinforces the need for these numeracy skills by the middle school years.

5.7   MEASURING CHANCE: THE DISTRIBUTION OF REPEATED TRIALS

The tasks discussed in the previous section focus on a single outcome for an event—tossing a die, drawing a name from a hat, or drawing a marble of a certain color. The probabilities of these events are based on sample spaces that take into account all possible outcomes, for example the six sides of the die, the 29 names, or the total numbers of marbles in the boxes. If one were to imagine repeating these single events many times, for example repeatedly tossing the die or drawing names or marbles (with replacement after each draw), one would expect a distribution of outcomes reflecting the proportions of the events in the sample space—1/6 of each number on the die, 16/29 girls, or 40% blue marbles. The random nature of the process as noted by David Moore at the beginning of this chapter suggests "a regular pattern" in many repetitions but this does not mean a perfect match with theory. Although this issue of the tension between expectation (of theory) and variation (from the random process) is dealt with in considerable detail in Chapter 7, an extension of one of the tasks in the previous section is presented here as a starting point. Considering many single outcomes early in work with chance is likely to lay a useful foundation for considering probability distributions formally in later years.

Consider the task presented in Fig. 5.9, which extends the question in Fig. 5.6 and asks for a distribution of the outcomes for 60 rolls of a die.[33] Using an activity such as this is a good beginning and motivation for classroom trials, which can then be recorded and compared to the estimates.

Of interest in students' responses are not only the values given but also the reasoning shown in justifying those numbers. Some students, responding at the prestructural level, have difficulty conceiving of the task and making up a set of six numbers that sum to 60.

- {1, 60, 0, 0, 0, 0} [no reasoning]
- {31, 5, 10, 29, 10, 10} One comes up a lot of times, six comes up a few times, and the rest come up all over the place.

At the unistructural level are responses that appear to understand one aspect of the task. They may, for example, provide numbers that sum to 60 but display idiosyncratic patterns, which have too much or too little variation, or which display strict probability accompanied by incomplete or illogical reasoning.

- {10, 20, 10, 10, 0, 10} Because you mainly get lower numbers than higher numbers.
- {15, 15, 15, 2, 3, 15} Because most of them are opposite each other so you get them the same amount of times.
- {10, 10, 10, 10, 10, 10} Because they're numbers I think would come up easy.

Imagine you threw the die 60 times. Fill in the table below to show how many times each number might come up.	
Number on Dice	How many times it might come up
1	
2	
3	
4	
5	
6	
TOTAL	60
Why do you think these numbers are reasonable?	

FIG. 5.9. Task to suggest the distribution of 60 tosses of a single die.

Some students have a strict (or nearly strict) view of the theoretical model involved, which appears to be in transition in terms of the requirement of the task.

- {9, 10, 10, 10, 10, 11} Because the numbers have the same chance of coming up.
- {10, 10, 10, 10, 10, 10} Because they all use equal space on the dice.

Other students show an appreciation of variation in either the numbers presented (considered reasonable based on a statistical criterion[34]) or in the verbal reasoning expressed but not both. These are considered multistructural in that they are not consistent across both aspects of the task.

- {15, 8, 9, 13, 10, 6} Because I think that's how many times they come up.
- {11, 19, 11, 10, 5, 4} There is a chance in it being all numbers.
- {5, 10, 10, 10, 15, 10} The dice could roll anything.

At the relational level students produce both appropriate variation in their estimates and in their reasoning.

- {8, 12, 10, 10, 7, 13} It's random but there is more chance of getting around 10 or at least a few.
- {9, 11, 12, 8, 10, 10} Because they add up to 60. All numbers are around 10 and each number has equal chances. It would be unlikely for every number to come up exactly 10 times.

The importance of tasks like this one is that they allow students to display several aspects of their understanding, from their basic appreciation of the mathematics of the task requiring the table values to sum to 60, to their resolution of the dilemma about the expected theoretical outcome and the expected variation from it. From the elementary to the middle grades, the fraction of prestructural responses is likely to fall from about 1/2 to 1/6, but at the same time the fraction of strict probability responses increases from about 1/20 to 2/5. It would appear that teaching about probability may override the consideration of random variation, which is why tasks like that in Fig. 5.9 should be used in classrooms across these years. Consistently across the years, about 1/8 of students provide multistructural responses, struggling with acknowledged variation, whereas at the middle school level about 1/20 students integrate the ideas of expectation and variation appropriately for the distribution of 60 outcomes.[35]

An additional classroom or assessment activity related to asking students to create their own distributions is suggested by David Green.[36] He presented middle school students with three bar graphs showing the frequencies of outcomes for 60 trials of a regular die like the one used in Figs. 5.6 and 5.9. One graph had a peak in the middle at 3 and 4, one was uniform with a frequency of 10 for each outcome, and one showed varying frequencies from 8 to 12 across the six outcomes. Although the largest group of students chose the appropriate graph as representing the 60 outcomes, 36% chose the peaked graph and 20% chose the even distribution. He believed that choices of the peaked graph reflected beliefs that 1 and/or 6 were more difficult to throw. It is also possible that students were confusing experiences of outcomes for a single toss with experiences where two dice are tossed and the two outcomes summed. This context is considered in the next section.

5.8   MEASURING CHANCE: INDEPENDENT EVENTS

The next step in increasing the complexity of tasks involving chance is the consideration of more than one event. These events might occur simultaneously, such as tossing two coins, or in sequence, such as observing nonmultiple births in a family. Implicit in such events is the condition that the outcome of one event does not influence the other. Termed "independence of events" in the later years of the curriculum, the link is not usually made in the elementary years. It is taken for granted that when two dice are tossed simultaneously and the outcomes summed to create an outcome, there is no influence of one die on the other. This is a matter that should be discussed at all levels, even if the term "independent" is not introduced. It is not easy at the elementary level to suggest alternative scenarios where independence does not hold but which appear similar enough to warrant distinction.

The main focus when studying compound events is working out the combinations of outcomes of the single events in order to find probabilities of particular events or determining a complete set of equally likely outcomes to use for calculating probabilities. In a theoretical sense this can be seen as working out the cross product of two sample spaces, but without that structure, devices such as tree diagrams and lists assist in documenting the possible outcomes. The fact that the process mimics a multiplicative process is not always obvious when making a list and the connection should be made explicit whenever possible. Notable difficulties that arise in early problems relate, for example, to obtaining two sums to equal 3 when two dice are tossed using a 1 and 2 from each die, or appreciating that when two coins are tossed, a head and a tail can occur in two ways whereas two heads can only occur in one way. Intuitions in this regard generally do not reflect the appropriate model until many experiences have accumulated and been linked to more formal presentation of outcomes.

Providing opportunities to explore various models for compound events from the upper elementary level can give insight into students' progress in picking up ideas associated with independent events and their documentation. Three examples are discussed in this section and illustrate the different models available. It should not be assumed that understanding of one model will automatically transfer to another. Summing the outcomes of rolling two ordinary dice provides a number between 2 and 12. Spinning two half-black-half-white spinners to produce a "win" with two blacks produces a yes-no type outcome, whereas observing the outcome of four coin tosses in a row produces many different possible sequences of heads and tails.

There are many classroom activities suggested for exploring the outcomes when two dice are tossed and the outcomes summed. Usually the appreciation of the nature of the entire distribution of outcomes is one of the goals of these activities. Sometimes a physical distribution is created from outcomes, say with chips. At other times, games with a board provided for chips begin with a child-chosen arrangement of chips that are removed as associated sums are obtained from the dice. Once such activities have been completed and discussed, more specific tasks can be employed to explore the overall understandings of students and their application to specific cases. Consider for example the two questions in Fig. 5.10. These focus on different aspects of the summing of two dice than considering the overall distribution but focus on important features that should be derived from work with the distribution.[37]

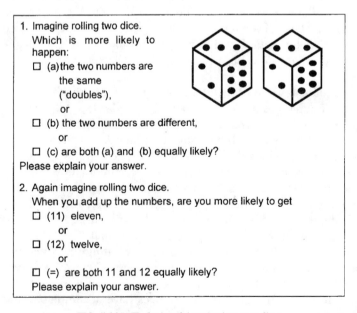

FIG. 5.10.   Tasks involving tossing two dice.

The levels of response to these questions are likely to depend to some extent on exposure to experiences with two dice but much can be learned from reasoning associated with inappropriate or partially correct responses. Previous experience, for example, may not reinforce the desired understanding, as the following justifications for the first question illustrate.

- (c) Because when I have played a game, I got lots of doubles and lots of numbers.
- (c) Well it happens like [. . .] both ways, it can sort of like have two numbers, then it can be different, then it can go like that again and it can go on like that for three times and then change for about one time and then go back to numbers that are different.

The single chance mechanism of "anything can happen" is also used to justify a decision of equality.

- (c) Well it is both possible in that they could come up.
- (c) Because you're not really certain what is going to happen, where the dice is going to roll.

As might be expected the influence of equal likelihood for the outcome from a single die sometimes interferes with thinking about two dice, for students of all grades.

- (c) Because there's the same chance of the number coming up on each separate dice. So it would be the same chance.
- (c) Because both dice have the same numbers on it and they would probably come up the same.

It is very unlikely that any students who have had even limited experience with dice choose the option (a) that doubles are more likely.

Experience, however, can lead to intuitions about the appropriate choice of different numbers being more likely, option (b).

- (b) Because in some games that I play with double dice you have to get double to start and so like it sometimes takes about 10 minutes to get a double.
- (b) Because it's sort of pretty rare that you roll the dice with two numbers the same on it.

At the next level of response students begin to qualify the opportunities to get each type of outcome from the dice.

- (b) The two numbers would maybe be different because there is more than one number so it would be likely that a different one would turn up.
- (b) [. . .] So if you get a two it's not as likely to get another two, but it is possible, 'cos you've got a lot of other numbers that could also come up with it.

As attempts at quantification increase, there is often confusion about how many possibilities exist. The following is a typical response of students with limited experience.

- (b) Because if the two numbers are the same it would be a 1 in 12 chance because there's two dice. And if two numbers are different it could be any two numbers and it wouldn't have to be the same numbers that come up.

Some do not quantify the comparison of outcomes.

- (b) There's six chances that it would come up doubles. There's more chances that it would come up uneven.

Others begin to appreciate the numerical relationship of the outcomes.

- (b) Because if I roll [a die] and get a 2, I've got a 1 in 6 chance of getting a 2. And so five chances I won't get a 2 and one chance that I will get a 2.

This response shows evidence of thinking through the situation with the dice. The next response may reflect similarly on a two-way table of outcomes or may be a "learned response."

- (b) Because there is a 6 in 36 chance of rolling a double and 30 in 36 of not getting a double.

This final response, although mathematically pleasing and "correct," is quite uncommon for students who have not recently experienced work with lists and proto-sample spaces to explain experimental results tossing and recording sums from two dice.

   The second question in Fig. 5.9 is more specific and designed to distinguish the understanding of students in relation to the number of possible outcomes when two dice are tossed. Choosing 11 and 12 allows for the distinction between beliefs that there is one way to get 11 as 5 + 6 and that there are two ways, taking into account the 5 and the 6 on each die. Eleven and 12 are chosen for this question because there is also the possibility of a nebulous "more" answer based on 11 and 12 being larger numbers than say

3 and 2, which would have the same theoretical probabilities associated with them.

Similar to the responses for the first question, some students rely on personal experience or an "anything can happen" view of chance.

- (12) Sometimes when I roll them I usually get maybe with two [dice], 12, because mostly at home I do get a 12.
- (=) Because you don't know what can turn up or it might not even be 11 or 12.

Ideas associated with beliefs about the difficulty of getting a six on a single die often produce a correct choice but based on an inappropriate justification.

- (11) Because sometimes it's a bit hard to roll 6 all the time.
- (11) I think you would be pretty lucky to get two 6s, so I reckon you are more likely to get an 11. You could get a 12 only if you get two 6s but not many people roll two 6s.

The more complex responses that claim the outcomes 11 and 12 are equally likely are based on allowing for too many possibilities for both without actually considering what they are, or neglecting the two combinations for 11.

- (=) Because you can add up—there are lots of different ways you can add up to 11 and 12.
- (=) Because there's only one way you can get an 11, which is a 5 and a 6, and only one way you can get a 12, two 6s.

The later response is quite common and shows that students are concentrating on the appropriate features of the context. "Correct" responses are often stated implicitly by those with prior experience with two dice.

- (11) Because there are two ways of rolling 11 and only one way of rolling a 12.

Others are more explicit.

- (11) Because the possibilities of adding up to 11 are a 6 on one and a 5 on the other, or a 5 on one and a 6 on the other, whereas to get a 12 you need to get a 6 on both.

Overall there are many levels of interaction and response for two-dice problems. As an initial activity rather than a culmination, class debate on the virtues of obtaining 11 in one or two ways can lead to trials and activities to create the entire distribution of outcomes from 2 to 12.[38]

A different type of compound event is seen in the task presented in Fig. 5.11.[39] Here an area model of probability is presented and although the area of 1/2 of the spinner is appropriate for translation to a probability of 1/2 of obtaining a "black" outcome, the visual presentation of two spinners side by side with 1/2 of their total area colored black is no longer appropriate for translating to a probability statement when both spinners are spun. Presenting students with a task such as this after they have worked with two dice (or some other random generator) but before they have carried out actual experiments with spinners, is a good way to judge transfer of understanding, as well as to motivate the exploration to follow.

For those not explicitly taught or who have had difficulty with comprehension, the range of sophistication of responses to the task in Fig. 5.11 provides valuable information for teachers and starting points for discussion and activities. The majority of students agree with Jeff that he has a 50-50 chance of winning in Part (a). When asked to translate their chance expectation into the number of games Jeff would win out of 10, students are required to make connections to the part–whole concept as well as to their appreciation of what 50-50 means.

Some students, often younger ones, appear not to recognize some of the salient connections in making their estimates.

- [Agree with Jeff] Part (b): 9 out of 10, because I'm turning 9 this year.
- [Agree with Jeff] Part (b): 4 out of 10, because the arrow stops where it wants to stop.

Some estimates reflect agreement with Jeff but without the expected reasoning.

- [Agree with Jeff] Part (b): 5 out of 10, [it] could be right over on the right and you don't knock it enough.

Others suggest variation from the translation of 50-50 but without a mathematical reason.

- [Agree with Jeff] Part (b): 7 out of 10, it depends on how hard he spins it.

This is a single idea and related to the general idea of "anything can happen" but with a physical mechanism described. Other responses are similar to those observed in different contexts.

- [Agree with Jeff] Part (b): 5 out of 10, you don't know what will happen with a 50-50 chance.
- [Agree with Jeff] Part (b): 5 out of 10, but it's chance, it could go either way.

The two fair spinners shown below are part of a carnival game. A player wins a prize only when both arrows land on black after each spinner is spun once.

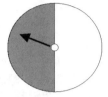 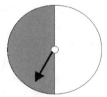

(a) Jeff thinks he has a 50-50 chance of winning. Do you agree? (Circle one)   Yes   No   Explain your answer.

(b) If he played the game 10 times, how many times would you expect him to win? Why?

(c) Now play it 10 times and record your wins and losses.

	WIN	LOSS
GAME 1		
GAME 2		
GAME 3		
GAME 4		
GAME 5		
GAME 6		
GAME 7		
GAME 8		
GAME 9		
GAME 10		
TOTAL		

(d) How does this compare with what you thought in Part (b)?

FIG. 5.11.   Task involving two spinners.

Of those who attempt to quantify their explanations, some focus on fewer than the total number of possibilities, whereas a few realize all possibilities.

- [Disagree with Jeff] Part (b): 3 or 4 out of 10, the luck of getting one is a 50-50 chance but the luck of getting the second one is even less of a chance.
- [Disagree with Jeff] Part (b): 3 or 4 out of 10, because both arrows have to be on black and one could land on white. There are 3 combinations to get and 2 of them are losses.
- [Disagree with Jeff] Part (b): 2 or 3 out of 10, 25% chance, that's a division of 4 parts—[I] divided 10 by 4 to get around 2 or 3.

Of interest for later discussion of variation in Chapter 7 is the tendency for about a third of students to qualify their estimates with some acknowledgment of possible variation, using phrases like "about 5" or "4 or 5." Fewer follow this with qualifications in their explanations.

- It would be a fluke if it happened on every spin.
- Because it's a 50-50 chance, there is no way of telling exactly.

One of the issues for the classroom is how much experimentation is required before students adjust their estimates to the appropriate expectation. Again, about a third of students who perform 10 spins of the two spinners and obtain three or fewer wins, are likely to change their estimates to 2 or 3 wins out of 10. Most however, although appreciating the necessity for the number of wins to be smaller have difficulty expressing this in quantified terms. A response such as the following is rare for students who have not had an introduction to sample spaces or their prototypes.

- Part (d): It compares badly because if you get white on the first one, it's an immediate loss; change [after trials in Part (c)] to 25%.

A traditional way of considering more than two independent events is to set tasks that look at a sequence of two-outcome events, such as tossing a coin a number of times or observing the gender of a sequence of babies born at a hospital.[40] Whereas the complete distribution of such compound outcomes is described in the senior school curriculum by a binomial distribution for a given n, many intuitions can be explored and built with simpler questions. Although many of the problems set with random generators appear far removed from the world outside of the classroom, there are occasional links with media reports that suggest that aspects of statistical literacy depend on chance understanding. Consider the questions presented in Fig. 5.12 that are set in the context of tossing a coin at the start of an international cricket match.[41] Such "unusual" events as losing the toss 8 out of 9 times are commonly reported in the news media. They provide motivating starting points for discussion of the likelihood of outcomes.

Although to many mathematics teachers Part (a) in Fig. 5.12 is a quite straightforward question, requiring a calculation that relates to the multiplicative nature of independent events ($1/2 \times 1/2 \times 1/2 \times 1/2 = 1/16$), most students, even many expected to have been exposed to the ideas, are not likely to appreciate this aspect of the problem. Of the inappropriate responses some would challenge a teacher to find useful starting points for instruction, whereas others would illustrate the great disadvantage to students of not making appropriate connections to the numeracy skills that are part of the mathematics curriculum. Of particular concern are responses greater than 1/2, such as "4/4" or "probable." The single-faceted

During the recent Australian cricket tour of South Africa, the Australian captain Allan Border had lost 8 out of 9 tosses in his previous 9 matches as captain. Imagine his situation at this point in time.

(a) Suppose Border decides to choose heads from now on. For the next 4 tosses of the coin, what is the chance of the coin coming up tails (and him losing the tosses) 4 times out of 4?

(b1) Suppose tails came up 4 times out of 4. For the 5th toss, should Border choose

☐ Heads   ☐ Tails   ☐ Doesn't matter

(b2) What is the probability of getting heads on this next toss?

(b3) What is the probability of getting tails on this next toss?

FIG. 5.12.   Task involving independent coin tosses based on a media report.

response of the "anything can happen" type occurs in two forms, without and with an accompanying numerical answer.

- Part (a): Anything is possible.
- Part (a): Doesn't matter, it's the luck of the toss.
- Part (a): It's both half and half because you can't predict what's going to come up.

Some students have elaborate but misguided concepts that may take some time to work through.

- Part (a): P(half+half+half+half). The chances of Border losing the tosses 4 times out of 4 are 4/8 or 2/4. There is a 50-50 chance he will lose on each of the 4 tosses.

Many students provide a response equivalent to a value of $1/2$, 0.5, or 50%; in fact this type of response is more likely than a value less than $1/2$ for all grades from upper elementary through high school. The fact that many responses may reflect, as in the preceding case, a summing of numerators and denominators before "reducing to lowest terms," is particularly disturbing. These responses are also as likely to represent an "it is possible" approach as a calculation. This is an issue of statistical literacy in the use of language, both verbal and numerical, to express ideas.

With increasing grade, students are more likely to have a qualitative appreciation that the probability should be less than $1/2$ since a single coin toss has that chance. Just as in the case of two spinners, however, many have difficulty with quantifying this appropriately.

- Part (a): unlikely
- Part (a): 25% [1/4]
- Part (a): 12.5% [1/8]
- Part (a): $1/2 + 1/2 + 1/2 + 1/2 = 1/8$
- Part (a): 1 in 5 chance {HHHH TTTT HHHT TTTH TTHH}

The last response in particular provides an interesting place to begin discussion of the possible outcomes.

The second set of questions in Fig. 5.12, Parts (b1), (b2), and (b3) focus on the next toss and explore the influence of previous outcomes on the next toss, perhaps reflecting the gambler's fallacy, which expects a head to occur to balance a run of tails.[42] The majority of students at all levels reject both a positive or negative recency belief and say it does not matter what choice is made next in Part (b1). Approximately equal percents of students, across grade levels, say the next choice should be "heads" or "tails" but of these a third revert to a probability of $1/2$ in Parts (b2) and (b3). Beliefs about "heads" and "tails" may be confounded by the usage of $1/2$ or 50-50 to signal the impossibility to determine the answer.

Even at higher grade levels where theoretical probability is introduced, discussion is required in order to be sure that the model for independent events is understood in context and previously held beliefs are considered. It is possible that some students will find it very difficult to forget a belief that "tails" is lucky for them but they must learn to balance that belief with a statistical appreciation of independent compound events and the numerical likelihood they present. This is an essential part of statistical literacy as students enter a world of gaming and lotteries.

The three models introduced in this section are very different although they all involve repeated independent use of a random generator. The two dice each present six possible outcomes and whose sums produce 11 possible outcomes; these 11 however are not equally likely and manipulation with numbers is required to sort out the structure and likelihood of outcomes. The two spinners each present two equally likely outcomes, visually modeled with areas, which lead directly to part–whole understanding and to probability rather than working with numbers. Working out all "possible" outcomes may not be as intuitive in the spinner context as in the dice context. The four coins again each present two equally likely outcomes, this time associated with a "yes-no," Head or Tail, type of outcome rather than an area model. That tossing two such coins and requiring two heads for a win leads to an identical probability model to the spinner task is not obvious to most students. Activities combining more than two events are usually built on single events with two outcomes in order to simplify the compound probabilities. It is of course possible to consider tossing three or more dice, leading to 16 or more outcomes but this is not often done.[43]

It is important for classroom activities to include a range of models and not to assume that understanding of independence or the relationship between single and multiple outcomes transfers automatically from one context to another. Working with tree diagrams is often useful in creating connections among different task contexts. They are also adaptable to situations where unequal probabilities are involved and can be appropriately labeled on the branches of the tree.

5.9 MEASURING CHANCE: CONJUNCTION AND CONDITIONAL EVENTS

It is likely that in school contexts students meet non-simple events presented as compound independent events, as discussed in the previous section, more often than they meet events made up of the conjunction of two other events or events of a conditional nature depending on another event. Because conjunction and conditional contexts arise commonly in social discourse, however, one of statistical literacy's goals is to be able to interpret events in such contexts appropriately. Traditionally when conjunction or conditional events were introduced as theoretical probability topics, they were accompanied by Venn diagrams, examples that involved removing balls from urns, and formal symbolism such as $P(A|B) = P(A \cap B)/P(B)$. The goal was likely to be a statement of Bayes Theorem with associated problems requiring the careful distinction of $P(A|B)$ from $P(B|A)$. Recent recognition of the importance of developing an appreciation of conjunction and conditional events expressed in common language, however, has motivated an interest in these events before their introduction in formal courses.

> Concepts of probability, such as independent and dependent events, and their relationship to compound events and conditional probability should be taught intuitively. Formal definitions and properties should be developed only after a firm conceptual base is established . . .[44]
> - Estimate the probability that an arbitrary student at the school plays on a sports team and plays a musical instrument. How is this related to estimates of the separate probabilities that a student plays a musical instrument and that he or she plays on a sports team?
> - Estimate the probability that a student who plays on a sports team also plays a musical instrument.[45]

Although the language and context of the conditional and conjunction events used with college students in early research projects was intended to be complex, it is possible to ask more straightforward questions in contexts that students understand. It is then possible to concentrate on the meaning of language in order to interpret the events. Consider two conjunction questions shown in Fig. 5.13.[46] The first question is asked in a frequency form based on a sample (set) of 100 men. The second is asked in a probability form and hence includes no numbers. The first form encourages, in fact explicitly asks for, a number between 0 and 100 to be provided for each part, whereas the second allows for any type of expression that can convey the chances of the events occurring. Giving students the opportunity to respond in both formats allows an assessment of which is more difficult for them. It also allows for comparison and perhaps debate about whether the goals of answering the two questions are similar. It may appear that the probability form of the second question is closer to the chance curriculum and in terms of language this is true. The frequency form of expressing conjunction relationships, however, is quite common in the media based on statistical reports from governments and other agencies. Both forms are hence important in activities aimed to build statistical literacy skills.

Judging the appropriateness of answers to the two questions involves the relationship of the answers provided to all three parts of each question. In each case the answer to Part (c) of the question must be less than or equal to the minimum of the answers to Parts (a) and (b). If expressed in words rather than numbers, as might happen for the second question, then the meaning of the terms used must imply the inequality previously noted. There are two other possible relationships among the answers to the three

---

1. A health survey was conducted in a sample of 100 men in Australia of all ages and occupations. Please estimate:

    (a) How many of the 100 men have had one or more heart attacks.

    (b) How many of the 100 men are over 55 years old.

    (c) How many of the 100 men both are over 55 years old and have had one or more heart attacks.

2. Please estimate:

    (a) The probability that you will miss a whole week of school next year.

    (b) The probability that you will get a cold next year.

    (c) The probability that you will get a cold causing you to miss a whole week of school next year.

FIG. 5.13.   Conjunction events in context.

parts that are of interest here. The answer to Part (c) may lie between the answers to Parts (a) and (b), or it may be greater than them both. The middle option may represent some form of averaging of likelihood in the response, whereas the answer to Part (c) being the largest of the three probabilities is the antithesis of an appropriate interpretation and may reflect giving too much attention to the extra information that defines the conjunction event.

What is initially frustrating for some students about these questions is that there is no "correct" answer to each part but that it is the overall relationship of the responses to the parts that is significant. For some the cognitive load of keeping the relevant information in mind is too much and aids such as Venn diagrams or two-way tables may be useful when frequencies are involved. What is surprising to some students is that they are allowed to make up their own numbers related to 100 (for the first question). Working out sensible values for the combination of conditions is an interesting exercise and can be the source of class debate.

For the first question, responses satisfying the criterion that the frequency for Part (c) be less than or equal to the minimum of the frequencies for Parts (a) and (b), are generally given by the majority of students (50–60%) in all grades from upper elementary through high school. Although the likelihood of giving a meaningless answer diminishes with grade, the frequencies of the other two alternatives, "averaging" answers to Parts (a) and (b) to obtain Part (c) and suggesting an answer to Part (c) that is the greatest, vary little across grades or with each other. It appears that there is a general ability to interpret the language of conjunction events in straightforward contexts. Although many students, perhaps a third, answer the first question in terms of percents and fractions rather than frequencies, those who respond in frequencies are more likely to show an appropriate relationship. Other complicating features can be added to this kind of conjunction question to form links to other areas of the curriculum, particularly science and social science.

Turning to the second question in Fig. 5.13, the context is based on personal experiences and the questions are stated in terms of probabilities rather than frequencies. Students appear to have more difficulty in deciding what form of response to give in this context. More often they give answers in percents but fractions, words, and mixed forms are common, with some also providing frequencies. The following are examples of appropriate responses expressed in the different forms.

- [Percent] (a) 75%, (b) 100%, (c) 65%.
- [Fraction] (a) 50-50, (b) 50-50, (c) 40/100.
- [Word] (a) likely, (b) most likely, (c) unlikely.
- [Frequency] (a) 30, (b) 90, (c) 10.

It is difficult to tell whether the last response is intended to reflect percent. Responses reflecting the "averaging" notion of the conjunction probability also appear in all forms.

- [Percent] (a) 25%, (b) 95%, (c) 50%.
- [Fraction] (a) 1 out of 10, (b) 99 out of 100, (c) 5 out of 10.
- [Word] (a) maybe, (b) certainly, (c) probably.
- [Frequency] (a) 50, (b) 90, (c) 60.

Similar types of response occur for the inappropriate view that the conjunction event is the most likely of the three.

- [Percent] (a) 10%, (b) 85%, (c) 95%.
- [Fraction] (a) 0.4, (b) 0.3, (c) 0.7.
- [Word] (a) unlikely, (b) unlikely, (c) likely.
- [Frequency] (a) 20, (b) 50, (c) 75.

In terms of discussion of students' responses, all forms of answer should be accepted and discussed to discover the meaning intended. Linking expressions to part–whole representations typical of formal probability can be an exercise that follows student discussion. Being aware of appropriate alternatives is also important in terms of building statistical literacy skills. Interpretation of language at this point can be linked to the type of discussion suggested in Sections 5.3 and 5.4. Responses presented in percent or fraction form in which the answers to Parts (a) and (b) are summed to give the answer to Part (c), should attract particular discussion to find out why this strategy is employed and why it is inappropriate.

Overall students are likely to improve in their performance on questions such as the second one over the years from upper elementary to secondary with the percent of responses satisfying the appropriate criteria rising from about 40% to 70%. Because the context appears equally understandable to all ages, it is likely that it is the use of probabilistic rather than frequency language and its translation into the complex structure of the events, which causes problems for younger children. Although again the tendency to choose an answer to Part (c) between or greater than the answers to Parts (a) and (b) continues to be constant across grades, the percent of undefined responses decreases markedly.

In terms of theoretical probability, the calculation of conditional probability requires an understanding of conjunction events. As noted at the beginning of this section, however, it is now accepted in curriculum documents that a conceptual base for conditional events is needed and should be developed before formal definitions and properties are introduced.[47] The two questions presented in Fig. 5.14 reflect this interest in laying a

---

1. Please estimate:

   (a) Out of 100 men, how many are left-handed.

   (b) Out of 100 left-handed adults, how many are men.

2. Please estimate:

   (a) The probability that a woman is a school teacher.

   (b) The probability that a school teacher is a woman.

FIG. 5.14.   Conditional events in context.

foundation and building intuitions in familiar contexts.[48] Similar to the two questions in Fig. 5.13, the first question asks for a response in frequency form out of 100 and the second asks for a probability. In this case both questions present contexts that would be expected to be familiar to students, acknowledging that some students may have more experience with left-hand people being left-handed themselves and some elementary school students may have more experience of female teachers than high school students have. Again however, it is not the absolute values of the numerical values that are judged for correctness (although this may be an interesting point for class discussion). What is of interest is the relationship between the two responses within each question and whether they satisfy the appropriate condition that the answer to Part (b) should be larger than that to Part (a), reflecting the higher proportion of men among left-hand adults than of left-handed men and the higher proportion of females among teachers than teachers among females.

For both of the questions in Fig. 5.14 there is likely to be improved performance with grade level. The first question, being in frequency form, is more accessible, with very few undefined responses and success rates from just below 50% at the upper elementary level to about 70% at the senior high school level. Giving equal answers for the two parts is more common than suggesting a larger answer for Part (a) than Part (b), but both of these types of response diminish with grade. At all grade levels about two-thirds of students respond with frequencies related to 100, about 20% translate to a percent form, and a few present fractional forms. Frequency and percent forms are more likely to be correct.

Interpretation of the second question in Fig. 5.14 is much more problematic with few students at the upper elementary level (about 10%) providing appropriate responses. By the senior high level this is likely to rise to around 40%. What is consistent across grades is the tendency to give the same value for each part of the question, which is done by nearly half of students. Given the context it is likely to be the language in which the conditions are expressed that is the source of difficulty. Many students may believe that they are answering the same question twice.

Again as for the probability-based question in a conjunction event, the conditional probability form allows students to respond with many representations: percents, frequencies, fractions, words, "yes/no," and mixed forms. Performance is likely to be slightly better for percent and fraction forms (around 30% success). The following are examples of appropriate responses to the two parts of the second question in Fig. 5.14.

- [Percent] (a) 10%, (b) 70%.
- [Fraction] (a) 0.05, (b) 0.68.
- [Word] (a) rare chance, (b) likely.
- [Frequency] (a) 5, (b) 85.
- [Mixed] (a) 50/50, (b) more than likely.

Although the final response shows the appropriate relationship between Parts (a) and (b), discussion might be useful in interpreting the understanding of what is required in Part (a). Many who respond with the same values to Parts (a) and (b) also choose values associated with a half and discussion should sort out whether these responses are meant to represent frequency or an "anything can happen" view of chance.

- [Percent] (a) 60%, (b) 60%.
- [Fraction] (a) 5/10, (b) 1/2 and 1/2.
- [Word] (a) very likely, (b) same as above.
- [Frequency] (a) 50, (b) 50.
- [Mixed] (a) 50-50, (b) 50%.

Responses with values for Part (b) greater than Part (a) are stated in similar forms to those just mentioned.

Both types of tasks discussed in this section, conjunction and conditional, are handled more easily by students when presented in frequency rather than probability form. These observations support the views of Gerd Gigerenzer[49] in his explanation for why college students did so badly when presented questions in probability form in the early work of Amos Tversky and Daniel Kahneman.[50] Classroom work with questions such as these should focus directly on links to the conjunction and conditional language used, and can be seen as applying literacy skills across the curriculum as well as developing statistical literacy skills that provide a foundation for those who go on to study formal probability. For those who do not go on with further study, the skills are important when interpreting public statements made by politicians and medical experts, where decision-making is to follow.

5.10   MEASURING CHANCE: ODDS

Making the connection between probability and odds is often notoriously difficult for students. The connections to ratio and proportion and the part–whole understanding elsewhere in the mathematics curriculum are essential at this point. Although not central to the chance curriculum,[51] students are likely to meet odds in many out-of-school contexts, and exposure inside of school may assist in building appropriate understanding. In most media situations not only is it important to understand the mathematics of odds, as "against" to "for," but also it is necessary to be able to read the surrounding text for nuances to assist in interpretation. The headline and questions in Fig. 5.15 offer an opportunity for a meaningful discussion of both aspects.[52]

Because the questions in Fig. 5.15 are based in a specific context, some students may have out-of-school experiences that greatly assist them, whereas others may have backgrounds that mean they have never been exposed to odds. If using the task as the basis for a classroom discussion or group work, a teacher should be careful in making initial assessments of students and engender a collaborative attitude toward sharing understanding. As students discuss their responses and reasoning, three perspectives are likely to emerge in dealing with the context. These perspectives are reflected in probabilistic (P) language, frequency (F) language, or social (S) language. The last involves use of terminology like *odds, votes, favorites,* or money. For each of these perspectives, increasing levels of response are likely to be observed as more sophisticated proportional reasoning is incorporated in the explanations.

North at 7:2

But we can still win match, says coach

What does odds at 7:2 mean in this headline about the North against South football match? Give as much detail as you can.

FIG. 5.15. Newspaper headline containing odds.

Some responses demonstrate no appreciation of any aspect of the context.

- 7 a.m.–2 p.m.

Others may indicate a reading of the accompanying language.

- That North lost by 5 points. [F]
- I think it's a bit like betting on the horses. [S]

At the next level responses contain a single element associated with the meaning ascertained.

- That's North's chances of winning. [P]
- That is the predicted score. [F]
- The number of how many say they are for South football. [S]

Responses then attempt to qualify the perspective used.

- North has a 7% chance to win and a 2% chance to lose. [P]
- It means in their last game they lost 7 goals to 2 goals. But they think there is still a chance. [F]
- It means North are 7-2 favorites. [S]

These responses are followed by attempts at using ratios, some of which are idiosyncratic or incomplete.

- Their chance to win the game; for example, 2-2 would be an even chance. [P]
- It means North has won 2 games out of 7. [F]
- 7/2 means that the odds are against them. [S]

Consolidation of the ratio idea is then likely to be observed in several stages, at first misinterpreted as a part–whole, rather than a part–part, ratio or else not explicitly stated.

- 7-2 means they have a 2 out of 7 chance to beat South. [P]
- It means if they play 7 games, they win 2. [F]
- For every $2 you put in, you get $7 out (if they win). [S]
- It means that 9 people or something were asked who would win the match, and 7 people said North would and 2 people said South would. [S]

At the next level responses interpret the part–part relationship appropriately but, perhaps due to lack of personal experience, get the direction wrong.

- 'Experts' believe North has a 7/9 chance of winning and South has 2/9. [P]
- Out of 9 games North would probably win 7 and South would probably win 2. [F]
- 7-2 means that if you place $2 on the game (probably with bookmakers), you will receive $7 plus your original $2 back if North win. These prices (7-2) are called odds. North expected to win. [S]

Finally responses reflect both the appropriate part–part relationship, and direction.

- North hasn't got a good chance, like ratio 7:2. A 2/9 chance to win. [P]
- These are the odds that North will win, these aren't very good. It means that out of 9 games, North will lose 7 and win 2. [F]
- 7-2 are the odds or chance the team has of winning. For every $2 you bet, if they win you get $7 back plus your $2. South are more likely to win. [S]

Responses to tasks like the one in Fig. 5.15 are likely to display a wide range of understanding of both the mathematics and the context. The three perspectives on interpreting the context can provide material for classroom discussion and debate about possible ways to consider odds. Connections to ratio, fractions, part–part, and part–whole understanding are obvious and should be made clear on many occasions.

5.11   CHANCE AND LUCK

If the consideration of independent and dependent events is the most sophisticated expectation of the chance curriculum at the school level, then dealing with the connection of chance to luck might be considered to come at the other end of the spectrum. The term *luck* has different meanings depending on context. It can be an explanation for an "anything can happen" view of chance outcomes: "it's just luck." But it can also be a causal mechanism in explaining the same outcomes from a different perspective: "this is my lucky number." Although luck is dismissed in considerations of frequency or theoretical probability settings, it may play a role in considerations of subjective probability. One of the questions for teachers in the light of a hierarchical curriculum is whether luck can be handled and dismissed at the lower grades. Evidence from interaction with adults in casinos around the world every day suggests that for many people a belief in luck as a causal mechanism continues to explain chance outcomes. It is likely that discussions of luck should occur periodically throughout the years of schooling in various contexts, perhaps motivated by a report of a "lucky winner" of a recent lottery.

Consideration of luck is likely to occur naturally, for example in relation to simple chance events, like the rolling of a die as discussed in Section 5.6. It is also possible, however, to address issues of luck directly by putting forward scenarios for debate. Two such examples are shown in Fig. 5.16.[53] The first is totally subjective whereas the second involves lottery numbers where it is possible to consider descriptively the likelihood of outcomes.

Considering first the question in Fig. 5.16 about getting out of bed, students' responses are likely to reflect several levels of belief. The lowest level of response agrees with the statement.

- I think he's right.
- I get out the same side too. It's bad luck getting out of the other side.

The next level of response is a straightforward disagreement with the statement.

- Not true.
- It's just superstition.
- It doesn't matter what side of the bed he gets out on. You still could fail or pass the test.

Other students provide more complex responses by including supporting arguments.

- It won't help him get better marks. You only get good marks if you study and try hard.
- I don't think he would unless there's a wall on the right hand side.

Perhaps the most sophisticated are explanations incorporating a psychological element. Because the nature of belief in luck is sometimes difficult to fathom, such arguments may prove useful in the classroom.

1.	Every morning, James gets out on the left side of the bed. He says that this increases his chance of getting good marks. What do you think?
2.	One day, Claire won Tattslotto with the numbers 1; 7; 13; 21; 22; 36. So she said she would always play the same group of numbers, because they were lucky. What do you think about this?

FIG. 5.16. Questions involving luck and chance.

- I think he is wrong because whether he gets good marks or not depends on him, the test, whether or not he is concentrating, etc. Getting out the left side might possibly help a bit, though, because if he *thought* he would get good marks, he might.
- It could if he thinks he could, and that would make him more confident in his work. Also it could affect the right and left side of the brain in some way.

From the elementary grades (about grade 3) to the end of middle school (about grade 9) the percent of students identifying the luck fallacy rises from about 50% to nearly 100%, with about 30% of students able to present alternative arguments.

In the more mathematical context of the second question in Fig. 5.16 about lucky numbers in the lottery, similar levels of response to the previous question are likely to occur and some students can include chance justifications. Again however, at the lowest level is an agreement with the belief in lucky numbers.

- I think it would be lucky. I will pick the same numbers too.
- I don't think many numbers are lucky. But I think 4, 7 and 9 are, so I guess I'd agree in a way you can have lucky numbers.

At the next level there is disagreement with the statement but it is either unsupported or supported in a fashion that is statistically inappropriate.

- There is no such thing as 'lucky numbers.'
- I think she shouldn't go for the group of numbers again because you can't get the same numbers after numbers after numbers, you always get different numbers all the time.

Some responses disagree and provide the beginning of an appropriate argument but without completeness. As is seen in the first of the next statements the meaning of luck is changed.

- It was just a stroke of luck because any number could of come up.
- There is no such thing as a lucky number, things like Tattslotto are picked at random.

More sophisticated responses include an appreciation of likelihood.

- She was fortunate for the numbers to come up but it is impossible for one number to be 'Luckier than another.'
- There is equal chance for all combinations, but she's already won once, so why keep gambling, why not invest the money, you would get more out of it.

Very occasionally psychological features appear in responses.

- It is a good idea to use the same numbers all the time but there is as much chance as getting any other six numbers.
- I'd kill myself if I changed my numbers and the old sequence came up.

In the last statement it is probable but difficult to discern if the student understands the equal likelihood of outcomes.

For the second question in Fig. 5.16 the separation of performance between elementary (e.g., grade 3) and middle school (e.g., grade 9) is not likely to be as extreme as for the earlier question. Although just over half of the younger students are likely to disagree with the idea of lucky numbers, very few can begin to suggest appropriate reasons why. About 90% of older students are likely to disagree, with about half of these able to expand their justifications.

Allowing students to react to others' statements is a good vehicle for initiating discussion on topics that may involve controversial beliefs. In fact, as is seen in the next section conflicting beliefs sometimes surface that students do not recognize as contradictory.

5.12 CHANCE, FAIRNESS, AND BIAS

The connections between chance and fairness can be more complex than might be expected by many teachers. A popular activity in many classrooms involves determining whether games whose rules are based on the use of random generators, such as dice, spinners, or coins, are fair. Fair in this context means that each player has the same theoretical chance of winning the game. The assumption in all of these activities is that the random generator upon which the rules are defined is itself fair. To ask students about their beliefs concerning the mechanisms of random generators, such as dice, can lead to some interesting discoveries. Some students appear to have "in school" beliefs about fairness of dice or coins, while at the same time holding contradictory beliefs in "out of school" situations. A student for example may know that the probability of obtaining heads or tails on a coin is 1/2, and yet still always choose tails in a game because "it is lucky for me."

Exploring students' beliefs about the fairness of random generators before studying the fairness of games created using them is essential if the full potential is to be gained from a study of fairness in the curriculum. Using dice as a starting point, there are several ways to initiate discussion, most likely based on a question about playing games with dice outside of school. Both frequency and chance forms of questions are appropriate.

- Do some numbers come up more often than others?
- Do all numbers have the same chance of coming up?
- What does it mean for dice to be fair?[54]

Surprising to some teachers is the situation where the answers to the first two questions are both "yes." When this is the case it appears that students are answering the frequency format in the first question based on their own personal experience in the past, whereas they see the chance format in the second question as a test of the theoretical model upon which the tossing of a die rests. This latter belief influences the future behavior of the die but cannot influence the past. Here is a point where the frequency view of probability meets, and may conflict with, the theoretical view. The resolution is important to how students deal with probability generally and how they deal with fairness in particular.

When asked questions like those previously mentioned, students are likely to display various levels of response that mirror to some extent those exhibited with respect to questions on lucky numbers discussed in Section 5.11. At an initial idiosyncratic level, responses reflect belief in specific outcomes happening more frequently. Some students use personal experience to answer the frequency form of the question about numbers on a die.

- Yeah, 3s, 4s, and 2s . . . Or the ones that you don't want to come up.
- Yes, 6 and 5 for me.

Others put their beliefs in the context of wanting a particular outcome.

- Sixes don't come up as often as smaller numbers. [So that's when you are playing games?] Yes, especially when you want a 6 to start.
- Yes. My mum always gets 6s and I always get 2s or 1s. [. . .] My hand just must be not very good at throwing the dice.

Young children, as noted earlier with respect to a specific question about obtaining a 1 or a 6 in Section 5.6, are likely to impart causal mechanisms to attributes of the die.

- Six. [Do you think a 6 comes up more often?] That's the most in the dice. Well, it's the most number in the dice.

Younger children also show the tendency to contradictions previously noted.

- Yes, number 3 because in fairy-tales there's 3 wishes and there's 3 fairy godmothers and there's 3 wishes and there's all sorts of 3 things. [Do you find

that 3 comes up a lot, or do all of the numbers come up?] Well 6 comes up
not the most because it's the biggest, and for me 2 comes up usually. [Do
you think that they all have the same chance of coming up?] Yes, I think
that's just because you turn the dice differently every time.

Although less imaginative, students through to high school are likely to
show similar ambivalence with frequency and chance.

For students who believe that dice are fair there are increasing levels of
sophistication in the explanations used to justify the belief. First is the single statement where the student feels no further need to explain.

- No, I think that they all have the same chance of getting rolled than all of
  the rest of the numbers.

At the next level some students feel the need to qualify their beliefs in fairness based either on a condition related to rolling the die or on the physical
conditions of the die itself.

- [Some more chance?] Not really. [They all have about the same chance, do
  you think?] Yes. It depends how you roll them. [Right, how does it depend
  on that?] If you roll it so that you roll it that way, it could land on any number along there, but if you rolled it along that way, it could land on any of
  those numbers.
- Well, if they had huge holes, then 6 would probably come up the most because 1 is set heaviest and it's got the least numbers, but this looks like it
  won't happen that much . . . and that [it's] random.

Finally at the highest level are those who acknowledge the conflict between
short-term variation and overall expectation.

- No. Umm . . . it sometimes seems that the other person always gets a 6, but
  it's just the luck of the draw really. It's just that you might get a row of 6s,
  but then probably in the next game you'll get a row of 1s [laughs]. And, but
  usually it just depends, sometimes it might come up more often, but then
  the next time it won't. It's just the luck of the draw.
- Well, if it was, if you had to say, sort of like the chance, you would say that all
  numbers have the same chance, but sometimes it doesn't turn out that way.
  Because sometimes we do, in our class [. . .] we make our own dice, and
  then we have to roll them 60 times, and see which comes up the most, out of
  all the numbers.

The question then arises as to the strategies students have at their disposal to check whether random generators, in this case dice, are fair or biased. To some extent strategies reflect beliefs in fairness but the relationship is not exceedingly strong. Some students at the elementary level have

difficulty with the idea of fairness even if they appear to agree with a frequency or chance description related to all numbers. When presented with several dice—one biased to the number 2 and one with repeated numbers—and asked to determine which are fair, some see fairness as a characteristic across dice related to similar outcomes.

- [Sitting on the table, the White die shows 2, Red and Blue show higher numbers] This one [White] is a bit unfair because you don't get much like these two [Red and Blue]. [The dice are turned so all show 2] [. . .] [Does that make any difference?] Yes. That is fair if they were all on 2.

Others see fairness in terms of the individual numbers rather than the dice.

- [Dice on the table showing Red 6, White 2, and Blue 5] Well, I reckon number 6 isn't fair, because it just doesn't really come up as much as the others. I just think that it doesn't come up. I reckon a 2 does. I reckon it sort of lands on it most of the times. And the 5, well, it's in the middle really.

When challenged with a statement such as "Suppose someone came along and said one number keeps coming up more often; how would you test out if they were right?" many students still do not suggest performing trials.

- [Could you test out if they were right?] No, not really, you couldn't really say that there wasn't [fair dice]. It's probably just a lucky chance that it came up on that one all the time.

There are also students with an unassailable belief in fairness expressed in a single statement.

- [Picks up each die] They all look pretty fine to me.
- [Does not pick up dice] They would all be the same.

In this situation however, more students are likely to engage with dice and consider multiple features of the dice. One aspect attracting attention is the number of outcomes that are possible, for example if a die contains repeated numbers with some of the usual ones missing.

- This [White] isn't a fair die. [. . .] Because it doesn't have 4, 5, or 6, like these two [Blue and Red]. [. . .] Those two are fair and that one isn't.

A few students are likely to conclude that such a die with repeated numbers is fair if considered on its own without reference to dice with six numbers.

Other characteristics of dice used by students to consider fairness are the symmetry of the cubic shape and the weight distribution.

- [Manipulates each die] Those two [White and Red] are fair, and that one [Blue] is unfair. [. . .] By putting them on an angle and seeing if they swung around. You could feel the weight, that it was at the top, like that [demonstrates swinging]. With the other ones, they didn't swing or anything.

Some students roll the dice as a means of considering their beliefs about physical characteristics rather than as a systematic means of providing data. For other students, often younger, there again seems to be confusion about the nature of the task.

- [Rolls each die once, then once again, and considers all dice together] Six came up more times than all the others. [Did it? How many times did you throw them?] I threw them twice, and 6 came up twice, and the other numbers only came up once. [Right. Could that help you decide whether they were fair or not?] They're unfair.

For others documenting the variety of outcomes appears to be the goal of a few trials rather than recording their frequency.

- If you roll them each 3 times. [Rolls Red die once, then Blue and White] Well, I suppose that's a kind of . . . they're all different, so they've all got a chance of . . . [Rolls each once more] They're all still different again, except 1 keeps coming up [points to White die]. [Rolls each once more] That one [Red] is the fairest because all different ones come up, and these two have had the same.

At the highest level of engagement with the task of determining whether dice are fair, are the responses that suggest and carry out trials, recording outcomes in a systematic way that allows for decision-making. The connections with students' experiences of sampling may play a part here, particularly in determining an appropriate sample size.

- [Without comment, rolls each die 20 times and records in a tally table: White: 4×1, 9×2, 7×3; Blue: 1×1, 3×2, 8×3, 6×4, 1×5, 1×6; Red: 2×1, 3×2, 4×3, 4×4, 3×5, 4×6] I definitely think the Blue one's weighted. You can feel it's heavier, and the White one possibly, but I don't think the Red one is at all, because it's fairly even across . . .

Having an idea of students' beliefs about fairness and how it can be determined for specific dice, or other random generators, is important when beginning to do trials in the classroom. In the context of testing fairness of dice, some students have a long way to go in being convinced that trials are necessary and if so how many are sufficient to draw a conclusion. Jumping into work with sampling trials without discovering students' initial beliefs may exacerbate the divide between out-of-school beliefs and those that are imposed by the mathematics teacher in school.

Students' beliefs and intuitions about random behavior can sometimes display an over-reaction to the variation that it produces. The "anything can happen" approach to outcomes, discussed for example in Sections 5.6, 5.7, 5.8, and this section, acknowledges variation that cannot be predicted. Students with such an appreciation are unlikely, however, to be able to go on to suggest what form potential variation might take.

There are times when expectation of variation can interfere with an understanding of an underlying random model. Consider for example the questions shown in Fig. 5.17. The task is designed to gain an appreciation of students' understanding that all possible combinations of six numbers have the same chance of being chosen in a lottery.[55] Personal beliefs about and observations of variation in such contexts are likely to overwhelm other considerations.

When asked to fill in their own numbers in the boxes in Fig. 5.17, students choose a wide spread of numbers rather than sequences. Some state this separation as a criterion for selection.

- {27, 8, 15, 32, 44, 21} [Why?] Because they are . . . about at least 5 numbers away from each other.

When asked to declare which set of numbers is more likely to win, only a few students from the elementary level up are likely to give idiosyncratic answers.

- Ruth is cheating.

The overwhelming majority of elementary students (e.g., grade 3) and even about 40% of high school students (e.g., grade 9) choose Jenny's numbers

Ruth says that choosing consecutive numbers like 1, 2, 3, 4, 5, 6 increases your chances of winning Tattslotto. But Jenny says that there is a larger chance of getting a random set of numbers.

Write six random numbers (between 1 and 45) that Jenny might choose.

☐ ☐ ☐ ☐ ☐ ☐

Which ticket is more likely to get all 6 numbers right (Ruth's or Jenny's)?

Why?

FIG. 5.17. Task about random numbers in a lottery.

(their own) as more likely to win the lottery. Some of the reasoning is based on personal experience.

- I've never seen the lotto get 1, 2, 3, 4, 5, 6.
- Single numbers hardly ever turn up, more "two numbers."

Some responses are more explicit in suggesting variation as a reason for choosing their own set of widely spread numbers.

- It has a better range of numbers.
- Because they're not in a row, they're all different, in a random order.

Whereas the first statement is a true observation, it does not increase the chance of winning, and the second statement is false.

At the next level of sophistication in responses are those that cannot resolve the dilemma of equal likelihood and variation, or state generally that it does not matter because "anything can happen" with no further comment.

- Probably equally likely but Jenny's a higher possibility since you don't normally get consecutive numbers.

This response appears to reflect the same kind of conflict experienced in the context of determining fairness of dice described at the beginning of this section.

With increasing grade level and exposure to chance activities in the curriculum, students are more likely to respond appropriately about the equal likelihood of Ruth's and Jenny's numbers winning the lottery. Some justifications however are likely to be more qualitative in nature.

- Both have the same chance.
- Doesn't matter, you probably have an even chance of getting either.

The most sophisticated justifications are those that recognize the equal likelihood of each number.

- The tattslotto thing isn't biased, there's the same chance of getting every number. So it's just as likely to get consecutive numbers as different numbers.

The extent of the misunderstanding of the relationship of chance and perceived variation in lottery outcomes, points to tasks like this being a focus of discussion at all grades from upper elementary school. In conjunction with questions on drawing names from a hat in Section 5.6, extended focus on the set of possibilities may assist in building appropriate views of equal likelihood. Producing many simulations with software packages is also useful in building intuitions, one of which may be the futility of buying lottery tickets at all.

5.13   CHANCE AND RISK

The acknowledgment that school students are exposed to all kinds of risks has brought many issues to the classroom that in years past would have been considered taboo. There is now considerable discussion among sociologists and educational researchers about adolescents' decision making in situations of risk. Of concern are drug abuse of various sorts, unprotected sex in the face of the HIV/AIDS threat, deaths of young males in car accidents, sun baking leading to high incidence of skin cancer, youth suicide, and dietary habits that risk health problems in later life.[56] Research has shown that risk-taking behavior may be related to adolescent feelings of vulnerability or invulnerability, levels of self-esteem, and perceptions of the locus-of-control of events in the adolescents' lives.[57] Research also has shown, however, that in areas such as the threat of HIV/AIDS, education programs that increase knowledge levels in students are not always accompanied by a reduction in risk-taking behavior.[58] What is missing from the research on risk beliefs and risk-taking behavior is the consideration of students' ability to assess risk in basic likelihood terms and to interpret and question claims made in various contexts.

Curriculum documents across different subjects suggest goals for students involving risk. The following objectives are from a health and physical education curriculum statement.

> Students examine the concept of risk, including real and perceived risk, and how this relates to different situations. They identify factors that influence risk-taking, and explore how inappropriate risk-taking presents dangers. They learn about the causes and consequences of different behaviours and the potential risks to safety related to, for example, substance use, sexual practices, participation in physical activities, and road behaviour.[59]

There is no specific mention in the statement however, of the mathematical aspects of evaluating or interpreting risk. Turning to mathematics curriculum documents there is at least some recognition that there are links between mathematics and risk. "Making informed choices will often require a general understanding of the mathematics underlying the analysis of costs and risks."[60] The chance part of the curriculum is fundamental to building the understanding that assists in the decision making process. Part of this is related to the interpretation and evaluation of language as discussed in Sections 5.4 and 5.5; part is related to basic numeracy skills required to quantify risk; and part is related to the ability to understand conditional language and to distinguish independent from non-independent events when they are stated in social rather than abstract random contexts (cf. Section 5.9). Combining these aspects to be able to make decisions or question claims made is one of the important goals of statistical literacy.

Examples abound in the media of claims that challenge readers with conditions and numerical claims that tell a partial story. Consider for example the extracts from a newspaper article on smoking and wrinkles shown in Fig. 5.18. Four conditional statements are presented, including quantitative information on number of years of smoking and increased risk.[61]

Before decisions can be made about potential action to be taken in relation to risk statements, it is necessary to interpret the statements and decide what further information might be necessary. For middle school students it is a reasonable exercise to ask them to write each of the statements in the article in Fig. 5.18, in "if . . . , then . . ." form. The first statement is the easiest and about two-thirds of students, say at grade 9, are likely to be able to interpret it appropriately.

- "If": Smoking a packet of smokes a day for less than 49 years. "Then": Doubled risk of premature wrinkling.

The second and third statements are slightly more difficult, most likely because of the inversion of the sentence structure, which places the conclusion before the condition. Also in the third statement there are two "ifs," which is difficult to decipher for those who only use "if" as a criterion for

> A study found that those who smoked a pack of cigarettes a day for less than 49 years doubled the risk of premature wrinkling.
>
> For more than 50 years, the risk was 4.7 times greater than those who do not smoke
> ...
> He said he was not sure if the wrinkling could be reversed if people quit smoking.
>
> "'You're going to be old and ugly before your time if you smoke,' may be just the message that leads them to throw away their cigarettes for good," he said.

FIG. 5.18. Conditional language in a newspaper article reporting on risk.

the setting of a condition. Slightly less than half of students are likely to provide reasonable interpretations of these sentences.

- "If": Pack a day smoker more than 50 years. "Then": Premature wrinkling is 4.7 times more likely.
- "If": A person stops smoking. "Then": Wrinkling could be reversed.

The final statement is quite structurally complex because it contains one conditional statement within another; that is, the "message" is both a complete conditional statement itself, as well as the condition for the larger conditional statement.

- "If": Old and ugly if you smoke. "Then": Maybe help people quit smoking.

Only about a quarter of upper middle school students are likely to interpret the conditional statement appropriately in its complete context.

The understanding of claims like those in the article in Fig. 5.18, is a goal of the second tier of the Statistical Literacy Hierarchy in two senses. First, the conditional language must be interpreted appropriately in the context. From a mathematical perspective this is likely to involve some first tier work with random experiments, but also some transitional second tier exercises such as discussed in Section 5.9. As well, students need to have had enough exposure to likelihood in terms of probability to appreciate what it means for the risk or likelihood to be doubled or increased 4.7 times. Talking about probabilities in multiplicative terms is not unusual in media reports but is less common when random generators are used in the classroom. Given a basic appreciation that all probabilities lie between 0 and 1, there are restrictions on what the unknown chance of having wrinkles is for non-smokers. Being able to put first tier statistical understanding to work in making sense of claims in contexts such as this one is at the heart of second tier understanding.

The ultimate goal is to reach the third tier goal of questioning, where appropriate, the claims made in articles such as the one in Fig. 5.18. Although the statements in the article are made in terms of risk and likelihood, there are obvious connections to the sampling and inference parts of the curriculum. What was the sample size upon which the claims were made? Why was a cutoff placed between 49 and 50 years? What statement could have been made if the cut-off were placed between 39 and 40 years of smoking? Or at some other arbitrary place? How did the cut-off split the sample? What proportions of the sample were in each group? What criteria were used to define "premature wrinkling"? Is a term like "premature" relevant for people who have been smoking for over 50 years? The questions go on.

Students need to develop a repertoire of questions when presented with media reports.[62] People who wish to warn students of risks—and this should certainly be done—need to state them in meaningful ways that communicate clearly all of the information needed for decision making. Excuses can be made for not heeding excellent advice if it is not adequately communicated. Having high level statistical literacy skills should assist students in discriminating between true and false information. Those who wish to influence students to "good" causes without appropriate arguments are guilty of a disservice, no matter how hazardous the risk.

5.14 IMPLICATIONS AND RECOMMENDATIONS

Uncertainty is part of life and the world students will enter. No matter what one's philosophical view of the underlying mechanisms, observations are consistent with models based on random processes. Students hence need to be aware of how the models operate and their long term implications.

Those who have suggested that the school curriculum needs to acknowledge the three aspects of probabilistic thinking—subjective, frequency, and theoretical[63]—are correct but the progression through the years of school is not linear. Connections and reinforcements among the three should be made over and over again, and made explicitly. Beliefs and intuitions about chance continue to exist throughout life. Sometimes they are appropriate and can be useful; often however they are misleading and can lead to misjudgments. Continuing to discuss and confront them not only helps to keep them in perspective but also may motivate the classroom-based investigations based on frequencies or theory. It is not always appropriate to introduce an experiment to find relative frequencies before suggesting a theoretical model based say on geometry or counting possible outcomes. Often material links exist and these should be developed as required to reinforce learning. Again the idea of "reaching" the environment of theoretical probability where collected data can be left behind is no longer adequate. Hands-on simulations, as well as software simulation packages now available, make it imperative to explore the nature of probability distributions, especially in light of the opportunity to refine understanding of variation.

Three overall aspects of chance have been discussed in this chapter. Chance language has been introduced into the curriculum in early grades as a preliminary step to quantitative measurement. Its importance, however, does not diminish throughout the years of schooling. Newspaper headlines and claims of risk and likelihood can and should be considered into the high school years to keep reinforcing links between qualitative and quantitative chance, between subjective and objective chance, and between chance and the rest of the school curriculum. The more traditional aspects of elementary probability measurement are still important but need to be introduced in ways that acknowledge students' starting points and to build increasingly complex structures for understanding. Activities should include many different models and these should be specifically linked to each other where appropriate, as well as to underlying numerical chance outcomes. Activities with dice or spinners, however, are not the end of the chance part of the curriculum. These must lead to consideration of fairness and bias, of the important part played by variation, and of interpreting statements of risk. These are the areas where sophisticated understanding and application of chance can be useful to students in decision making outside of the mathematics classroom.

In terms of the Statistical Literacy Hierarchy referred to throughout this book, the experiences planned for chance over the years of schooling are likely to revisit all three tiers over and over, and perhaps all three in each activity. First tier appreciation of terminology can be straightforward or complex and may depend to some extent on the context within which a certain activity takes place. What must not be forgotten then is the link between the first and second tier and the reinforcement of the meaning of terms as they are reintroduced. Words such as *random* and *variation* may have different connotations when used in different settings and these should be a matter for discussion. Terminology includes informal language as well as technical terms such as *independent* or *conditional.*

Looking at the second tier of statistical literacy and considering terminology in context has important implications because of the many wide-ranging contexts within which meaning can be made for chance experiences. As noted earlier, it is imperative to consider many contexts, both abstract in nature, divorced from the social milieu, and related to actual data that occur in the world outside of school. The potential immediate link to the third tier of the hierarchy and questioning claims and suspecting bias is obvious once social issues are included in activities related to chance. Introductory activities, however, related to abstract settings such as the fairness of dice, can be used to challenge students' trusting belief structures and get them to begin questioning in every context presented to them.

If the chance part of the curriculum is to go beyond playing games with dice as a Friday-afternoon fill-in activity, the connections illustrated in Fig. 5.1 need to be made explicit and reinforced over and over again with many activities based in varying contexts. Students should come away with a foundation that allows them to study formal probability and statistics if they desire with a deep appreciation of where the building blocks come from, or that allows them to make statistically literate decisions in contexts they meet outside of school, from decisions about gambling to decisions about medical treatments.

Over the years much anecdotal evidence has accumulated to support a belief in the importance of many repeated experiences in chance environ-

ments to reinforce the connections among ideas of fairness, equal likelihood, variation, and distribution. Confusion among these ideas has been
mentioned in several sections of this chapter. One repeated experience
with two 6-sided dice has led me to suggest a situation of cognitive conflict
that may assist in several regards.[64]

The classic assumption is that young children do not realize that when
summing two 6-sided dice, all sums to 12 are not equally likely. This belief is
exploited in a drill-and-practice activity for early childhood where students
are given a rectangular grid labeled 2 to 12 along the longer side and 20
chips to place opposite the numbers on the grid in a pattern. A chip is removed when the appropriate sum is achieved when the two dice are tossed.[65]
Either as a competition or as an individual activity, it does not take students
long to realize that the middle numbers are more likely to occur than the extremes, and they change their patterns accordingly. Although such appreciation is built through experience, without it many adults are in the same situation as young children. This came home to me in two contexts working with
adults. One was a public Math Expo where I ran a games stall at which parents and children were given the chance to play this game against each other.
Not only were parents generally less able to suggest "optimal" placements
than their children but also several parents were heard to chastise their children for not placing the chips evenly from 2 to 12. It was delightful to observe
parent after parent lose to the children. A more sobering observation, however took place during professional development with elementary teachers.
In modeling the random choosing of months of the year, a selection of random generators was provided—decks of playing cards, 6-sided dice, 12-sided
dice, blank dice, tokens and bags—and teachers asked which would be appropriate to choose a month. On several occasions at least one teacher, sight-
ing ordinary 6-sided dice, suggested using two of them. Luckily another
teacher always intervened with the observation that "two 6-sided dice don't
equal a 12-sided dice," before the idea was taken very far.

Although less frequently occurring, a complementary experience has
led me to believe that in some cases mathematics teachers have gone too far
in stressing the distribution of outcomes from summing two dice, while forgetting the importance of the uniform distribution associated with a single
die. In carrying out the individual interviews to explore students' understanding of fairness as described in Section 5.12, two grade 10 girls from the
same school were interviewed. When asked whether some numbers came
up more often than others on a single die, both suggested the 3 or 4 was
more likely to come up. When asked why, both replied that there is always a
peak in the middle when you throw dice and plot the results. I suspect that
their school had planned excellent activities on tossing two dice and summing the outcomes, but had taken for granted that students knew about the
expected uniform outcomes from tossing a single die.

These experiences have led me to take a direct approach with teachers in professional development sessions, asking them "When is 6 + 6 ≠ 12?" After discussions of the language of likelihood, including the nebulous nature of "50-50" and "anything can happen," and of the uniform expectations for a 12-sided die and peaked expectations for two 6-sided dice, teachers are set the task of building experimental distributions using grids and chips. Even working in groups this activity takes teachers some time to complete. For 50 tosses of two 6-sided dice teachers naturally talk about their expectations and the variation. Some distributions do not look very much like the "triangular" or "peaked" expectation. Then pairs of pairs of teachers combine their distributions of chips to display 100 trials. There is then talk of "the 5s coming up" or "the 8s evening out." When time and space permits, these distributions are combined in pairs to produce a display of 200 trials. Teachers are impressed with how the distributions look more like what they expected but are still not perfect. The procedure is then repeated for a 12-sided dice. Teachers are initially surprised with the unevenness of their distributions, which they expect to be uniform, and generally it is not until the whole group's outcomes are recorded on the white board that they are satisfied that the distribution is "nearly" uniform. The conflict of pattern versus variation replaces the original conflict of two 6-sided versus one 12-sided dice, as the major discussion point.

An encouraging outcome of these activities is that some teachers have had the confidence to develop such activities for their classrooms and are proud of their students' results. Fig. 5.19 shows the distributions and a report written by grade 7 students working in groups of three.[66]

Report

A 12 sided dice has more of a chance of rolling each number while 2 six sided dice, 7 is more likely to be rolled, one's won't be rolled because you have to roll two dice and there is no way of getting a one. A 12 sided dice has a 1 on it though and because you are only rolling 1 dice it will get a chance. A 12 sided dice has more chance of being equal with all of the numbers, two six sided dice are unfair to most numbers such as 1, 2, 3, 10, 11, and 12.

FIG. 5.19.   Classroom outcomes to show a case when "6 + 6 ≠ 12."

NOTES

1. Moore (1990, p. 98).
2. Moore (1997).
3. Scheaffer, Watkins, & Landwehr (1998).
4. Australian Education Council (1991); Department for Education (1995); Ministry of Education (1992); National Council of Teachers of Mathematics (1989).
5. Kahneman & Tversky (1972); Tversky & Kahneman (1971, 1974).
6. Gigerenzer (2002); Gigerenzer & Hoffrage (1995).
7. Fischbein (1975); Fischbein & Gazit (1984).
8. Green (1983b, 1986, 1991).
9. Shaughnessy (1992, 2003); Watson (2005).
10. Amir & Williams (1999).
11. Moritz (1998); Schwartz & Goldman (1996); Watson (1993).
12. Fischbein & Gazit (1984); Green (1984); Pratt (2000); Tarr (2002); Watson & Moritz (2003a).
13. Konold (1989); Konold, Pollatsek, Well, Lohmeier, & Lipson (1993).
14. Amir & Williams (1999); Fischbein & Gazit (1984); Green (1983a); Maher (1998); Truran (1995); Vidakovic, Berenson, & Brandsma (1998).
15. Shaughnessy, Canada, & Ciancetta (2003); Shaughnessy & Ciancetta (2002); Shaughnessy, Watson, Moritz, & Reading (1999); Shaughnessy & Zawojewski (1999); Zawojewski & Shaughnessy (2000).
16. Batanero, Serrano, & Garfield (1996); Cañizares & Batanero (1998); Lecoutre (1992); Li & Pereira-Mendoza (2002).
17. Fischbein, Nello, & Marino (1991); Fischbein & Schnarch (1997); Pratt (2000).
18. Tarr & Jones (1997); Watson & Moritz (2002).
19. Fischbein & Schnarch (1997); Watson & Moritz (2002).
20. Moritz, Watson, & Pereira-Mendoza (1996); Watson, Kelly, Callingham, & Shaughnessy (2003).
21. Watson & Kelly (2003d); Watson, Kelly, Callingham, & Shaughnessy (2003).
22. Australian Education Council (1991, p. 166).
23. Fischbein & Gazit (1984); Green (1984).
24. Moritz, Watson, & Pereira-Mendoza (1996).
25. Green (1984) found similar contexts used by 11–16 year old students.
26. Ernest (1984).
27. Watson & Moritz (2003a).
28. The phrase "no worries" is an Australian colloquial term expressing confidence that an event is certain to happen, as in "I'll be there, no worries!" The phrase "sure thing" is used as an expression for "a certainty; something assured beyond any doubt;" Delbridge & Bernard (1998, p. 1178, 1361).
29. Garfield & Gal (1999); Konold & Garfield (1992); Watson & Moritz (2003a).
30. Green (1983a); Varga (1983); Watson, Collis, & Moritz (1997).
31. Borovcnik & Bentz (1991); Watson, Collis, & Moritz (1997).
32. Green (1983b); Konold & Garfield (1992); Watson, Collis, & Moritz (1997).

33. Watson & Kelly (2003c); Watson, Kelly, Callingham, & Shaughnessy (2003).

34. The criterion used in Watson, Kelly, Callingham, & Shaughnessy (2003), was based on the simulation of 1000 outcomes in a spreadsheet, calculating the standard deviation of each, and choosing the 90% in the center as appropriate; this produced a range of 1.2 to 4.7.

35. Watson & Kelly (2003c).

36. Green (1983a).

37. Fischbein, Nello, & Marino (1991); Watson & Kelly (2004b).

38. Speiser & Walter (1998) discuss the dilemma for preservice teachers in considering the outcome for a sum of 11 on two dice.

39. Shaughnessy & Ciancetta (2002); Watson & Kelly (2004a).

40. Fischbein & Schnarch (1997); Garfield & delMas (1991); Konold, Pollatsek, Well, Lohmeier, & Lipson (1993).

41. Moritz & Watson (2000).

42. Kahneman & Tversky (1972).

43. Fenton & Watson (2001).

44. National Council of Teachers of Mathematics (2000, p. 171).

45. National Council of Teachers of Mathematics (2000, p. 332).

46. Watson & Moritz (2002).

47. National Council of Teachers of Mathematics (2000).

48. Watson & Moritz (2002).

49. Gigerenzer (2002); Gigerenzer & Hoffrage (1995).

50. Tversky & Kahneman (1980, 1983).

51. Australian Education Council (1991, p. 175, p. 182).

52. Moritz (1998); Moritz, Watson, & Collis (1996).

53. Fischbein & Gazit (1984); Watson, Collis, & Moritz (1995a).

54. Watson & Moritz (2003b). Students answering these and the following questions had access to three large dice: White with repeated numbers 1, 2, 3; Red with six numbers; and Blue, weighted with six numbers.

55. Fischbein & Gazit (1984); Watson & Caney (2005).

56. Pfeffer (1989); Plant & Plant (1992).

57. Mann, Harmoni, & Power (1989).

58. Roscoe & Kruger (1990).

59. Australian Education Council (1994b, p. 14).

60. Australian Education Council (1991, p. 6).

61. Watson (1998e); "Wrinkles ultimate smoking deterrent" (1991).

62. Gal (2002).

63. Hawkins & Kapadia (1984).

64. Watson (2002d).

65. Kirkby & Short (1991).

66. Watson (2002d).

6

Beginning Inference:
Supporting a Conclusion

Instructional programs from prekindergarten through grade 12 should enable all students to develop and evaluate inferences and predictions that are based on data. In grades 6–8 all students should—

- *use observations about differences between two or more samples to make conjectures about populations from which the samples were taken;*
- *make conjectures about possible relationships between two characteristics of a sample on the basis of scatterplots of the data and approximate lines of fit;*
- *use conjectures to formulate new questions and plan new studies to answer them.*[1]

6.1 BACKGROUND

Inference is a term that is usually associated with chapters near the end of introductory statistics texts where formal statistical tests are introduced with p-values to judge significance. At the end of secondary schooling some students meet z-tests, t-tests, chi-square tests, and correlation coefficients. These techniques are used to evaluate formally stated hypotheses and are based on quite a few underlying assumptions and complex calculating formulas. For students who have not been introduced to ideas of inference in less complex circumstances, the big picture is often lost in the procedural details, and arithmetical errors can result in absurd conclusions because there is no intuition about the story the data are telling. Although in this circumstance teachers may encourage students to sketch graphs of data sets before rushing to calculate statistics, students are notoriously reluctant to follow such advice.[2]

One of the big advantages of following advice such as that given at the start of this chapter by the National Council of Teachers of Mathematics is that students are more likely to learn good habits of data handling and analysis before they learn the details of hypothesis testing or forming confidence intervals. The fact that in middle school they cannot satisfy a criterion based on a p-value, as required by a statistician, is not relevant. What is relevant is building intuitions that sound warning bells if distributions look unusual or too many outliers appear. Although sometimes data sets, particularly those collected by students themselves, are such that it is difficult to make a decision about a conjecture, this is an experience also encountered by professional statisticians and to meet these situations early will help develop a realistic approach to statistical investigations. The focus of this chapter hence is on beginning inference: the issues that need to and can be considered at the middle school level.

Because of the limitations of class time it is often not possible, even if desirable, to allow students to control all aspects of a statistical investigation, from asking a question and designing a data collection process, to collecting, recording, graphing, and summarizing the data, to making a decision on the question. Although it is important to have some experiences of this complete type, it is also feasible to move in and out of the investigation process to illustrate aspects of what is involved in drawing inferences. Such activities can be used to illustrate and reinforce the components of the inferential process. At one time it may be appropriate to present students with a raw data set and ask them to formulate hypotheses. This can then be extended in some cases by asking students to use the tools at their disposal, such as graphs, to support their hypotheses. At another time it may be appropriate to present students with a graphical representation and ask a question requiring an inference to be made from the graphical presentation of the data. One variation on this theme asks for predictions to be made on the basis of graphical presentations, even as early as when pictographs are used (cf. Section 3.2 and Section 4.6). Another is to ask for evaluation of forms of representation to support a story being told (cf. Section 3.8). As well as graphical forms, two-way tables can be used to present data and request inferences be drawn. It is also important to expose students to inferential claims made with little or no justification in order for students to gain experience in questioning inferences of others. These related but varied aspects of the inferential process can be used to help students develop a broad foundation for what is involved in inference, long before they meet specific statistical procedures.

The research that could be classified under the general heading of beginning inference is quite varied in nature. Some researchers, such as Richard Lehrer and his colleagues[3] or collaborators Lyn English and Helen Doerr,[4] have allowed students freedom to develop their own models for answering questions of a statistical nature. Although at times including naïve considerations, these studies have illustrated the importance of allowing students the opportunity to explore ways of drawing inferences. In her study of elementary students while they planned and carried out a science experiment, Kathy Metz documented interesting beliefs about the kind of evidence that influences decision-making (see Section 2.1).[5] Precursors to some of the research that forms the basis for this chapter include the work of Lionel Pereira-Mendoza in asking young students to make predictions from pictographs,[6] of Iddo Gal and his colleagues in asking students to compare two groups,[7] and of Carmen Batanero and her co-workers in analyzing students' responses to tasks related to association of variables, in two-way tables[8] and in two data sets.[9]

The relationships among the stages of the statistical investigation process and the inference component are illustrated in Fig. 6.1, where it is seen that the data collection, data representation, and data summary aspects relate directly to the inference stage as well as sequentially to each other. The entire process is involved when reaching a conclusion or inference. Various types of inference-related activities such as predicting, hypothesizing, supporting, and criticizing are relevant during the middle school years. The influence of variation on drawing inferences is important from the very beginning of discussion with elementary children, despite the only mathematical tools likely to be available being averages or proportions. Although

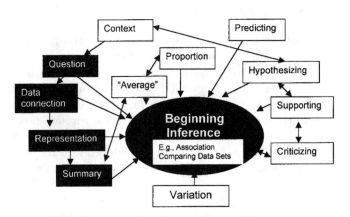

FIG. 6.1.   Links among the ideas and statistical elements associated with beginning inference.

there are many possible statistical contexts within which to consider inferences, the main focus in this chapter is on tasks based on association questions and on comparing two data sets. These are potentially motivational in terms of the types of questions asked and are precursors of the types of questions encountered in later study of those who continue who pursue statistics. Section 6.2 considers prediction based on a pictograph as a setting that is accessible to students at all years of schooling. Inference as hypothesizing is the focus of Section 6.3, following on from the discussion of students' representations of relationships of data related to fast food consumption in Section 3.3. In Section 6.4 comparison of two data sets illustrates links to data representation, data summary, and specific ideas of proportion and average. The data set comparison tasks also provide a connection to the underlying importance of variance in decision making, which is amplified further in Chapter 7. Section 6.5 turns to the consideration of associations and considers examples with links to non-linear graphical representations and two-way tables. The skills required to question or criticize inferences of others are considered in Section 6.6, again in connection with a claimed association of two variables.

The following sections of this chapter consider tasks completed by students throughout the years of schooling to illustrate the development of understanding that takes place with respect to drawing inferences. The final section relates the development to the Statistical Literacy Hierarchy introduced in Chapter 1, suggests some activities in line with the recommendations at the beginning of this chapter, and presents two articles from the media for possible use in the classroom.

6.2   INFERENCE AS PREDICTION

Initial experiences with inference can be linked with predictions from data sets presented in graphical form, whether these are prepared by the students themselves or prepared by the teacher for class discussion. An example of the former is given in Section 3.2 in the creation of pictographs with concrete materials to represent children and the number of books they have read.[10] A first step toward inference is the interpretation of what has been created. Then, as is discussed in Section 4.6, it is possible to ask for predictions of the number of books read for children who are not currently shown in the pictograph. The development from inability to predict because the information is not explicitly given, to suggesting middles, means, ranges, or consideration of gender, occurs from early childhood through middle school and students' responses can form the basis of productive classroom debate. It is important to notice how students begin to respond to the variability in representations and build on this in discussion. At the same time it is also essential to help students appreciate the assumptions that they bring when making predictions from a data set. This ranges from young students making up stories about why children read books, to stating a belief, without support from the data, that girls read more than boys.

A related task can be based on what is sometimes called a "travel graph" or a "transport graph," which represents the way that children in a class come to school. Figure 3.15 shows a bar graph form of the representation and in practice the bars each have a tab at the top and are moveable through slits at the base line of the graph.[11] After initial discussion to ensure that children understand how to read values along the left scale, it is possible to move the bars up and down to make predictions about different days under different conditions. How would a new student come to school on the first day? After a few weeks how would the student come to school? A pair of questions like these acknowledge the likelihood that elementary students will predict from personal experience for the first question but are then given the opportunity to consider the information in the graph for the second question. How would the graph look on a day when the bus did not come? This question allows for the graph to be manipulated, the bus column to disappear, and compensation to be made in the other bars. This task can be used to confirm conservation of number, as well as counting skills, for younger students. The associated explanations indicate the degree to which students rely on their personal experience and on the information in the graph. What would the graph look like on a day when it was raining? This is a more complex question in that potentially two columns can be changed and hence there are more numbers to keep in mind. For students in the middle elementary grades (say, grade 3), this can be a challenging task but one that displays several aspects of understanding: one-to-one correspondence, counting, conservation of number, contextual understanding of the implications of the condition set, the representation form using the bars and grid, and willingness to predict in a situation when explicit information is not available.

The pictograph is another representation that can be used to display information about how children travel to school. The graph shown in Fig. 6.2 again allows for basic questions on counting and comparisons.[12] The questions accompanying the graph in the figure provide starting points for speculative discussion and prediction. Part (a) is a very basic question but it allows for contextual reasoning about why the graph might not look the same everyday, introducing the idea of variation. The question in Part (b) about the new student is set differently from the earlier question for the bar graph because in Fig. 6.2 the pictograph allows the depiction of both boys and girls. Part (c) addresses the issue of zero-data categories and their meaning.[13] Finally Part (d) is the most open-ended question allowing for speculation based on imaginative storytelling or various attributes in the graph.

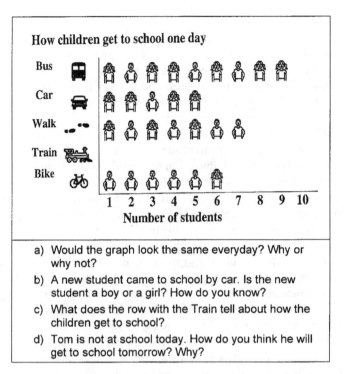

FIG. 6.2. Task asking for inferences from a pictograph.

The majority of responses for Part (a) reflect students' understanding that changes are likely to occur and language like "might" and "could" is commonly used.

- No, someone could be sick.

Part (b) provides a rich context for discussion where alternatives that are more statistically appropriate can be contrasted with other reasoning. A question like this with no certain "correct" answer needs to be handled carefully as some students have an expectation that in a mathematics class there are always right answers. Four levels of student response reflect increasing involvement with the graphical representation. At the lowest level are responses that include personal experience and inability to speculate based on the pictograph.

- Girl, because at our school more girls come by car.
- Girl, it is just a guess.
- Can't say, impossible to tell, because there isn't enough information on the graph.

These responses deserve further discussion to encourage consideration of the possibilities when full information is unavailable.

At the next level are responses that engage the context and graph but in a non-statistical fashion. Some reflect basic uncertainty.

- Girl or boy, there is a 50% chance of each.

Many students interpret the order represented on the pictograph as significant.

- Girl, because she is the last one on the graph.
- Boy, because it goes two girls, one boy, and then two more girls, so then it should be a boy.

These are interesting responses in that they may reflect other influences in the mathematics curriculum, for example the early emphasis on detecting patterns. A few students follow this line but include an element of uncertainty.

- I can't tell, maybe a boy because he's the only boy to come in a car but you can't really tell.

Two frequency approaches are seen at the next level of response, one that might be considered proto-statistical and the other more conventional. Some students appear to consider the frequencies of boys and girls (either in the row with the car or overall) and feel the need to balance the genders. Some responses are vague and it is not possible to determine which group is being considered.

- Boy, because there are more girls.

Others specifically state a comparison.

- Boy, because there are 14 girls and 13 boys so they need one to make it even.
- Boy, because there's only one boy in the cars.
- Boy, 4 girls, 1 boy! The odds are on another boy.

The last response reflects the "gambler's fallacy" of compensating for previous outcomes in a context expected to produce an even outcome. This is a topic for classroom discussion. The contrasting use of frequency in the graph is to view the majority of girls, either in the car row or the class overall. Again some responses are likely to be vague and others specific.

- Girl, because there are more girls than boys.
- Girl, the majority of people who come in the car are girls.

Although without other information this observational approach is likely to be considered the most appropriate, it is not very common even in the upper middle school grades.

The highest level of response combines the focus on the majority with appropriate uncertainty.

- 4/5 chance girl, because there are 4 girls and 1 boy.
- Probably a girl but could easily be a boy. It's a guess, more girls currently travel by car.

Very few students include such qualifications but it is the type of consideration that needs to be encouraged from the beginning of prediction and decision-making with data.

The Part (c) question in Fig. 6.2 offers somewhat less scope for answers but again the most appropriate responses allow for variation and uncertainty about the information given. At the lowest level of response a few students appear to misinterpret the question or provide brief responses without further explanation. Answers of "0" and "none" appear to refer to frequencies, whereas "nothing" is inappropriate as the blank row does provide information on how children get to school. The vast majority of students respond at a level that makes a definitive statement about the situation with no qualification. Some students justify the absence of children with personal preference.

- Children don't like going to school by train.

Others suggest geographical explanations.

- No one lives that far away to need to catch a train.
- There are no trains close to the school.

The most common explanation is a straight declaration.

- No one catches the train.
- They all walk or go by bike or car or the bus.

The most complete responses imply a degree of variation or uncertainty of what might happen on other days.

- No one caught the train that day.
- They might take the train.

The final question in Fig. 6.2 is another prediction question on how a student who was absent when the pictograph was constructed would get to school the following day. This type of question again elicits many levels of response reflecting increasingly appropriate reasoning in relation to the information in the graph. Quite a few students have difficulty in engaging with the information presented.

- Car, it's just a guess.
- Don't know, because it doesn't say anything about Tom.

A few rely on assumptions about previous behavior without making a choice.

- The same way he normally comes. There is no need to change.

The next level of response includes a large percent of students who make up stories for Tom.

- Bike, because it might be a nice day.
- Car, because he has been sick and might be too weak to walk or ride anymore.
- I don't know, he might not come tomorrow.

A few students at this level make suggestions based on the patterns in the graph.

- Car, because he would complete the car row pattern.

As with Part (b) some students use Tom to balance other features in the graph.

- Car, because there is only one boy in the car list.
- Train, train would not be included if no one used it.

A few also take an "anything can happen" view.

- I don't know, because he could come any way.

A frequency approach is shown in responses at the next level in two ways.

- Bus, because most people catch the bus.
- Bike, because lots of boys come by bike.

Finally at the highest level of response, a few students include an element of uncertainty in their predictions.

- Probably bus, because it is the most popular.
- Bike, given the data, more boys go to school by bike, so Tom is more likely to go by bike.
- Bus or bike, because the bus is the most popular way and most boys take the bike.
- Probably bus or walk, because that's how most kids do.

For all parts of this task there is the opportunity for debate and consideration of likelihood based on the information presented. That students suggest contextual explanations from their own experience or explanations based on patterns should not be condemned. In both cases students should be encouraged to begin to see these explanations as assumptions that contribute to the prediction made. Even students who predict based on the frequencies shown in the pictograph need to be aware that they are assuming the pattern of class behavior that produced the graph will continue. Students should be encouraged to incorporate all types of information available and come up with balanced alternatives that include the possibility of variation and uncertainty.

6.3   INFERENCE AS HYPOTHESIZING

The task suggested in Section 3.3 is based on a set of 16 data cards containing the name, age, favorite activity, eye color, weight (in kg), and number of fast foods eaten per week for children aged 8 to 18 (data in Appendix to Chapter 3). The discussion in Section 3.3 focuses on the representations drawn by students to support hypothesized relationships in the data set. The connections among hypothesizing, representing, and then interpreting a relationship are complex, and depending on the tools available, students may not display the same levels of understanding for each component of the overall task.[14] In contexts such as the one with the 16 data cards, where students have some intuitions about fast foods, exercise, and weight, it is likely that elementary students can interpret raw data and make hypotheses at a higher level than they can produce graphical representations. This may of course be due to lack of exposure to appropriate graphing methods.

The levels of response when students are asked to find and justify interesting features in the data set of 16 data cards generally reflect their ability to consider increasing numbers of features and data values, and to relate them in increasingly complex structures. At the prestructural level are students who have difficulty in separating themselves from the data set and cannot get past their own personal experience. Discussion centers about how many fast food meals a week they themselves eat and perhaps what these are, such as pizza or fish and chips. Often these students can be persuaded by other students to consider other features of the data set but left on their own, their interest is in comparing others (in the data set or working group) with themselves.

At the unistructural level are responses that engage purposefully with the data on the cards but focus on single aspects, for example suggesting reasons for the results on a single card at a time. Most students by the elementary grades (say, grade 5) can consider several aspects of the relevant information at the multistructural level of understanding. This is often done in a sequential fashion. Some students consider all of the data but only one variable at a time, perhaps noting that more people like television than any other activity. This can be supported by a bar graph of frequency for each activity (see Fig. 3.4(c)) but does not suggest connections among variables. In explaining the results for an hypothesis about eye color, the following response is typical of this level of response.

- I was surprised because I thought most people would have brown eyes, not blue, except it turned out that most people had blue eyes and green eyes were the same as brown.

At the relational level, responses show an integrated understanding of the relationships among various aspects of the information and are likely to propose cause and effect relationships between two variables, for example, between fast food consumption and weight. For a small data set this inference may be drawn without an accompanying ability to produce a graphical representation.

- We noticed that the people who eat a lot of fast food seem to also like watching television too. Also they are the heaviest of their age and sometimes over their age.

There are a few students who can go beyond this level to speculate about the fit of the data to their hypotheses. These students require access to a graphical representation that displays the variation in the data set and lack of a straight linear trend. Depending on their experience in observing and explaining variation in data sets, some are prepared to reject their hypothesis due to a seemingly poor fit. Discussion of such observations can lead to a deeper appreciation of what it means to fit data to a model. For many students graphs are confirmations of beliefs or hypotheses rather than starting points for future speculation.

Data sets such as the one discussed in this section allow for consideration of both types of questions noted at the beginning of this chapter. Although hypothesizing about an association of two measurement variables—weight and number of fast food meals—is perhaps the most natural for those with contextual experience, it is also possible to hypothesize in relation to the categorical variables. The observation reported about television watchers liking fast food for example, could be checked by averaging the number of fast food meals per week for television watchers and those in other favorite activity categories. Also some students naturally want to consider outcomes for boys and girls. In reporting on a group's work on this data set, the following response shows the potential for supporting hypotheses of this kind.

- [Ted] added up all the weights of the [8] boys and all the weights of the [8] girls and he only found that there was a difference of 35 kilograms between girls and boys. And with this one we discovered that boys—these boys—ate more fast food than the girls.

For many students at the elementary and middle school level specific instruction is required to distinguish both the types of variables that are involved when hypotheses are being proposed and the appropriate tools needed in supporting the hypotheses. Finding averages, for example for different groups, is likely to be appropriate for categorical variables (such as gender), whereas scattergrams are likely to be useful when looking for an association of two measurement variables. Introducing a basic graphing package at this stage[15] may assist the students who are having difficulty creating their own representations, to bridge the gap from making hypotheses to supporting them with evidence.

6.4 INFERENCE IN COMPARING TWO GROUPS

In making decisions about differences between two groups, there are various places where an activity can enter the statistical investigation model. The tasks in Fig. 6.3 are linked to the presentation of data in graphical form to allow the comparison of two classes of students based on results from a test of quick recall of mathematics facts.[16] The representation is meant to be straightforward to encourage students to focus on differences rather than complicated graphs. After a suitable introduction, students are asked, for each of the four pairs of graphs, which class did better (Blue or Red, Green or Purple, Yellow or Brown, and Pink or Black). From grade 3, students have little difficulty with the story being told in the graphs. All students conclude that the Red class did better than the Blue class in Part (a), mainly by observation, although a few, often older students, calculate the totals of

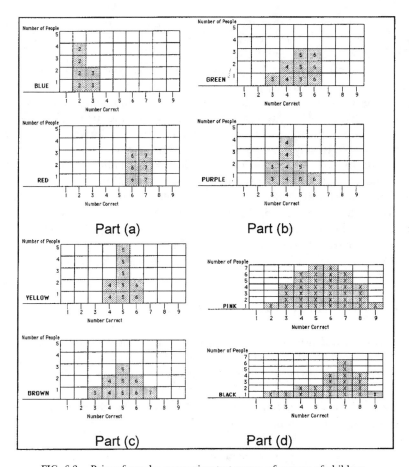

FIG. 6.3.   Pairs of graphs comparing test scores of groups of children.

scores for the two groups. Not all of these students explicitly state that the number of students in each group is the same, the criterion that makes calculating totals a valid exercise. Similarly for the Green and Purple classes in Part (b), most students conclude that the Green class did better by considering the shape of the graph or by again calculating totals. Errors in finding totals are not uncommon and for those who do not also consider the shapes of the graphs, the errors go undetected. Part (c) is more problematic because although the totals for the Yellow and Brown classes are the same and each is symmetric in shape, one distribution is more spread out than the other. Arguments are possible supporting any of the three hypotheses: the Yellow class did better, the Brown class did better, or the classes did equally well. Finally Part (d) presents two classes with different numbers of students, where the larger Pink class has a lower mean score than the smaller

Black class. The visual appearance of the graphs, however, can be misleading for some students because of the larger bulge in the middle of the Pink class with higher frequencies than the Black class.

The differences in the presentations of the parts of the task in Fig. 6.3 make the overall task an excellent hierarchical context within which to explore students' understanding from the middle elementary to high school years. Over a range of students six levels of outcome are likely to be observed when performances on the four parts are considered together. The levels are split into two groups depending on whether students are able to cope with the unequal class sizes in Part (d) or not. The first three levels exhibit increasingly complex reasoning for sets of equal size, whereas the second three levels mirror this increasing complexity for sets of unequal size.

For students who can deal successfully only with comparing two sets of equal size, there is still increasing structural complexity shown in the reasoning displayed. At the unistructural level students focus on single aspects of the graphs in making decisions. "More" is a significant feature of many responses to Part (a).

- [The Red class did better because] Red got more points.

For Part (c) individual values could be the basis of decision making.

- [The Brown class did better because] Brown got a 7 and no one else did.

These students are much more likely to be susceptible to the visual appearance of the Pink class in Part (d).

- [The Pink class did better because] Pink has got more.
- [The Pink class did better because] Pink is nearly filled right up to the top.

At the multistructural level responses tend to focus either on a numerical totaling strategy for comparing the pairs of groups or on a visual strategy comparing different parts of the two graphs. Components chosen are usually considered in a sequential fashion. Typical are responses to Parts (b) and (c).

- [The Green class did better because] By adding the scores up . . . [Purple] added up to 34 and . . . [Green] added up to 36.
- [The Yellow and Brown classes are equal because] By adding them up they both got 45.

For Part (d) the decision is again likely to be based on totals, without consideration of the numbers in the classes.

- [The Pink class did better because] Pink got 198 and Black got 130.

Visual strategies are similar in the sequential approach shown at this level.

- [The Green class did better because] There are more 6s and 5s than . . . over in the Purple class.
- [The Pink class did better because] Just by looking at it you can tell a lot more, but 9 and 8 are a lot like the same but then, the 6 and 5 and 4 and just all the rest are much bigger than these ones down here [Black].

At the relational level students are able to integrate visual and numerical strategies successfully for equal-sized data sets.

- They're even [The Yellow and Brown classes]. These people, the Brown class, they had kind of more people in the 6 and 7 in the higher scores, but these people [Yellow] had a lot more people in the middle, which kind of added up, so they're even. Well by looking at it, you can sort of see that it's kind of even, because it's kind of the same. There's those there and those there . . . they add up to the same as those two . . . 5 and 5 is 10, and 7 and 3 is also 10, so if you moved those two [3 and 7] up there [5 and 5] they're the same . . . so they're even, the Yellow and Brown class.

The second group of three levels of response again reflect increasing structural complexity in the justifications provided but these deal success-fully with the unequal sizes of the data sets in Part (d). At the unistructural level justifications appear based on intuitions related to the visual presenta-tion of the data in the graphs.

- [The Black class did better because] Black have got a higher amount for the number of people.
- I think that Black would have done better. They have got, for the amount of people in their class, they have got a higher number, a highest percentage or something.

At the multistructural level responses are sequential in nature based either on numerical or visual strategies but not both. The mean is the usual nu-merical strategy.

- [Writes $198/36 = 5.5$ for Pink and $130/21 = 6.19$ for Black] This one's [Black] got a higher average . . . Because there's a higher number of people in the [Pink] class then it would make the average lower because you are di-viding by more. But they scored more so it really doesn't change it. So I think they are comparable.
- The people in this class [Black] have done well for how many people there are, whereas this one [Pink]: more than probably about half of them are on the lower side, whereas this class [Black] hasn't got as many people on the lower side, more on the higher side.

Finally at the relational level students are able to integrate numerical and visual information to reinforce arguments favoring the Black class in Part (d).

- [Calculates the means for each group and concludes that Black has the higher average . . .] So that [Pink] is an average of 5.5 and I suppose I would expect that because obviously there is the same amount of people between 5 and 6 and so most of them are in 5 and 6 so you would probably expect that . . . So their [Black] average is just a little bit higher, 6.2. Even though they had less people it still averages, so you work out the average so it's still fairer . . . that makes it equal averaging, but these people [Black] had a little bit higher, which I expected because they had more people in 7. Actually they didn't have more people in 7, they had less people that got lower. [Points back and forth between the two graphs throughout the discussion.]

To have students able to produce integrated arguments that appreciate the proportional nature of comparing two groups of different size with averages is a goal of the statistics curriculum. The connection to proportional reasoning elsewhere in the mathematics curriculum is crucial and should be reinforced explicitly.[17] The connection with the arithmetic mean or other measure of average is also critical. For a statistician the mean is probably the obvious statistic to employ in comparing two groups such as those in Part (d) of Fig. 6.3 but this is not necessarily the case for middle school students. It takes a long time for averages to become natural tools to be used in investigations. Unless recently taught in a similar context, the mean is not the usual choice of students. They are more likely to look at visual features, such as humps and clumps, in making decisions about which group has done better. Although it is also important to consider visual characteristics of data sets, they should be used in conjunction with measures of central tendency. Very few students, even at the high school level, naturally consider all three measures—mean, median, and mode—in comparing two data sets.[18] Many experiences are needed to reinforce the usefulness of the link between averages and inference.

The visual impression of the graphs in Fig. 6.3 and how the variation they represent is interpreted by students are features considered in a case study in Chapter 7.

6.5 INFERENCE IN ASSOCIATIONS

Drawing inferences in relation to association often focuses on one of two forms of variable: numerical or categorical. Both are considered in this section. For two numerical variables it is possible to draw a scattergram of the variables and use it to justify the strength of the association. In Sections 3.3

and 6.3, a task based on 16 data cards including both numerical and categorical variables is used to consider students' developing appreciation of
the hypothesizing process and the need to create graphical representations
to support these hypotheses. The highest level of graphical representation
discussed in Section 3.3 is associated with the creation of a scattergram and
the highest level of hypothesizing in Section 6.3 is associated with hypothesizing cause-effect or other associations among numerical variables.[19] Associations of this type are also considered in the Section 6.6 when questioning
of associations is the focus.

Although the associations that students meet first in school when learning to plot scattergrams are likely to be linear, many actual studies in the sciences and social sciences produce non-linear associations. Becoming ac-
quainted with such contexts is important to avoid building a stereotype of
linear graphs being the only ones that can show association and to learn to
draw inferences in the non-linear setting.

The graph and questions in Fig. 6.4 deal with data from a context familiar to students, that of time spent on homework and score obtained in

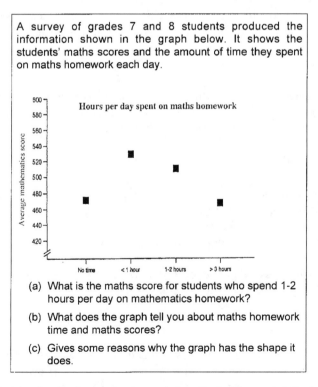

FIG. 6.4.   Graph of a non-linear association. Used with permission of the
Australian Council for Educational Research.

mathematics.[20] The questions are graded in order to encourage students to engage with the graph, then to explain the story told by the graph and hypothesize reasons for the shape. The final question allows for the suggestion of a non-linear cause-effect relationship that may be counter to what students have been told by their teachers who want to encourage them to do their homework.

The range of responses to Part (b) in Fig. 6.4 is likely to demonstrate increasing appreciation of the association portrayed in the graph. For some students the task is very difficult and they misinterpret what the graph is telling.

- More students studied for an hour.

The use of "more" here in interpreting the highest value on the graph is reminiscent of the "more" response in suggesting why the Pink class was better in Part (d) of the task in Fig. 6.3. Although sometimes pertinent, discussion needs to take place to raise students' awareness that "more" needs to be considered in context and is not always better. At the next level, responses often provide a basic single reading of the axes labels to set the context without any further interpretation of the trend displayed.

- It shows the total maths scores / total homework time.

When students begin to interpret the association shown, several further levels of response are likely to occur. Some students suggest an incorrect association that may be influenced by their own personal experience.

- [The] more homework you do, the better your scores.

Others, perhaps only recognizing the significance that a linear association would imply, respond as follows.

- It doesn't matter how much homework you do.

At the next level are responses of students who do see an association but immediately take it too far and speculate on a cause-effect relationship.

- If you do 1 hour's homework you will get a better score.

At the highest level are responses that state the association as shown. The subtle difference in language between the next and the previous responses, can be a discussion point in the classroom in terms of the vast difference in implications.

- Those who did 1 hour got the highest scores.
- Scores go up to 1 hour and then decrease after that.

Some responses go further to draw conclusions in the interpretations. Again a subtle language change is seen in the first response.

- You are more likely to get good grades if you do an hour.
- Doing 3 hours can be just as bad as doing nothing.
- Those better at maths finished early.

In asking for reasons why the graph in Fig. 6.4 looks as it does, the question in Part (c) invites hypotheses to be formed. Again students are likely to display differing facility in responses. At the lowest level responses tend to focus on the graph itself rather than the data it portrays.

- Easy to read.
- It's the most appropriate type of graph.

At the next level, students engage with the variables but do not go on to suggest hypotheses.

- The shape is the result of different times.

Responses at the next level go further to tell a more detailed story of what the data represent, without hypotheses.

- The people that studied 1 hour got the highest mark, those that did not study or did too much study got a lower mark.

Finally, some students attempt to form hypotheses to explain the data shown.

- The struggling students take more time to do their homework.
- The drop in scores is due to stress and frustration.

Although statisticians would still quibble about the quality of some of the hypotheses stated, the suggestions could provide starting points for further investigation. For those without specific training the responses reveal willingness to become involved with the data and their meaning. It should also be noted that within the context of a classroom discussion of responses to the task in Fig. 6.4, some of the responses categorized in lower levels are not incorrect in a technical sense. They should be valued and contrasted with others in order to help build broader foundations for future reasoning in related situations. Similarly, discussion of the feasibility of testing the different hypotheses formed can be useful and some will be discarded along the way as "interesting but impractical."

Associations can also be considered between categorical variables. This is often done using two-way tables. The creation of such tables is within the capacity of most students but interpretation (with a statistic such as chi-square) requires skills of proportional reasoning, which may be difficult for some students to apply without specific instruction. Again the connection to the study of proportion in the mathematics curriculum is strong.

The two-way table and question in Fig. 6.5 provide an opportunity to gauge student understanding in this context.[21] Presenting data, as this table does, with no association present is a challenge not only to students' ability to handle the proportions but also to students' previously held views about the relationship between smoking and lung disease.

Students through the high school years find this type of question demanding for the reasons noted in the previous paragraph. At the lowest level are responses based on students' beliefs. These responses make no reference to the data in the table.

- Yes, smoking is known to cause lung cancer—it is a fact.
- No, it could be hereditary.
- Yes, there is more chance if you smoke.

Some responses continue to ignore the data presented but consider the context and suggest potential limitations of the study or its reporting.

- We don't know how they collected their sample. It could be biased.

These responses are not actually addressing the question in Fig. 6.5. At the lowest level of engagement with the data, responses focus on single cell values.

The following information is from a survey about smoking and lung disease among 250 people.			
	Lung disease	**No lung disease**	**Total**
Smoking	90	60	150
No smoking	60	40	100
Total	150	100	250
Using this information, do you think that for this sample of people lung disease depended on smoking? Explain your answer.			

FIG. 6.5.   Two-way table of "association" of smoking and lung disease.

- There is a lot of non-smokers [60] with lung cancer.

Some are influenced by the 90 in the upper left cell to agree with the statement that lung disease depends on smoking; 90 is the largest number and it is in the cell with these two characteristics as labels.

- Yes, 90 who smoked got lung disease.

At the next level, usually two or three cells are considered.

- Yes. [The] difference between 60 (smokers) and 40 (non smokers) is big.

Relative sizes apparently play little role in these responses. Of the students who disagree with the statement for the data presented, differences rather than proportions are likely to be the focus of attention.

- For lung disease, with 60 no smoking and 90 smoking, the difference is not much.

Similarly, lack of difference across categories with different totals is sometimes offered as an explanation.

- 60 "no smoking lung disease" and 60 "smoking no lung disease" are the same.

At the highest level, responses appreciate the proportional reasoning involved; there are however, very few of these responses.

- No, because if they surveyed 150 people who smoked and didn't smoke it would be the same—90-60 each.

The difficulties in considering the proportions of smokers for the two different conditions of lung disease or of lung disease for the two different conditions of smoking, are similar to those encountered by many students in solving the proportional events problem presented in Section 5.6, in Fig. 5.8. Differences rather than proportions are also often used in that context. In that problem, however, there is a visual presentation of two boxes, which some students use as a clue to consider proportions. In the case of the two-way table in Fig. 6.5, the distinction of conditions is not as obvious as for the two boxes with marbles in them. There are also two pairs of conditions to consider. Further the context of the problem in Fig. 6.5 is more complex in that it involves an issue about which students hold beliefs, whereas marbles in boxes are abstract in nature. Links among these parts of the data and chance curriculum and to proportional reasoning are strong and likely to require much reinforcement into the senior high school years.

6.6 QUESTIONING INFERENCES

Learning to make predictions, to form hypotheses, and to justify conclusions are exceedingly important to those who are going to be involved in data collection and studies of their own. For everyone, however, it is essential to learn to be sensitive to the inferences made by others and to develop the ability to question claims made without proper justification. A suspicious attitude to extravagant media claims is a useful attitude in many social contexts students will meet when they leave school.[22] From a claim that 9 out of 10 dentists recommend a certain toothpaste to a claim that beer causes crime, citizens need constantly to ask for the hard evidence that supports the claim. Students can be exposed to such advertisements and news stories and then asked to find their own to bring to class for discussion.

The article in Fig. 3.6 claiming "an almost perfect relationship between the increase in heart deaths and the increase in use of motor vehicles" is a case in point. The article is introduced in Section 3.4 in relation to a graphing task that asks students to provide a labeled sketch of what a graph supporting this claim would look like. A further question for students is to consider what questions they would ask Mr. Robinson about his research.[23]

The levels of response to this question clearly illustrate the Statistical Literacy Hierarchy and the increasing structural complexity in the third tier. The terminology associated with cause–effect relationships can be subtle if students are not familiar with it or if they have difficulties with literacy. "Family car is killing us" and "motoring is a health hazard" send a "motoring causes deaths" message. Some students, however, appear unable to decipher the messages and their responses indicate no questions for Mr. Robinson. It is hence not possible to tell if they are able to engage in the first tier of statistical literacy.

- None. He would do that for a living. He'd know what he's talking about.

Some responses appear to understand the claims, appropriate for the first tier, and accept them as true.

- What can be done about this problem? Can it be prevented?
- Is there a chance of technology so we don't have to use fuel?

At the next level students appear to appreciate the context of the claim as a statistical one where data are involved, and questions reflect this in the second tier of statistical literacy.

- How many people has he researched?
- What age group did he research on?

Some responses question single aspects of the study whereas others consider multiple aspects.

- What area the survey was in, what age, was there a wide variety of people?
- What physical conditions were people in? The type and condition of their cars?

Although these students may have an underlying concern about the claim, it is not explicitly stated in second tier responses.

In the third tier of statistical literacy, the questioning of the claim itself occurs. Some students make single comments, whereas others are structurally more complex.

- Is it true?
- Can he prove it?
- What are the numbers?

These questions signal a warning of disbelief but with no indication of why. Others are more explicit relating the question to the context.

- How can driving increase these things?
- How do you know for sure it is the motor car?

Further, some ask specifically for additional factors.

- Is anything else likely to cause a heart attack anyway?
- How was it obtained? Could there be other contributing factors? Just because there is a correlation does not mean that there is a direct link.

At the highest level responses go on to suggest different variables that could be involved in explaining the health hazards.

- Has he considered other causes, smoking, pollution, and so on?
- Surely something else could have contributed to this information? More junk food? More stress?

- How old were the sampled people; what pressures did they have on them, loans, house, car, any other debts?

The goal of statistical literacy in schools is for students to be able to express concern about the claim, ask questions about the procedures followed in the research, and suggest alternative hypotheses. The connections to literacy generally and to other areas of the curriculum where contextual understanding is consolidated are very important. This is an area where students cannot be allowed to hide behind the "mathematics is numbers" excuse.

6.7   IMPLICATIONS AND RECOMMENDATIONS

Inference is often thought of as the end point of a statistical investigation: after the question is asked, the data are collected, the graphs are drawn, and the statistics are calculated; then the conclusion is reached, the inference complete. As the examples in this chapter show, however, inference being the goal means it is closely tied to every part of the process of statistical investigation. When each aspect is being taught, it is not an isolated topic but must be seen to be related directly to a question and the goal of coming to a conclusion. This is sometimes forgotten in the presentations of textbooks. The asking of questions, making of predictions, and stating of hypotheses are stages in the inference process that can be entered into by quite young children, even if they do not have extensive experience in all stages of the process. As the previous section stresses, it is also important to be able to evaluate the inferences made by others and have the motivation and ability to ask questions if required.

In terms of statistical literacy, the third tier of the hierarchy that highlights critical questioning would commonly be identified with the questioning of inferences made without proper justification. The earlier chapters, however, give examples where questioning is appropriate in all other areas as well: in sampling, in graphing, in averaging, and in likelihood statements. The fact that questioning can occur at every stage may then mean that by the time the conclusion is reached, it is felt that the job is finished. Neither situation is the case. Questioning, both by the researcher and others, should take place continuously throughout the investigation process.

Knowing the terminology of inference implies having an appreciation of conditional statements and language associated with cause–effect claims, even if they are not explicitly stated. The demands of the first tier of the hierarchy can hence be quite difficult to meet for younger children. The second tier, putting this language into some context, may also place special demands on students. If a hypothesis is stated about a medicine or a treatment, it is necessary to know quite a bit about the medicine or treatment in order to consider challenging a claim made. This must be accompanied by motivation in order to move to the third tier and begin to question the authority involved.

Even in the third tier of the Statistical Literacy Hierarchy less and greater sophistication of questioning is observed. It is possible to question a claim with a statement like, "That's rubbish!" Whereas such a comment may be true, it may be reflecting the bias of the observer as much as the strength of the argument. Students must be encouraged to build structurally complex arguments into their questioning processes, in order to create credibility. The final responses presented in the previous section are examples of good starts in this direction.

The building of good habits related to inference and prediction can begin in the middle school, as suggested by the National Council of Teachers of Mathematics at the beginning of this chapter. Anecdotal evidence from work with teachers and their students supports the contention that students are naturally drawn to questions related to comparing groups and to explaining relationships seen in data sets. This is shown in the suggestions of some of the students dealing with the data cards discussed in Sections 3.3 and 6.3. Classroom work beginning with an activity such as introduced in Section 3.10 to create connections between stacked dot plots and box-and-whisker plots can easily lead to questions and predictions generated by the students themselves. The data in Fig. 3.23 for example represent the foot lengths of 20 people. The question is likely to arise as to whether the males have longer feet than females. What is meant by "longer" for individuals and groups is an important part of the discussion before attempts are made to make a prediction or draw an inference. The decision about what the reference group (or population) is, is also important. In the first instance, however, students are usually mainly interested in the boys and girls in their class. Allowing students freedom in what they choose to represent and how they present it, is important because many realistic suggestions are likely to arise in middle school classrooms.

Building on the ideas presented in Fig. 3.23, it would be possible to mark the females with a different symbol or color and to create two separate box-and-whisker plots. The representation created in Fig. 6.6 is typical of the ideas of middle school teachers meeting these ideas for the first time and suggesting what would be likely to arise in their classrooms. Discussion of the variation within the subsets, the overlapping values, and the shapes of the box-and-whisker plots, is important in reinforcing ideas and helping to make a decision about whether there is a difference between male and female foot lengths in the data in Fig. 6.6. Given the likely size of samples in classrooms, quite striking, or even disappointing (in terms of difference), outcomes may occur. Teachers need to be able to discuss many possibilities and explanations. Basing hypotheses, predictions, and inferences on graphical representations rather than numerical statistics alone is essential

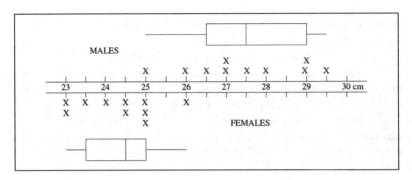

FIG. 6.6. Foot lengths of 20 males and females.

in the middle school and establishes good habits for later statistical investigations.

A similar situation arises in questions of association. When measuring both hand span and foot length for a class, students are likely to suggest a relationship between them when observing that people with wider hand spans tend to have longer feet. Representing both measurements on a stacked dot plot such as in Fig. 6.6 does little to display the relationship, although some students try side-by-side value bars, perhaps ordered in pairs along the horizontal axis to show an association: as the shorter bars (hand span) rise, so do the longer bars (foot length). At the middle school level students are likely to need an introduction to the form of a scattergram but then can be quite motivated by the relationships they see, such as that shown in Fig. 6.7. The fact that the individual points represent two measurements needs constant reinforcement and the fact that these points do not lie on a precise straight line also requires discussion. At this stage it is important to develop intuitions about the appearance of strong and weak associations, not an awareness of the values of correlation coefficients and their statistical significance. If students learn to plot points as part of their initial analyses, they may not be so easily misled later by "significant" correlations for large sample sizes that explain virtually none of the variation seen in the scattergram.

Although it does not happen every day, there are often headlines in the newspaper that suggest cause-effect inferences that could initiate useful classroom discussion. Attention-grabbing headlines may start discussion and argument even before the details are read. The article in Fig. 6.8 is humorous and yet illustrates a simple design that can form the basis of a classroom discussion.[24]

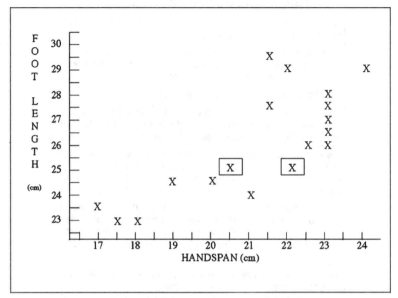

FIG. 6.7.   Scatter plot of foot length and hand span for 20 people.

The article in Fig. 6.8 is useful for several reasons. First, the outcome of the study is "no association." Usually media organizations report on studies with significant positive, or negative, associations. This as a point for discussion with students in terms of building skills for critical reading of media reports. Second, aspects of the study itself, in terms of sample size and length of time the cream was applied, warrant discussion. Some students could be asked to take the side of the cream manufacturer and criticize the study. Students must be careful of bringing their pre-conceived ideas about a topic to their consideration of whether an appropriate statistical investigation has been carried out.

The extract from an article shown in Fig. 6.9 is more typical of the type of headlines newspaper sub-editors create to attract the attention of readers.[25] Judging from the professor's quoted comments within the article, he acknowledged not understanding completely the direct link between beer consumption and rates of violence, but the person who wrote the headline had no such qualms. Classroom discussion could focus on whether the report justifies the claim in the headline, on what possible lurking (hidden) variables could be causing both beer drinking and violent crime, and on the difference between two variables being correlated and change in one causing change in the other. It is likely that class discussion will unearth "sample of size one stories," such as, "We once had a neighbor who drank beer with his friends every Friday night and then came home and beat his wife." The suggestion of personally known examples illustrating a claimed

Thin thighs don't come from a jar

San Francisco. Happiness, at least in the form of thin thighs, might not come in a jar.

Two studies released yesterday at a plastic surgeons' convention here raised questions about the much touted creams which are said to melt fat from thighs.

And according to the plastic surgeons, they don't work.

"We found that if you just apply the cream and don't change your diet or exercise, there's no difference," said Dr. Leroy Young of St. Louis's Washington University.

He and his colleagues had 17 women apply cream on one thigh and one side of their stomach for eight weeks. Half the women used the fat-melting cream and half used a placebo.

In addition to the objective evaluation – thigh measurements and before-and-after photos evaluated by outside observers – 16 out of the 17 women themselves saw no differences in the thighs treated with the $US30 ($A41) jar of cream.

The 17th woman was convinced, however, even though her weight and measurement were unchanged.

FIG. 6.8. Newspaper article useful in considering inference.

Beer gets blame for violent crime rate

Australia's high incidence of violent crime and domestic violence was directly linked to the population's massive beer intake, a crime expert said yesterday.

Speaking in Adelaide at the eighth International Symposium on Victimology, Professor Jan Van Dijk from the Netherlands said an international study he had made found a link between drinking beer and violent crime.

The study found a particular link between beer drinking and sexual and domestic violence.

"There is a direct correlation between beer consumption in countries and levels of violence, so where people drink more beer the rates of violence tend to be higher," he said.

"In countries where people drink less, or drink wine, there appears to be less violence.

"We do not fully understand the direct link between these two, but the link is certainly there.

"In typical beer-drinking cultures like Holland, Germany, England, Canada and Australia there is more violence than in Italy or Greece or Spain, where people drink wine."

FIG. 6.9. Newspaper article with cause–effect claim in headline.

cause–effect relationship need to be appreciated for what they are—a biasing influence that may be totally atypical of the association and have no cause–effect nature. Explicit discussion is needed to help students appreciate the psychological but non-statistical influence they can have.

These two articles are intended to be illustrative. As mentioned in other chapters, the breakthrough comes when students bring their own examples to class, perhaps from the television news, from popular magazines, or from the internet. They may be incensed with what they find as statistical detectives but they also need to be encouraged next to look for good examples of studies and their reporting. Knowing when to believe the valid reports is just as important as knowing when to disregard the others.

NOTES

1. National Council of Teachers of Mathematics (2000, p. 248).
2. Outhred & Shaw (1999).
3. Lehrer & Romberg (1996); Lehrer & Schauble (2000).
4. Doerr & English (2003).
5. Metz (1999).
6. Pereira-Mendoza (1995); Pereira-Mendoza & Mellor (1991).
7. Gal, Rothschild, & Wagner (1989, 1990).
8. Batanero, Estepa, Godino, & Green (1996).
9. Estepa, Batanero, & Sanchez (1999).
10. Watson & Moritz (2001a).
11. Watson & Moritz (1999c).
12. Watson & Kelly (2003b); Watson, Kelly, Callingham, & Shaughnessy (2003).
13. Pereira-Mendoza & Mellor (1991).
14. Chick & Watson (2001).
15. For example *Tinkerplots*, Konold & Miller (2005).
16. Watson (2001, 2002b); Watson & Moritz (1999a).
17. Watson & Shaughnessy (2004).
18. Watson & Moritz (1999a).
19. Chick & Watson (2001).
20. Lokan, Ford, & Greenwood (1996, p. 169); Watson & Callingham (2004).
21. Batanero, Estepa, Godino, & Green (1996); Watson & Callingham (2004).
22. Gal (2002).
23. Watson (2000b).
24. "Thin Thighs" (1995).
25. "Beer gets blame" (1994).

Variation—The Underlying Phenomenon

Variety's the very spice of life,
That gives it all its flavor.[1]

7.1 BACKGROUND

For more than 200 years people have been quoting variations on this adage. As discussed in Section 1.6, variation is the underlying reason for the existence of statistics. It comes in many forms and the purpose of probability and statistics is to describe it in meaningful ways. Probability distributions exist, for example, to describe the theoretical random variation that occurs when trials of random generators are carried out many times. This might be called the expected variation from an expected value. There is also the issue in statistics of unexpected variation, that is, variation that does not fit an expected distribution. Unexpected variation may be caused by non-random behavior, or perhaps variation is related to an identifiable cause such as a treatment or an association among measured characteristics (or variables). When students reach formal statistics courses they will use hypothesis testing or confidence intervals to assist in making decisions about how extreme the difference or variation is in problem situations and whether a particular conclusion is acceptable or not. These formal procedures are based on rules related to probabilities, for example, "Is there an overlap of two 95% confidence intervals?" or "Is the probability of this outcome less than 1 in 20 or 1 in 100?" Teachers have observed, however, that often students in beginning formal statistics courses rely so heavily on the

rules that they fail to consider the data themselves, in particular the variation shown if data are plotted.[2] It is hence essential, from the middle years
of schooling, that students are given opportunities to handle many kinds of
data sets, to explore ways of presenting data, especially visually, and to begin making decisions about reasonable and unreasonable variation, about
large and small differences within and between data sets. The fact that the
criteria used to make these decisions may not meet all of the criteria of statisticians is not important; what is important is that students come to an appreciation of the need to explore and understand the stories that data can
tell.

Variation has been mentioned at various points in the preceding five
chapters and these connections are summarized in the links shown in Fig.
7.1, both with respect to the overall investigation process and to particular
aspects such as interpreting media reports or detecting bias. Instead of focusing on particular links in the figure, this chapter presents a description
of students' general understanding of variation followed by four case studies of investigations of student understanding of variation across grades 3 to
9. Three of the cases are based on individual interviews and seven six-year-
old children are included in two of the case studies, with occasional note
made of their levels of understanding. No case study encompasses all of the
links in Fig. 7.1, however the major features of the investigation process are
included within the four.

Although David Green made an explicit plea for research into students'
understanding of variation at the International Association for Statistical
Education Roundtable in Canada in 1992,[3] interest in the following decade
remained focused mainly on other aspects of the data and chance curriculum, those covered in the preceding chapters. Mike Shaughnessy made a
similar call for interest in variation in 1997 in New Zealand[4] and began with

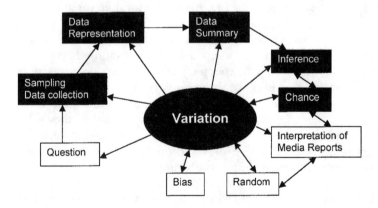

FIG. 7.1.   Links among the ideas and statistical elements associated with variation.

his co-workers to investigate scenarios that would allow students to display their understanding.[5] This work influenced three of the case studies discussed in this chapter. The fourth grew out of early work by Iddo Gal and his colleagues in Philadelphia.[6]

7.2 VARIATION: HOW TO DESCRIBE IT

In contrast to terms such as *sample* and *random*, which are very well defined in the literature (e.g., by D. B. Orr in Section 2.1 and by David Moore at the beginning of Chapter 5), it is difficult to find definitions of *variation*. David Moore, who provides the excellent discussion of the importance of variation to statistics in Section 1.6, in fact does not provide a definition of the term. Many curriculum documents do not even mention the word except in connection with the introduction of the standard deviation.[7] It is hence of interest to explore the appreciation for the term variation built up by students in the middle years of schooling. Asking a series of questions, such as those in Fig. 7.2, allows students a range of opportunities to display understanding about this nebulous idea of variation.[8]

Considering the responses to the questions in Fig. 7.2 holistically, middle school students generally respond in surveys at one of four levels. At the lowest level, students do not know the term or give idiosyncratic prestructural responses, perhaps confusing the term with another one.

- (b) Jayden varies from place to place.
- (a) It means exactly.
- (a) It shakes. (b) I have a big car that has variation.

At the unistructural level responses reflect a single idea that could be construed as appreciation of the concept, although often this is awkwardly expressed.

- (a) You get a choice. (b) A car varies from sizes and colors.
- (a) A variation of something like food, etc. (b) The variation of food was amazing. (c) Food, shoes, events, shops.

> (a) What does "variation" mean?
>
> (b) Use the word "variation" in a sentence.
>
> (c) Give an example of something that "varies".

FIG. 7.2. Survey questions on variation.

- (a) Something varies from the other. (b) The variation between a cat and a dog. (c) Cat and dog.

At the multistructural level, responses provide a straightforward explanation of the term with an appropriate example.

- (a) How something changes. (c) The weather.
- (a) Lots of different things. (b) The variation of chocolates that were on the bench. (c) Days in school (subjects).
- (a) Not the same things. (b) There was a large variation in the score. (c) A team's score.

Finally at the highest level, responses relate the subtle idea of change with appropriate usage and examples.

- (a) Slight change or difference. (c) People vary in size, some are short, some are tall, some are medium.
- (a) Something that differs from its previous state. (b) There's a big variation in the results. (c) The weather varies.
- (a) Not always the same. A little change in something. (b) Last week we had a small variation in our timetable . . . (c) The time the sun goes down varies from day to day.

Less than 10% of middle school students are likely to be able to respond at the highest level with about a quarter at each of the middle two levels.[9]

As might be expected, when similar questions, such as those in Fig. 7.3, are asked in an interview setting, students tend to respond at higher levels.[10] Perhaps this is due to the presence of a person interested in their responses or to the time allowed to think about what they say. Including the word *variable* assists some students in searching for meaning, as does the prompt about the wind.

The lowest level of response is likely to reflect total unfamiliarity with the term. This is typical of students in the elementary rather than middle

---

Here are some words.

(a) Do you know what the word "Variation" means?

(b) Have you heard the word "Variable"? Do you know what it means?

(c) Sometimes I hear on the weather, "The winds are variable." What do you think it means?

FIG. 7.3. Interview protocol questions on variation.

school grades. At the unistructural level the hints are likely to assist or reinforce single ideas of change.

- [Variation?] Umm, variation, like a variety, got a few things to choose from. [Sentence?] No. [Variable?] Heard of it on the radio. [What were they talking about?] Not sure now. ["Winds are variable"?] Yes. They are going to change [uses hands] any moment.

At the multistructural level, responses adequately reflect one of the terms, usually variation, but struggle with the other, and often are assisted by the hint.

- [Variation?] I have heard of it sort of and used it before . . . to say variation between the colors in the rainbow is big. Because there's all different, sort of. [Variable?] I have heard of it but am not sure how to put it. ["Winds are variable"?] Oh yes, I've heard of that but, they could change.

At the relational level of response, all terms are used with meaningful descriptions, often involving complex contexts.

- [Variation?] Yes we use it in science and it means differently. It is like you can have a variation of foods—this is different foods, but they do the same thing, like they give you vitamins and things. [Variable?] Yes it means like if you take with science we had a test strip and put eno in it and we had a balloon over it and we took it out cold—we had it in a cup of cold water and then we took it and put it in a cup of boiling hot water and the eno started to fizz differently when it was in the hot water. [Sentence?] The water was variable. We had variable water temperatures. ["Winds are variable"?] Yes it means sometimes the wind can be higher and then one minute and then like the next minute the wind can [be] really . . . soft.

Up to a third of middle school students are likely to give a response at the relational level in such discussions with slightly more at the multistructural level. It would appear useful, then, to include such general discussions as part of introductions to units of work involving data and chance, particularly to work on using the language with ease.

7.3 CASE STUDY ONE: THE WEATHER

The development of intuitions about variation can be explored in familiar contexts where people talk of change and where change is often attributed to observable causes. Such is the case with the weather. The questions in Fig. 7.4 are designed to elicit students' understanding of variation in rela-

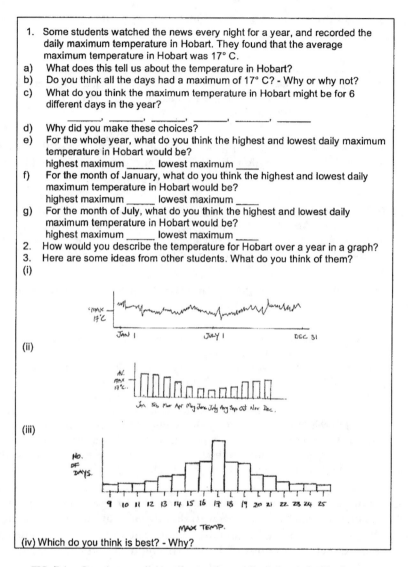

1. Some students watched the news every night for a year, and recorded the daily maximum temperature in Hobart. They found that the average maximum temperature in Hobart was 17° C.
a) What does this tell us about the temperature in Hobart?
b) Do you think all the days had a maximum of 17° C? - Why or why not?
c) What do you think the maximum temperature in Hobart might be for 6 different days in the year?

      _____, _____, _____, _____, _____, _____
d) Why did you make these choices?
e) For the whole year, what do you think the highest and lowest daily maximum temperature in Hobart would be?
    highest maximum _____ lowest maximum _____
f) For the month of January, what do you think the highest and lowest daily maximum temperature in Hobart would be?
    highest maximum _____ lowest maximum _____
g) For the month of July, what do you think the highest and lowest daily maximum temperature in Hobart would be?
    highest maximum _____ lowest maximum _____
2. How would you describe the temperature for Hobart over a year in a graph?
3. Here are some ideas from other students. What do you think of them?
(i)

(ii)

(iii)

(iv) Which do you think is best? - Why?

FIG. 7.4. Questions to elicit student understanding of variation in the context of maximum daily temperatures.

tion to the reporting of an average maximum temperature for a year for a city familiar to students and in relation to possible representation of a year's data in a graphical form.[11] It is clear that some contextual understanding, for example related to seasonal fluctuation, is required for full appreciation of the questions. It is likely, however, that students from grade 3 have some understanding and that the weather is among the most acceptable topics available to school age children. Scenarios based on the characteristics of the children themselves, such as height, hand span, or foot length, are also possibilities[12] but care must be taken to avoid measurements that may threaten students' self esteem.

Students' developing ability to describe variation spontaneously is seen in responses to questions about what it means for a city, such as Hobart, Tasmania, to have an average daily maximum temperature of 17°C over a year. Of interest in classifying responses is the degree to which students appreciate the variation in daily maximum temperatures that contributes to the yearly average. At the lowest level, responses appreciate the meaning of the average and make a single comment but do not mention its representation of many different temperatures; that is, they do not explicitly acknowledge variation.

- It is probably not that hot.
- It is pretty cold.
- It is sort of mild.

The next level of response, multistructural, reflects comparison of other places with Hobart, indicating an aspect of geographical variation rather than the variation that produced 17°C.

- That it is not really high like in Darwin but it is not absolutely freezing like Antarctica or something.
- It is reasonably cold—not very hot like Queensland and not really cold like England.

At the highest level are responses that use language relating the variation in Hobart's temperature to the average presented in the question.

- That it is most normally around about 17 degrees.
- That it is not very warm. That 17 came up a lot.
- That is cold and it was probably a little above it or under it—they just found the average.
- The temperature in summer would be around the 20s and the temperature in winter would be below 17 probably, and they range around.

When asked specifically if all days have the same maximum temperature, all students from the elementary grades are very likely to disagree. In fact all but the youngest students (some grade 3 and below) are likely to suggest reasonable temperatures for 6 days of the year. The explanations for the choices, however, display differing levels of ability to explain the variation in the six choices made. Some students appear unable to verbalize a reason for their choices. At the unistructural level, there is a refusal to predict or a focus on a single aspect, perhaps related to the outcome approach of predicting single specific outcomes without the necessity to consider the distribution of possibilities.[13]

- Just around 17.
- Sometimes it is rainy and cold.
- Because I have lived through these temperatures.
- They are hot days.

At the multistructural level often a dichotomous explanation is used or reliance on chance.

- I put some of them in summer and some in winter.
- Because Hobart's got very random weather.
- Because sometimes it might be foggy and cold and sometimes it might be nice and sunny, some days it might be inbetween sort of.

Finally, at the relational level responses feature variation around the center, sometimes with explicit recognition of average, range, or distribution.

- Just estimating, just a chance type of thing, because the average temperature was 17, so I put them around that.
- To give a wide range of the possibilities because quite often you have a very cold day but then you have very hot days and so the rest are just spread out through the middle to show that . . . you can get different temperatures.
- Probably all over numbers. We have quite varied weather down here, so I wouldn't put anything exactly around 17 all the time.

Over the middle school years there is a wide range of usage of language to show an appreciation of variation and its relationship to an average.

In a similar fashion there is a range of ability to describe the maximum daily temperatures over a year in a graph, as requested in Question 2 in Fig. 7.4. At the prestructural level (with respect to the task) students produce pictures, weather maps, or axes without context. Two such representations are shown in Fig. 7.5, produced by students in grade 5 and grade 3.

In the transition into a meaningful representation, responses are likely to focus on relevant features but not create a graph that makes sense in terms of the task. The two representations in Fig. 7.6, by students in grades 3 and 5, attempt to use numbers with days or months but do not present the story of a year.

At the unistructural level, focusing on a single aspect of variation, responses either discuss its nature in relation to a picture or produce a graph

FIG. 7.5.   Representations of the maximum daily temperature throughout the year in a weather map and a picture.

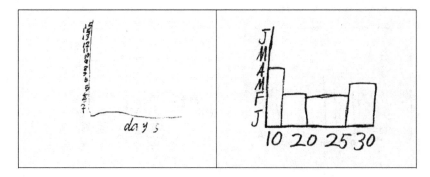

FIG. 7.6.   Attempts to engage the task of representing maximum daily temperatures for a year.

with variation, although not appropriate for the task set. The former is likely to be done by quite young children who may draw pictures of summer and winter, whereas the graphs in Fig. 7.7 are from grades 3 and 7.

At the multistructural level responses include variation and indicate a start on a yearly representation but are not complete. Examples are shown in Fig. 7.8 from grades 5 and 7.

Finally at the relational level, responses appreciate the need for completing a representation of the variation in temperatures across the year, in this case accounting for a drop in the southern hemisphere winter in the middle of the calendar year. Usually students choose a monthly "average" representation, as shown in the graphs in Fig. 7.9, drawn by students in grades 3 and 7. The horizontal representation by the grade 3 student probably represents a variation on a pictograph form learned in the classroom but is perfectly adequate for the task.

For a task such as this students are likely to show increasing ability to complete the task with grade level. A grade 3 response such as in Fig. 7.9 is

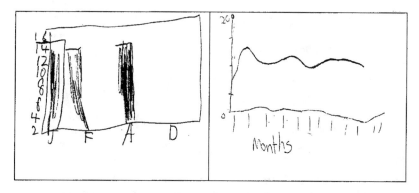

FIG. 7.7. Graphs indicating change but not appropriate variation in maximum daily temperature throughout the year.

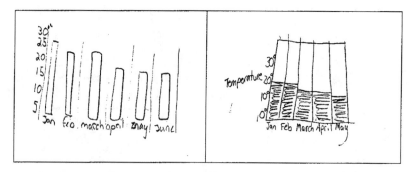

FIG. 7.8. Graphs with appropriate but incomplete representations of the maximum daily temperature throughout the year.

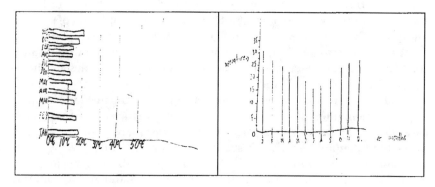

FIG. 7.9. Representations of the maximum daily temperatures for a year with realistic variation.

unusual and by grade 9 about half of students can be expected to perform at the highest level.

Turning to interpretation of the three graphs in Question 3 of Fig. 7.4, the middle bar graph is the easiest for students to interpret because it is most likely to be the form used by students themselves, for example in Fig. 7.9. The first graph, a squiggly line, potentially representing daily maxima for the year, is somewhat more challenging with less change in response level likely across grades. At the prestructural level students are totally unfamiliar with the representation.

- Not very good because you wouldn't know because it's too squiggly.
- It could climb and then go down.

At the next level, a transition occurs, where students have general ideas about the graph but not specific to the context of the task.

- They have used a pointy sort of graph . . . the further up the hotter.
- It goes up and down a lot. [Can you interpret?] It looks like how the temperature goes up and down.

At the unistructural level, responses provide a single mention of 17 as relevant in the interpretation of the graph.

- It does get over 17 degrees—if it is winter it doesn't really . . . kind of cold.
- The average is 17 and sometimes it is a little bit higher over the bar and not very often—not very, very much over 17.

At the multistructural level there are statements involving contrasts in context or comments on variation without context, often implicit and requiring some prompting.

- It's a bit over 17. [The line?] I know that type of graph but can't remember its name. They use it for volcanoes. This is high and this is getting low, and this is the same amount [flat part] and that's below it.
- Every day is different. [The line?] The heat every day, it could go up one day and down the next.
- The higher bumps are the hot days and the smaller ones are the cold days . . . [The line?] A matter of chance, high ones and low ones.

Finally, at the highest level are responses that relate the variation across time and the context.

- It varies a lot. It starts off above 17, that's the average and then it will go up a little and down, moving slowly around—so then it was probably the same for a few days and then slowly it goes up a little more and then a sudden drop which means the temperature has gone down and will slowly rise again which is strange because it is winter then—then it will drop for winter and go back up and down and stay low through winter and then it will slowly rise because of summer.

- The maximum for each month—all the temperatures for that month [points to month] and then all the temperatures for that month [points to another month]—July in the middle, so it goes January, July, December [to show] they change.

The most difficult graph to interpret in terms of the weather context is the frequency bar graph in Question 3 (iii) of Fig. 7.4. Although it is centered on the average value students have difficulty moving away from a time-based representation. Students are also unlikely to present a graph like this themselves because of the causal association with seasons that they would want to represent, which is not possible in this type of graph. A majority of students up to the middle school level are likely to misinterpret the representation, either ignoring the label on the horizontal axis and thinking in terms of dates, or ignoring the label on the vertical axis and continuing to interpret height in terms of temperature.

- The 17th was a hot day and the 9th a cold day.
- Over a period of days that have been chosen, the temperature has got hotter and then it has started to decrease again. [What do the numbers mean?] They are the days, so between day 9 and day 25, at day 17 it was fairly hot and then after it decreased again.
- Tells you on Monday it could be 9, and on Tuesday then it could be . . . each bar shows the degrees.

Of the responses that appear to adopt a frequency approach, at the unistructural level they only consider a single feature without appreciating the context or purpose of the graph.

- It is going lower and lower like that one [points] and really high at 17, and it goes up to 25 and gets lower at the ends and higher in the middle. [Why high at 17?] That's what is on the other page [the reported average].
- The least was 9 and 25, the most was 17, going up to 25 and then down again, making an average day.

At the multistructural level, responses recognize the purpose of the graph in terms of the frequency represented (two ideas) but there is no acknowledgment of the importance of 17.

- Scale of different temperatures from 9 to 25. It shows how many days it was like that.

- They have done the temperatures along the bottom and the number of days up the side and they recorded it like that.

At the highest level, responses are able to relate the frequency information with the context and appreciate the importance of the 17 degrees, the average maximum temperature.

- It is most likely to be 17 within the whole year.
- The most days had 17 and the least had 25.
- Saying how many number of days they should have got up to that temperature—the temperature and which days got them. Not many days got a maximum of 9 but it shows a lot more days got 17.

Although sophisticated reasoning is not often shown either with respect to explanation of variation in relation to the average (early questions in Fig. 7.4) or with respect to graphing (later questions), middle school students are more likely than elementary students to perform at higher levels on the graphing tasks. There is likely to be improvement across the years for the graphing tasks due to exposure to various graphing techniques within the mathematics curriculum. It would appear, however that without explicit discussion of variation as a formal activity in classrooms, improvement is unlikely to occur in the ability to explain variation verbally, even in a context as familiar as the weather.[14]

7.4   CASE STUDY TWO: SAMPLING
IN A CHANCE SETTING

Although there may be advantages to considering variation in contexts such as daily temperatures where causal mechanisms like night and day or the seasons provide sources of variation, there are also advantages to considering variation in more abstract settings where a random mechanism is employed. It is intended that such a simplification allows for a focus on expected outcomes consistent with a theoretical perspective, followed by consideration of random variation from expectation. The exploration can have two components: suggestion of a sequence of individual outcomes and suggestion of a distribution of many outcomes. The latter is likely to involve graphical representations. Various random generators, such as spinners, dice, or coins, can be used to investigate variation, but the case study described in this section is based on drawing 10 objects from a container of 100, 50 of which are red, 30 green, and 20 yellow.

The protocol in Fig. 7.10, in which the objects just referred to are candies, involves quite a few tasks in order to allow students many opportuni-

1. Suppose you have a container with 100 candies in it. 50 are red, 20 are yellow, and 30 are green. The candies are all mixed up in the container. You pull out 10 candies.
   (a) How many reds do you expect to get?
   (b) Suppose you did this several times. Do you think this many would come out every time? Why do you think this?
   (c) How many reds would surprise you? Why do you think this?

2. Suppose six of you do this experiment.
   What do you think is likely to occur for the numbers of red candies that are written down?

   _____, _____, _____, _____, _____, _____ Why do you
   think this?

3. Look at these possibilities that some students have written down for the numbers they thought likely.
   (a) 5,9,7,6,8,7
   (b) 3,7,5,8,5,4
   (c) 5,5,5,5,5,5
   (d) 2,3,4,3,4,4
   (e) 7,7,7,7,7,7
   (f) 3,0,9,2,8,5
   (g) 10,10,10,10,10,10
   Which one of these lists do you think best describes what might happen? Why do you think this?

4. Suppose that 6 students did the experiment. What do you think the numbers will most likely go from and to?
   (a) From _____ (lowest) to _____ (highest) number of reds. Why do you think this?
   (b) Now try it for yourself: _____, _____, _____, _____, _____, _____
   (c) What do you think of these results? Do you want to change your estimates?

5. Suppose that 40 students pulled out 10 candies from the container, wrote down the number of reds, put them back, mixed them up. Can you show what the number of reds look like in this case?

FIG. 7.10. Tasks on variation in a chance sampling context.

ties to display understanding of variation in a sampling setting. First, expectation must be established in Part 1(a). Second, there is the opportunity to explore variation in a number of ways: by thinking about repeated trials (Part 1(b)), by naming a surprising outcome (Part 1(c)), by suggesting a sequence of outcomes (Part 2), by choosing a best alternative (Part 3), and by suggesting a range of outcomes (Part 4(a)). Third, actual trials are performed and students given the opportunity to change their initial estimates (Parts 4(b) and (c)). Finally in Part 5, students are asked to represent in some way what would happen if the experiment were carried out 40 times (with replacement after each draw).[15] How much scaffolding is provided for students in this last task depends on their previous experience and what teachers would like to know about their graphing abilities in this context.

For tasks like this it is possible to observe explicitly the variation that students display in their responses, as well as the reasoning they give for their responses and their final ability to provide a distributional representation of a large number of trials. There are connections here to the graphing part of the curriculum; knowing what graphical techniques have been previously taught may influence the weighting given to the representation and to the story that is told about distributional variation.

Considering first the estimates made in response to Part 1(a) in Fig. 7.10, about half of students across grades are likely to predict five red candies in a handful of ten. The other responses are split fairly evenly between numbers less than or equal to four, or greater than or equal to six. Very few students change their estimates after performing their own trials. When predicting the outcomes of six such trials of drawing ten candies for Part 2, about three quarters of students center their choices around five and about three quarters display reasonable variation about their estimates. These are not necessarily the same students, however, with just over half satisfying both criteria. Of those who do not produce centered estimates, they are more likely to predict a low center than high and of those who do not suggest reasonable spread they are more likely to produce a wide rather than a narrow spread of values. Few younger children use repeated values in their estimates, which can be a useful point for discussion. Overall again few students, perhaps 10%, are likely to change their six estimates after performing six trials themselves.

When asked to choose the most reasonable set of six outcomes from the seven alternatives in Part 3 of Fig. 7.10, consistently across grades about half of students are likely to choose the most appropriate alternative, (b) 3, 7, 5, 8, 5, 4. The second most popular alternative is (d) 2, 3, 4, 3, 4, 4, showing reasonable variation but a low center, attracting about a quarter of responses. Then about half again of the remaining responses are drawn to alternative (c) 5, 5, 5, 5, 5, 5 or alternative (f) 3, 0, 9, 2, 8, 5, both centered at five but the first with no variation and the second with too much. The request to provide a range (lowest to highest) of reasonable values in Part 4(a) is likely to produce great variation in student performance itself, with younger students more likely to provide a range reflecting all possible values rather than reasonable values, which is done by around half of older students. About 10% of students overall are likely to suggest ranges with appropriate spread but a high or low center. For both types of question few students are interested in changing their responses after trials.

In considering the reasoning students use to justify their numerical choices and the understanding displayed in their graphical representation of 40 trials, four levels of sophistication are likely to be shown across the elementary and middle years. At the prestructural level, generally observed in younger children, students are likely to display inconsistencies between their suggestions of the six outcomes and their suggested range of outcomes, or to suggest ranges of 0 to 10 or 1 to 10 that by their nature cannot be inconsistent but which do not reflect reasonable variation. The reasoning for the decisions made by these students is usually idiosyncratic or intuitive in nature, mentioning guessing, favorite numbers, location in the container, candies being mixed up, the number of candies that would fit in the hand, "you could get any," and "you wouldn't get all in one go." Occasionally students appear to show an intuitive appreciation of proportionality but this is generally mixed with more imaginative reasoning.

- [Part 1(a)] 5 red candies, because there's 50 and 5 like . . . 10. [Part 2] 4, 6, 5, 3, 8, 2, because $4 + 6 = 10$, $5 + 3 = 8$, . . . and 2 is my second best number.

Students at this level have great difficulty with graphs but many show their understanding of the context by drawing pictures of the candy-drawing scenario, as is illustrated by a grade 3 drawing in Fig. 7.11.

At the next level there is considerable variation in the responses to the estimating questions, with some students still producing inconsistencies in their suggested outcomes and ranges or making predictions on the low or high side of middle. The reasoning expressed to support choices is likely to focus on the single idea of there being "more red" in the container without explicit mention of the proportion involved.

- [Part 2] 7, 5, 9, 6, 8, 10, because there are more reds than any other color.
- [Part 3(b) 3, 7, 5, 8, 5, 4] Because there are more red than yellow and green.

FIG. 7.11. A prestructural representation of 40 trials of the candy (lollie) task in Fig. 7.10.

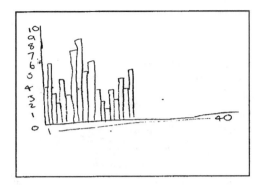

FIG. 7.12.   Representation of 40 trials of the candy task in Fig. 7.10 consistent with a unistructural response.

For the graphing task, most students at this level are likely to generate their own representations as drawings of numbers or candies, with a few drawing case value graphs (similar to time series) as shown by a grade 9 student in Fig. 7.12. These graphs tend to demonstrate wide variation. With assistance of a grid some graphs may show appreciation of variation in frequency but not of the location of center.

More complex reasoning associated with centering of outcomes based on "more" or "half" red is shown at the multistructural level. Students are more likely to be consistent in predictions among their responses and some students choose the option (c) (5, 5, 5, 5, 5, 5) from the multiple-choice list, supported with probabilistic reasoning.

- [Part 3(c) 5, 5, 5, 5, 5, 5] Because half the number is red, so there is 50-50 chance of getting red.

Although some students still focus on "more" rather than "half" red, there is an acknowledgment of some clustering near the center.

- [Part 1(b)] Mostly around 5 and mostly reds.
- [Part 2] 5, 6, 7, 4, 5, 5, some might go up higher, some might be lower, but half of them is red.
- [Part 3(b) 3, 7, 5, 8, 5, 4] All in the middle. [Other alternatives?] Mostly all high or low.

Although some students still experience difficulty with graphical representations, with the help of a grid, others can produce idiosyncratic representations that display an appreciation of variation about the middle. The graph in Fig. 7.13 by a grade 7 student interprets the vertical axis as individual students rather than frequency of students and appears to represent some sort

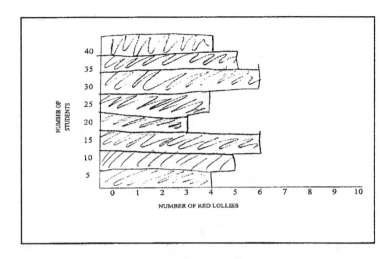

FIG. 7.13. Multistructural representation of 40 trials of the candy (lollie) task in Figure 7.10.

of "average" performance for each group of five students; these values are clustered about the middle. For students without vast graphing experience this is a creative way to tell the story.

Responses at the relational level from students who have not had formal instruction about theoretical distributions show a strong appreciation for the proportion of reds in the container as well as variation from this proportion.

- [Part 1(a)] *About* 5, because there's 50 red, so divide 100 by 10 and then divide 50 by 10 to get 5.
- [Part 1(a)] 5, because 50 is half of 100, so 5 is half of 10. [Part 3] (b) 3, 7, 5, 8, 5, 4] They're all *around* the 5 mark.

These students are also likely to draw reasonable distributions of 40 trials, as shown in Fig. 7.14, although the distributions are often wider than statistically appropriate. The representation is by a grade 9 student.

Depending on the situation in which the tasks in Fig. 7.10 are used, it may be useful as a final activity to perform classroom trials 40 times and plot the outcomes to compare with predicted values and distributions. This is particularly useful for students who hold a strong probabilistic view based on $(5, 5, 5, 5, 5, 5)$ being theoretically the most likely outcome in six trials of a handful of 10 candies.

Classroom investigations adapted from the protocol in Fig. 7.10 can cover all aspects of the data and chance curriculum from the discussion of how to sample to the suggestion of inferences concerning the long term be-

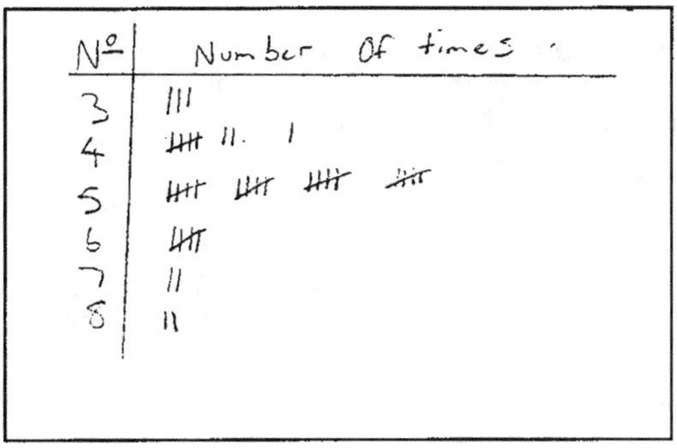

FIG. 7.14.   Relational representation of 40 trials of the candy task in Figure 7.10.

havior of outcomes. Throughout, however, the focus should be on variation as the underlying phenomenon.

7.5   CASE STUDY THREE: SPINNERS

Variations on Case Study Two include changing the random generator, requiring "trials" rather than sampling, and asking students to distinguish among graphs in terms of their appropriate representation of variation. When students are asked to imagine spinning a 50-50 (black-white) spinner 50 times and record the number of times it lands on black, most responses reflect the proportion of black on the spinner and say "25." When asked about repeated trials, however, students say the outcomes will not be the same every time and when asked for six such trials of 50 spins, most students produce values that lie within 90% of those produced by simulation.[16] When asked what sort of outcome would surprise them, most students again suggest appropriately extreme values, such as "all" or "none."

Although the idea of an outcome different from 25 (the expected value) is relatively straightforward with such a large number of spins, an appreciation of the shape and spread of the distribution is more difficult to grasp without many trialing experiences. Again classroom trials where students each perform 50 spins and record the number of times the spinner lands on black, are very useful in building a first-hand appreciation of what reasonable distributions look like. The connection to stacked dot plots, as discussed in Section 3.8, creates the opportunity to construct an easily interpreted display of the trials. A plot similar to that shown in Fig. 7.15 is likely to result. This can be used as a reinforcement of graph construction and meaning by asking, in this context, what is the lowest value, the highest value, the mode, and the range of the data set. Even after repeated experi-

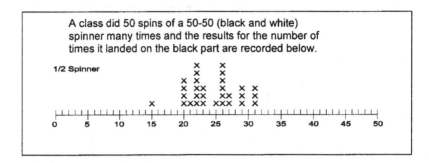

FIG. 7.15.   Stacked dot plot for 30 trials of spinning a 50-50 spinner 50 times.

ence, some students confuse the frequency with the values being reported, here the number of times the spinner landed on black. They hence may report the lowest value as 1 not 15, and the highest value as 6, not 31.

Following this experience a sense of students' appreciation of reasonable distributional variation can be gained by presenting them with graphs of similar sets of 50 trials performed by other classes, for example as shown in Fig. 7.16. In this task students are asked to decide whether the graphs show data that were actually collected by a class or were likely to have been made up.[17] Appreciations of understanding of the initial expectation (of 25 blacks), of reasonable variation from that expectation to create a distribution that theoretically would involve a pattern, and then of reasonable variation from that pattern, are needed to assess completely the three graphs presented.

For each of the graphs there are four levels of appreciation that students are likely to display in the middle school years. Some students choose an inappropriate alternative and give reasons that are vague or do not appear to appreciate the nature of the distribution.

- (a) Real—It looks real.
- (b) Real—It's random.
- (c) Made up—It looks wrong.

At the next level, students make appropriate choices without logical reasons or make inappropriate choices based on features of the graph that are not the important ones for decision making.

- (a) Real—Around 25, the average.
- (b) Real—Spread out.
- (c) Made up—Bunched up in the middle.

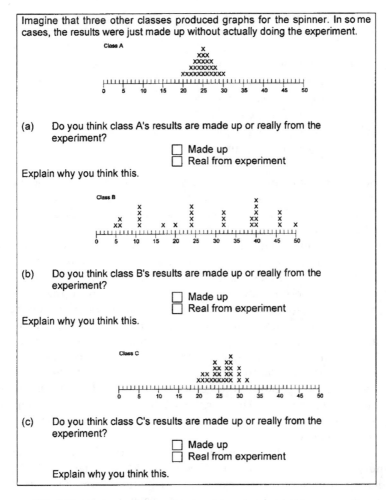

FIG. 7.16.   Tasks to decide on authenticity of trials involving spinners.

The highest two levels of response to the tasks in Fig. 7.16 reflect the sophistication of the reasoning given for an appropriate response. Penultimate responses provide vague justifications.

- (a) Made up—Because of the shape.
- (a) Made up—Because it's in a pattern.
- (b) Made up—Doesn't look real.
- (b) Made up—Unlikely to be like that.
- (c) Real—More stable graph.
- (c) Real—Doesn't look like a pattern.

Higher level responses are more specific in noticing salient features of the graphs.

- (a) Made up—Shape of a triangle.
- (a) Made up—Should have some under 20 and over 30.
- (b) Made up—The range is too big.
- (b) Made up—One got 50 and one got 5.
- (c) Real—Not even but around 25.
- (c) Real—Results between 19 and 32.

Middle school students are likely to find Part (a) of Fig. 7.16 the easiest, with around 3/4 of students giving responses at the highest two levels, and Part (b) the most difficult, with about 40% of responses at these two levels. Around 2/3 of students are likely to perform comparably on Part (c). It appears that much experience is needed to gain an appreciation for and be able to express appropriately the sort of variation in distributions that is reasonable, particularly when variation not pattern is the issue. A combination of producing classroom data sets and considering inappropriate alternatives, should assist in building intuitions. The examples given in Sections 7.4 and 7.5 have been based on counting occurrences of single outcomes— red candies or black half of a spinner—in a number of trials. Although as noted earlier, it may not be a trivial exercise for students to transfer understanding from one model to another, it is possible to draw direct links in this case, especially because as described here, the underlying theoretical distributions are the same. How far this linking process might go depends largely on the grade level and how close the curriculum is to making connections via theory.

Another extension to the spinner activity described here is to use two spinners as described in Section 5.7. For students who have studied independent events tasks to create expected distributions for many trials of two 50-50 spinners can then be compared with classroom trials or with potentially authentic or non-authentic examples.

7.6   CASE STUDY FOUR: COMPARING TWO GROUPS

Comparing the means of two samples, say with a t-test, to determine if a significant difference exists, is typically one of the exercises in the first formal statistics course students meet. Such tests are based on assumptions such as random assignment and data behaving as normal distributions, and rely on the relative difference in means compared to the measured variation shown in the two samples. Middle school students cannot analyze samples with this level of sophistication but they can understand the need to compare two data sets and can be motivated by the task, for example answering the question, "Who can tie their shoe laces faster, boys or girls?" It is encouraging to note that the National Council of Teachers of Mathematics recognizes the comparing of two data sets as a significant and motivating activity for students in grades 3–5 and 6–8.[18]

Section 6.4 considers a task to decide which of two classes had performed better based on a presentation of scores in two graphs. Four pairs of graphs are presented in Fig. 6.3 and students display three levels of increased sophistication in interpreting the graphs, depending on whether or not they have the proportional reasoning skills to deal with unequal-sized data sets. For these tasks it is also possible to observe students' tendencies to be aware of variation in two senses.[19] There are differences between the two sets that should be noted but these contrasts need to be made with respect to the shape and spread within the two sets themselves. As a starting point for building appreciation of these issues, several levels of student appreciation of variation can be observed in relation to responding to the tasks in Fig. 6.3.

Some students appear unaware that variation is an issue or occurs within the data sets. Particularly in calculating totals, but sometimes with means as well, the goal is "a number" and it is used as the complete representation of the information in the data. For many students this happens for Parts (a) and (b), where few data values are involved, and then transfers to Parts (c) and (d) without recognition that more complex issues of shape are involved. In this section, interest focuses on students' responses to the last two parts because of the presence of more data values and the potential for more complex interpretations. Parts (c) and (d) are hence reproduced in Fig. 7.17.

In beginning to appreciate the need to consider variation between data sets in decision making, students may consider individual or global features. Within these two ways of viewing the data sets, different levels of complexity are likely to be observed. The consideration of individual features is based on columns in the graphs. At the unistructural level responses are likely to focus on a single value and compare it across the two data sets, without any synthesis across columns.

- [Part (c)] Brown did better because the person who got seven was the only one in the two classes to get seven.

At the multistructural level of considering individual features, some students look at several columns in a sequential comparison.

- [Part (c)] I think that one [pointing to the Yellow graph] has got more than that one [pointing to the Brown graph]. [What makes you say that?] Be-

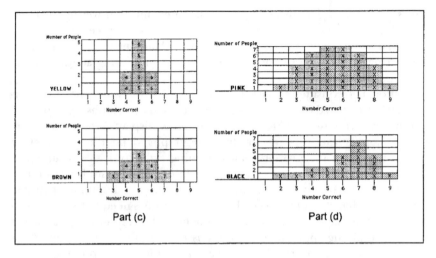

FIG. 7.17.   Pairs of graphs comparing test scores of groups of children.

cause they have got more people scoring 5 scores and they have got less people for the other ones except for 6 and 4 because they are equal on both of them.

- [Part (d)] Well, just by looking at it [Pink] you can tell a lot more, but 9 and 8 are a lot like the same but then, the 6 and 5 and 4 and just all the rest are much bigger than these ones down here [Black].

The global perspective in considering differences and variation can also be observed at several levels. The unistructural level is associated with the single observation of "more," usually in association with the Pink class in Part (d), as noted in Section 6.4. At the multistructural level, students consider multiple global features and may also include individual values as relevant.

- [Part (c)] The people in the Brown class, like one person actually scored a 7. Both classes have two 6s. I think . . . having more people with a score of 5 is actually better than having one person with a score of 7; there is more of like an average score. [. . .] But the 7 is obviously a higher mark. [. . .] And you know like this class [Brown] only has a few people and each side is sort of scattered around and this class [Yellow] is quite direct and has quite a few people getting a very good average mark.

One of the aspects of global comparison that would likely be dismissed by a statistician as trivial is the observation of variation in group size. This however is important for beginners and may trigger a realization of the need to employ the mean as a global feature of the data set. If students have enough prior experience the following approach may become natural.

- [Part (d)] Well there's more people in this class [Pink] so you'd have to take an average for this one, you can't tell just by looking at the graph.

The most sophisticated level of response, however, integrates and contrasts several global, and perhaps individual, features in reaching a conclusion. Sometimes a firm decision is avoided.

- [Part (c)] This one [Brown] is, umm, [a] more standard-deviation-shaped graph but that one [Yellow] has more of a solid average. [Uses calculator] That's 45 [Yellow] and that one [Brown] is 45 too. So they both seemed to have done well. But it is hard to really say because they are virtually the same shape, it is just that these seemed to have been evened out [pointing to Yellow columns] so the average of these two here [Brown initial and last columns] made another 2 for that one, that area [pointing to 5 column— Brown]. So I can't really say which one has done better. I suppose if you wanted students to go in a maths competition this one [Brown] would probably have done better because it has got more up that end [Brown 7] but on average that one is [Yellow] . . . well they are both the same on average actually, so [shrugs shoulders].

The following response is typical of a global view.

- [Part (d)] . . . Okay, by averaging it Black scored better. They got 6.2 and the Pink class got 5.5. So even though they [Pink] had more people, they have more people who scored lower, like it kind of goes in an archish kind of shape [points to Pink], like they had more people score around the middle kind of range. Whereas bearing on the numbers in the class, they had more people score around the middle kind of area [Pink]. The Black class had more people score around the top kind of area. So averaging it Black still scored better.

Not all such responses require the use of the mean.

- [Part (d)] Umm I can say that the Black class has done better because it's got higher columns the further up it goes, and it's got less people, so. Like they've sort of got more people doing well than people doing not so well. Whereas this class has sort of got say up to 5, it's got sort of the most number of people like there [points to Pink graph] doing, getting 5 or under to the same as getting 5 or over. . . . Whereas this class [Black] is better than that, . . . it's got more over 5 than under 5.

Although the focus on spread illustrated in these responses is not as strong as desired for building understanding of standard deviation, the responses show an appreciation for difference as a beginning idea. Class discussion can then start to move to issues of relative spread in the two groups.

7.7   IMPLICATIONS AND RECOMMENDATIONS

This chapter has provided four case studies to demonstrate the omnipresence of variation across the data and chance curriculum at the middle school level. Although intuitive understanding that "things change," like the daily temperature or the number of red objects drawn from a container, is present in very young children,[20] explicit discussion throughout the elementary and middle school years is essential to reinforce this fundamental concept before formal measures such as the standard deviation are introduced at the senior secondary level. This is particularly important for students who do not go on to study statistics in the final years of school.

In contrast to the other terms that feature in the titles of chapters in this book, variation does not feature widely in curriculum documents.[21] It is hence essential that with reference to the first tier of statistical literacy, the word, and its derivatives "variable" and "vary," become part of the everyday vocabulary of the classroom. Observations of variation in everyday life, on the sports page of the newspaper, or on the local weather report, can be discussed and tied to the specific activities taking place in the classroom. As is seen in Section 7.2, many students have difficulty expressing ideas about variation in words. It is likely that this is also a problem for some teachers. As in other areas of the mathematics curriculum, however, it is important to use language in appropriate ways to aid development of concepts.[22]

At the same time as language use is developing, progress on the second tier statistical literacy goal of understanding in context should occur. As noted throughout this book, variation occurs in context and is difficult to characterize without reference to some observations in a context. It is mainly a matter of reinforcing the connections whenever possible.

The third tier of statistical literacy in relation to variation focuses on developing an appreciation of the unusual, perhaps the outlier in considering individual outcomes or the inappropriate shape of a distribution of outcomes. Although appreciation of the exact degree of variation from a distribution required to produce a statistically significant difference is beyond middle school students, the appreciation of extreme cases, such as in the stacked dot plots in Fig. 7.16, is accessible to most students, especially if accompanied by classroom discussion. Identification of exaggeration of variation in graphs such as those in Fig. 3.24 should become second nature to students by the middle school level. Later, formal techniques such as analysis of variance and chi-square tests of goodness of fit, will make much more sense if based on sophisticated intuitions about and familiarity with "what looks reasonable."

Anecdotal evidence suggests that students from grades 7 or 8 can begin to appreciate the relationship of variation to average and random sampling, and its representation in graphical form, by repeatedly considering a data set that they have collected themselves, say from measuring their hand spans or foot lengths. If there is a sample of 24 measurements, say from the class, the usual classroom activity would be to calculate the mean. This might be done from a list of values, without any type of graphical representation, but a representation such as in Fig. 7.18, allows for a much more interesting discussion. Even with a stacked dot plot, however, the task is likely to be to calculate the mean and median, and mark them, and perhaps the mode, on the graph. Although this illustrates the relationship of the three measures, it does little to characterize the variation shown in the data except for the effect of outliers on the mean and median.

In connection with a discussion of random sampling it is possible to illustrate how increasing sample size reduces the variation in mean values, where in this case the least variation (none) occurs in the mean of the entire sample of 24 measurements. Assigning each measurement a number makes possible the random selection of pairs of measurements (perhaps from a "hat"). Drawing pairs of numbers identifies samples of size two, for which the 12 means can be calculated and placed on a stacked dot plot vertically aligned with the original plot. These 12 points will show less variation in the plot, certainly in terms of range, than the original 24. There are several ways to proceed in increasing the sample size, but randomly combining these samples of size 2 to create samples of size 4 is fine. Again, means are calculated and plotted to be compared with the previous two graphs. These 6 values again show less variation. It is important to label these values in a manner that indicates their increasing sample size. Now these six samples of size 4 are randomly sorted in pairs and the three means of the samples of size 8 calculated and plotted as before. Finally, the mean of all 24 values is plotted—it should be reinforced that this mean is also the mean of the means of the three samples of size 8. (The process could start with random samples of size three, leading to 8 samples, followed by 4, then two.) There

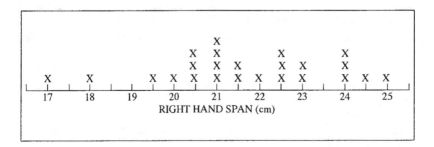

FIG. 7.18.　Right hand spans of 24 people.

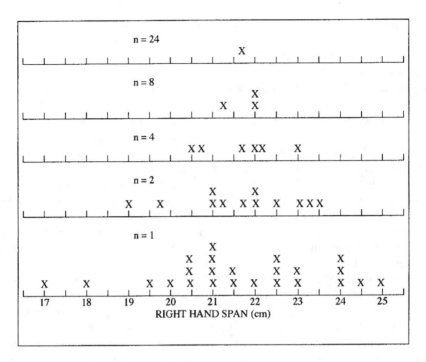

FIG. 7.19.   Decreasing variation in mean values with increasing sample size.

are many possibilities but the process needs to be kept relatively straightforward for middle school students. The final presentation might look something like in Fig. 7.19, illustrating the convergence of the smaller sample mean values to the mean for the sample of size 24. The decreasing spread in the ranges from graph to graph as the sample size increases is intended to show the decreasing variation in sample means as the sample size increases. The link to the population mean (perhaps measurements for all students in that grade in the school, city, or state) may be made at this time but it is likely that a complete appreciation will come only at the senior secondary level. Having actually carried out exercises like that shown in Fig. 7.19 is likely to build intuitions that will assist in understanding the Central Limit Theorem when it is introduced in formal statistics courses in later years.

NOTES

1. The *Chambers Dictionary of Quotations* (Jones, 1996, p. 293) attributes this quote to William Cowper (1785), *The Task, Book 2, 'The Timepiece,'* line 606–607.
2. Outhred & Shaw (1999).

3. Green (1993).
4. Shaughnessy (1997).
5. Reading & Shaughnessy (2000); Shaughnessy, Canada, & Ciancetta (2003); Shaughnessy & Ciancetta (2002); Shaughnessy, Watson, Moritz, & Reading (1999); Torok & Watson (2000).
6. Gal, Rothschild, & Wagner (1989, 1990); Gal & Wagner (1992); Wagner & Gal (1991).
7. Australian Education Council (1991).
8. Watson & Kelly (2003d); Watson, Kelly, Callingham, & Shaughnessy (2003).
9. Watson, Kelly, Callingham, & Shaughnessy (2003).
10. Watson & Kelly (2003a).
11. Watson & Kelly (2003a).
12. Torok & Watson (2000); Watson (2002c).
13. Konold (1989).
14. Watson & Kelly (2003a).
15. Kelly & Watson (2002); Shaughnessy, Watson, Moritz, & Reading (1999); Torok & Watson (2000).
16. Watson & Kelly (2004c); Watson, Kelly, Callingham, & Shaughnessy (2003).
17. Watson & Kelly (2004c); Watson, Kelly, Callingham, & Shaughnessy (2003).
18. National Council of Teachers of Mathematics (2000, pp. 180–181, p. 250).
19. Skalicky (2005); Watson (2001, 2002b).
20. Watson & Kelly (2002b).
21. Australian Education Council (1991); National Council of Teachers of Mathematics (1989, 2000).
22. Malone & Miller (1993); Miller (1993).

8

Statistical Literacy—A Global Goal

Statistical ignorance and statistical fallacies are quite as widespread and quite as dangerous as the logical fallacies that come under the heading of illiteracy.[1]

In particular, citizens must be able to read and interpret complex, and sometimes conflicting information.[2]

An understanding of probability and the related area of statistics is essential to being an informed citizen.[3]

A knowledge of statistics is necessary if students are to become intelligent consumers who can make critical and informed decisions.[4]

8.1 BACKGROUND

These quotes are a reminder of the need for statistical literacy outside of the classroom. The first quote dates from 1959 when the term *numeracy* was first being introduced. Its continued relevance today motivates efforts like those in this book to assist in the development of appropriate statistical literacy skills. The last three represent recognition by the National Council of Teachers of Mathematics in the United States of the importance of applying the school curriculum content in wider contexts.

This chapter takes a somewhat different approach to Chapters 2 to 7, where particular aspects of the development of understanding specific topics in the school data and chance curriculum are discussed. Some of the tasks introduced in those chapters are based on media sources and provide explicit links to the goals of adult statistical literacy as stated by Iddo Gal in

Section 1.3.[5] Other items are associated with the concepts that provide the building blocks for a critical approach to statistical thinking. Combining most of the survey items from the earlier chapters, this chapter proposes an overall model for the development of a construct of statistical literacy. Knowing that the goals of critical statistical thinking lie in the "correct" answers to tasks is not sufficient in an education context. It is also important to anticipate the growth steps taken along the way in order to know what to expect in the classroom and how to plan activities to move students from current levels to higher ones.

The next section introduces the components that contribute to statistical literacy in its broadest sense. The components arise from the analysis of responses from several thousand students who completed the survey tasks introduced earlier. Subsequent sections describe six levels of development in relation to statistical literacy involving most of these components. A final section comes back to the classroom and its contribution to building statistical literacy.

8.2 COMPONENTS OF STATISTICAL LITERACY

Figure 8.1 shows the links among the components contributing to statistical literacy that are considered important for the presentation in this chapter. Those that make substantial contributions are the ingredients of the data and chance curriculum—data collection, data representation, data reduction, chance, and inference—combined with appreciation of variation, understanding of context, literacy skills, general mathematical and statistical skills, the format of the tasks, and the motivation to engage with a task. The survey tasks that are described in earlier chapters cover the data and chance

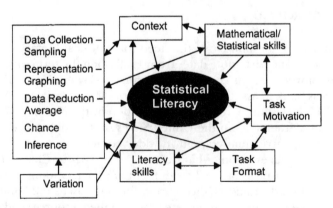

FIG. 8.1. Links among the components of statistical literacy.

curriculum, while at the same time requiring differing mathematical and statistical skills, providing a variety of contexts, requiring different reading skills, and offering different formats for response. Although task motivation cannot be gauged directly from written student responses it is acknowledged that the contexts of some tasks may have more appeal to some students, whereas some students may experience an "off day" and not be motivated by any of the items on a survey.

The components of the school curriculum and variation found at the left of Fig. 8.1 are discussed in detail in the previous chapters. This section focuses on the other five components surrounding statistical literacy in the figure.

As noted throughout the earlier chapters, the mathematical skills required for the tasks presented in this book do not go beyond the expectations of the middle school curriculum: understanding proportions, rates, percents, and part–whole relationships generally. The statistical skills are based on understanding and calculation of averages, basic numerical probabilities, and probabilities of compound independent events. Definitions of basic terms are also important. What is considered adequate mathematical/statistical reasoning for statistical literacy should be achievable by most students by the end of grade 10.

Context is a very significant component of statistical literacy. Although this is made evident in the discussion of the needs of adults by Katherine Wallman[6] and Iddo Gal[7] in Section 1.3, it may not be recognized in classrooms where tossing coins and measuring hand spans do not put many demands on appreciating the context in which an investigation is carried out. The tasks described in Chapters 2 to 7 generally represent one of three types of context. These three are considered increasingly complex because they place more demands on cognition in terms of familiarity with the situation presented within which a question is being asked. First, there are tasks, for example associated with dice or table-reading, that have mathematical, isolated contexts without added complications once the "rules" are understood. Second, some tasks are set in contexts considered to be familiar to students from their experiences in school, such as conducting local school surveys. Third, there are items based on extracts from the media, which involve potentially unfamiliar contexts from out-of-school environments. It turns out that engagement with increasingly complex or unfamiliar contexts is associated with higher level performance in terms of statistical literacy.

Given the reference to literacy in the phrase statistical literacy, it is appropriate to consider literacy itself as a component in Fig. 7.1, especially where critical literacy is involved. The Statistical Literacy Hierarchy, introduced in Section 1.4 suggests building an understanding of terminology (Tier 1), applying that terminology in context (Tier 2), and questioning claims related to the terminology that do not have a proper statistical foundation (Tier 3). Similar sorts of frameworks have been suggested for the development of literacy skills generally. Within the field of critical literacies, Alan Luke and Peter Freebody propose four roles for the reader and associated practices that are required to be able to carry out these roles when reading for social practice.[8]

- Coding practices relate to developing the learner's resources as a code-breaker: working out text, finding patterns, figuring out how text works. (Element 1)
- Text-meaning practices relate to developing resources as a text-participant: how texts string together, what cultural resources can be brought to the text and what meanings are possible. (Element 2)
- Pragmatic practices relate to developing resources as a text-user: how uses of the text shape meaning, what can be done with text and by whom and what are the alternatives for interpretation. (Element 3)
- Critical practices relate to developing resources as a text-analyst and critic: what interests lie behind the text, what action is intended to flow from the text, what is not said in the text. (Element 4)

Almost all information of a statistical nature in social contexts is presented in some form of text. Element 1 performance reflects the code-breaking aspects of getting into the field of data and chance, for example appreciating that a graph presents information in a visual form. Element 2 reflects the making of meaning in contexts, which in this case are social as well as cultural; an example is the appreciation of the various meanings "average" can have depending on context. Element 3 performance is closer to becoming a user of the information presented in appreciating what can be done with data, samples, outcomes, and graphs to create alternative meanings. Element 4 reflects the critical aspects that lead to a questioning attitude in relation to all claims emanating from data and chance contexts, for example considering who sponsored a study or what aspects of the results are presented for public consumption. Although these four elements are not seen as hierarchical by their proposers, they fit well within the Statistical Literacy Hierarchy with text-meaning and pragmatic practices falling within Tier 2 of applying understanding in context. The linking of statistical thinking and critical literacy through their shared concern for social issues and critical thinking is significant in considering the implications for improving performance during the school years.

There are two types of tasks used in the surveys that are the basis of the presentation in this chapter, open-ended questions and multiple-choice questions sometimes with explanations requested for the chosen response. By offering alternatives, multiple-choice questions can be more supportive of students, allowing them to show recognition rather than creation of an appropriate answer. This is a feature in some of the descriptions of what students are likely to be able to do at some levels of statistical literacy.

The final component shown in Fig. 8.1 is task motivation. This component is related to the dispositions that students bring to various statistical literacy tasks. In his model for adult statistical literacy, Iddo Gal suggests that a "critical stance" combined with "beliefs and attitudes" make up a dispositional dimension, contrasting with a knowledge dimension.[9] Chris Wild and Maxine Pfannkuch expand on these ideas in their four-dimensional model of statistical thinking, which includes dispositions as one dimension.[10] They describe specific dispositions including skepticism, imagination, curiosity and awareness, openness to ideas, propensity to seek deeper meaning, being logical, and perseverance. There is no doubt that all of these dispositions can assist in drawing conclusions in conjunction with the other components in Fig. 8.1. Specific measurement of the dispositions, however, is not a focus of the discussion in this chapter, although many of the tasks are intended to generate appropriate attitudes and stances.

8.3 SUMMARY OF STAGES OF DEVELOPMENT OF STATISTICAL LITERACY

For the individual tasks introduced in earlier chapters, the levels of performance generally display increased complexity with respect to single element starting points. The starting points of course may be different for different tasks and for different students depending on their personal background, exposure to the concepts and terminology involved, familiarity with the context, and numeracy skills. Looking at a selection of students across grades gives some indication of what improvement is likely to occur over time.[11] It can also provide an indication of the relative difficulty of tasks with respect to each other, especially when several levels of performance are observed. Given the variety of tasks it would not be expected that the lowest levels of each would be equivalent to each other. The context, for example its familiarity to students, may make a task accessible to more students, as may the format in which a question is asked. The mathematical and statistical skills required, for example knowledge of proportions or the arithmetic mean, may also exclude some students.

What is of interest for the discussion in this chapter is the analysis of the interaction of student performance and task difficulty that produces an ordering of both on a single scale that predicts the probability of each student achieving success at each level of each item.[12] For the purpose of describing the trend in performance from tasks found to be easier for students to tasks found to be more difficult, the large number of students surveyed across grades provides the variation required for a rich description of the progression observed in performance. At this point what is important is a description of the progression observed in terms of the tasks likely to be completed successfully by all, some, or few of the students in the pool. Although it is likely that grade 3 students would be found more often with higher probabilities of performing with "success" on levels of tasks at the lower end of the scale, a grade by grade description is not the purpose of this chapter. Also as noted in Chapter 1, younger students answer fewer questions than older students. The purpose is to describe the processes involved and the aspects of the tasks that are characteristic of the progression observed as statistical literacy skills become more highly developed among the students surveyed.

From the analysis performed, a continuous progression is observed in the difficulty of the items in relation to the ability of students. In considering levels associated with items that appear near each other in the overall scale of items, however, it is possible to suggest characteristics of the responses and the processes involved in six clusters. Although it is not possible to draw hard boundaries separating the clusters, generally internal consistency is seen. Because most tasks have several levels of response in reaching an optimal solution, the appearance of the highest level reflects the desired outcome. Lower levels, however, can provide important information on the progression taking place and expectations in relation to other tasks, perhaps focusing on different aspects of statistical literacy.

The six clusters of tasks reflect to a large extent the increased interaction with context as reflected in the second and third tiers of the Statistical Literacy Hierarchy discussed throughout this book. The top two clusters reflect performance involving critical thinking in increasingly unfamiliar and mathematical settings. The middle two clusters reflect performance that appreciates context but not in a critical questioning sense and is sometimes inconsistent. The bottom two clusters reflect performance that struggles with most contexts. There is of course more involved than context, and the influences of the other links shown in Fig. 8.1 are discussed in the following sections as descriptions of the six clusters are presented. To avoid confusion with the use of the term *level* to describe performance on individual tasks, the term *stage* is used in association with the six hierarchical clusters. A brief summary of the characteristics of the six stages in performance in relation to topics that are the focus of earlier chapters is given in Table 8.1.[13]

8.4   STAGE 1 OF STATISTICAL
LITERACY—IDIOSYNCRATIC

Observation of student performance on the lowest cluster of items suggests little engagement with the contexts of tasks. What is observed indicates responses made from personal, intuitive, and non-statistical viewpoints.

TABLE 8.1
Summary Characteristics of Six Stages
of Understanding of Statistical Literacy

Stage 1: Idiosyncratic
Context: engagement nonexistent, idiosyncratic, or personal
Sampling: inappropriate, personal beliefs
Representation: basic graph and table reading
Average: no engagement
Chance: idiosyncratic reasons, inappropriate interpretation for probabilities
Inference: imaginative explanations
Variation: no appreciation for chance, difference only for graphs
Math/Stat Skills: one-to-one counting, select largest number

Stage 2: Informal
Context: engagement colloquial or informal
Sampling: single elements employed
Representation: basic calculations from values observed
Average: single, colloquial terms used
Chance: idiosyncratic, colloquial interpretation, "anything can happen"
Inference: single, non-central issues considered
Variation: rigid predictions in chance settings
Math/Stat Skills: addition, subtraction

Stage 3: Inconsistent
Context: engagement selective or inconsistent
Sampling: focus on inappropriate features
Representation: interpretation of graphical details rather than context in graphs
Average: colloquial interpretation on recognition of need for a formula
Chance: limited interpretation of percent, conjunction, and conditional chance
Inference: mainly non-central issues
Variation: inappropriate attempts
Math/Stat Skills: little change, qualitative chance statements

---

Stage 4: Consistent non-critical
Context: engagement often appropriate but non-critical
Sampling: multiple elements but inconsistent
Representation: partial recognition of context
Average: straightforward application of mean and median
Chance: mixed success depending on context
Inference: inconsistent acknowledgment of central issues
Variation: success in chance settings
Math/Stat Skills: mean, simple probability, graph characteristics

---

Stage 5: Critical
Context: critical engagement
Sampling: critical thinking in familiar contexts
Representation: representation of bivariate association in context
Average: consolidation of mean and median
Chance: success on conditional tasks
Inference: little change
Variation: unsolicited acknowledgment in chance and graphs
Math/Stat Skills: little change

(Continued)

TABLE 8.1
(Continued)

Stage 6: Critical mathematical
Context: critical engagement including proportional reasoning
Sampling: critical thinking in less familiar, subtle contexts
Representation: summaries and rate calculations in context
Average: recognition of biasing effect of outliers
Chance: success when more sophisticated mathematics required
Inference: appreciation of subtleties of uncertainty and cause–effect
Variation: no change
Math/Stat Skills: proportional reasoning, rates, multiplication principle for independent events

---

These are illustrated in responses associated with several of the components of the data and chance curriculum.

With respect to sampling, it is likely that students cannot get started on a definition and instead share personal beliefs, for example indicating that "people should not have guns" in responding to the task in Fig. 2.7, asking for unusual features of an article about guns in U.S. high schools. In the multiple-choice task about buying a new car in Fig. 2.5 students are likely to respond, but inappropriately, choosing option (B2), "rely on friends," in making a decision. This may reflect difficulty in interpreting the wider social context. The lack of engagement with the tasks associated with surveying a school before selling raffle tickets shown in Fig. 2.4 is likely to indicate reading difficulty as the introductory comments explaining the task are quite lengthy and structurally complex.

In terms of data representation, students at this stage are likely to be successful at basic graph and table reading. They can for example read specific values from a simple two-way un-nested table and choose the highest value from a row or column of entries in a table. For a pictograph, such as that in Fig. 6.2, they are likely to be able to count accurately, for example to determine the number of children who come to school by bus and how many more come by bus than by car. The fact that many of the tasks upon which students are successful at this stage involve basic table and graph reading may indicate the less demanding literacy requirements of the questions asked. As well, interpretation of context does not play a role in answering direct questions of the "how many" type.

At this stage there is no apparent engagement with tasks related to average. This is likely to reflect the lack of exposure to the concept for younger children.

For tasks associated with chance, students are likely to provide idiosyncratic responses. For the question about the chances of drawing a boy's or a girl's name from a hat, shown in Fig. 5.7, responses like "a girl because the teacher is a girl" are typical. For the item asking for the interpretation of an odds statement from a newspaper article on a sporting event in Fig. 5.15, the interpretation may reflect aspects such as the current score in the game. In a task based on a 50-50, half-shaded spinner, responses to a question on the chance of landing on the shaded part, are likely to be inappropriate, such as "bad chance," "1 in 10," or "80%." Given the support of a multiple-choice format, however, in the question about interpreting "there is a 15% chance of getting a rash" in Fig. 5.5, students are likely to choose one of the colloquial responses, "good chance" or "hardly any chance." This response appears at the high end of the items at this stage and may reflect a transition in thinking between the two lowest stages of statistical literacy.

In terms of inference, non-engagement or imaginative storytelling is the feature at this stage. Again in relation to the interpreting and predicting from the pictograph of how children travel to school in Fig. 6.2, students are likely to suggest reasons for no students on the train (Part (c)) without acknowledging uncertainty, such as "the train broke down." For Part (d) about how Tom who was not in school when the graph was made, would come to school, students refuse to predict saying they cannot tell from the graph or "it will be the same as yesterday."

Basic acknowledgment of variation is likely, for example in Part (a) of the pictograph scenario where most students agree that the graph will not look the same every day. For chance tasks, for example predicting the number of times a 50-50 spinner will land on the shaded part in repeated spins or predicting the distribution of die outcomes in 60 tosses, estimates are inappropriate or accompanying reasoning is idiosyncratic, often suggesting "guessing." In determining which of the stacked dot plots in Fig. 7.16 represents real data and which made up data, students are likely to achieve partial success in recognition. This is another task response that appears high in the Stage 1 cluster of tasks and is likely to be an indication of transition to Stage 2 reasoning for middle school students.

With respect to the terminology associated with the curriculum it is unlikely that students can provide more than tautological or inappropriate responses. The mathematical skills likely to be displayed at this stage are associated with successful one-to-one counting, enough to work out a difference between rows in a pictograph, and determining entries in tables and summing two entries (e.g., "20 + 10") to achieve a column total. Overall the beginning of engagement occurs in simple contexts involving tables, pictographs, and chance environments, assisted by straightforward questions.

8.5   STAGE 2 OF STATISTICAL LITERACY—INFORMAL

At the second stage of statistical literacy the performance on tasks suggests that although engagement with context is taking place, responses still are likely to represent intuitive, non-statistical beliefs or focus on irrelevant aspects. In several areas, however, single elements of concepts are likely to be exhibited or employed in responses.

Responses to questions about what a sample is are likely to display a single idea, such as "a test," or provide an example, such as "cheese at the supermarket." In considering a school-based context, for example the planning of a school survey described in Fig. 2.4, responses indicate that literacy skills are sufficient for the context to be understood but suggestions again focus on single features of sampling, such as "ask 400," "ask everyone," or "ask the people I meet," without considering the need to represent the population. When asked to choose the best of the methods suggested in the task in Fig. 2.4, students are likely to make inappropriate choices and support them with idiosyncratic reasoning. When asked how a teacher could choose four children in a fair way to lead a closing parade at a school sports day, responses are likely to focus on single non-representative characteristics, for example "those that have been good all day." Responses to the item from a wider social context about buying a car, found in Fig. 2.5, are likely to be attracted to the multiple-choice option that "it doesn't matter whether a person uses friends' advice or data from a consumers' report."

At Stage 2 students are likely to be successful at basic comparisons and calculations in tables, for example comparing cells to determine the highest or most even counts and finding a total greater than 100. In a stacked dot plot they are likely to be able to identify the smallest data value. In a complex context from the media, for example the graph interpretation and calculation task in Fig. 3.17, they are likely to produce inappropriate, idiosyncratic arithmetic operations to work out prices as requested. If asked for a graph to show an association such as that claimed for heart deaths and car usage in Fig. 3.6, attempts are likely to be similar to those in Figs. 3.7 and 3.8.

When asked for the meaning of average, students are likely to respond with single colloquial ideas, such as "normal," or an example such as "he is average weight." Given the multiple-choice opportunity to define the term *median*, an inappropriate option, "the most accurate value," is likely to be chosen. For tasks involving applications of averaging concepts, there is unlikely to be any engagement at this stage.

In relation to tasks involving chance there is improvement compared with the previous stage in that students are likely to answer a straightforward question about a 50-50 spinner appropriately with chance statements involving a half or 50%. For the question in Fig. 5.7 about drawing a boy's or girl's name from a hat, the response is likely to be "equally likely boy or girl" with reasoning related to an "anything can happen" view of chance. Similarly for the task to compare two boxes of marbles in Fig. 5.8, students are likely to choose either a box for an idiosyncratic reason, such as "blue is my favorite color," or "equally likely" because "anything can happen." For tasks set in media contexts such as the tossing of coins at the start of a sporting match shown in Fig. 5.12, responses for Parts (b1) and (b2) are likely to be inconsistent within the question, for example choosing a head as more likely for the next toss but saying that the probability of each outcome is 1/2. Also for the task of ordering newspaper headlines found in Fig. 5.3, students are likely to place the headlines in the appropriate half of the number line but go no further in terms of realistic ordering. In what might be considered the more familiar context of considering left-handedness for men, the conditional task based on frequency found in Fig. 5.14, students are likely to respond with the appropriate relationship between the parts of the question. This item is on the boundary between Stages 2 and 3, and may indicate a transition into reasoning that is more comfortable with context, particularly when frequencies rather than probabilities are involved.

At this stage responses to tasks asking for inferences and decision-making are likely to continue to be inappropriate. For questions related to the pictograph on how children get to school in Fig. 6.2, responses are likely to focus on storytelling for how Tom gets to school the following day in Part (d), such as "walk, because he likes walking," or to focus on non-statistical aspects for whether a new student is a boy or girl in Part (b), such as "boy because there is a pattern in the row" or "it could be either since it doesn't say." For judging which of the two stacked dot plots in Figs. 3.20 and 3.21 better tells the story of how long the families in a class have lived in their town, students are likely to provide reasoning for a choice but both the choice and the reasoning are inappropriate, for example choosing the unscaled graph in Fig. 3.21 because "it is well set out."

The responses to tasks at this stage that potentially involve appreciation of variation are related to chance, either spinning a single 50-50 spinner many times or predicting outcomes for 60 tosses of a die as presented in Fig. 5.9. In considering a single spinner, variation is not likely to be expected if a repeated set of many trials are completed but reasonable "surprising" values for outcomes are given. In predicting the outcomes for six repeated trials of many spins, variation is likely to be either too wide, too narrow, or too lop-sided. For predicting 60 die outcomes, suggestions either follow patterns such as multiples of five, or follow a strict theoretical outcome of {10, 10, 10, 10, 10, 10}. Hence it appears that by Stage 2, students know in many cases that variation occurs in chance contexts but have difficulty in putting appropriate bounds on it.

The mathematical/statistical skills displayed at this stage relate to one-step table and graph calculation tasks and one-step straightforward chance evaluations, such as a half when it is visually displayed or an extreme frequency outcome from a number of trials. Although appreciation of some statistical terms is beginning, it is limited to descriptions involving single elements. In many of the tasks attempted single elements, often not the statistically appropriate features, are those upon which comments are made. Appropriate understanding of context is still very limited.

8.6   STAGE 3 OF STATISTICAL LITERACY—
   INCONSISTENT

At the third stage student responses display more engagement with context than at the previous two stages but it still remains selective often dependent on the format of items, which may provide added support. Although more features are taken into account than before, statistical ideas are represented qualitatively rather than quantitatively.

For open-ended tasks on sampling and judging bias in the context of surveying a school as set out in Fig. 2.4, students are unlikely to detect the salient features for fairness or bias. Shannon's random method in Part (a) is likely to be judged as bad because "more people are needed" or "the wrong people might be picked." Jake's method of choosing 10 from the computer club (Part (b)) is considered good, for example because "it isn't too many." Adam's choice of all 100 children in grade 1 (Part (c)) is likely either to be considered good or bad because of the "large sample size" or to be answered as unsure because "they're a bit young." Raffi's survey of 60 friends (Part (d)) is either judged as good because it is "easy" or "gives lots of reasons" or judged as bad for vague reasons such as "they all like him." Claire's method of a voluntary booth (Part (e)) is likely to be assessed as good because it is "easy" or "gives a wide range of people." Although a few of the suggestions for Adam's and Raffi's methods may be on the verge of expressing an appropriate idea, most of the comments focus on inappropriate features of the methods in making decisions on whether they are good or bad. In suggesting two methods of selection for four students to lead a parade, students may suggest representation, such as of boys and girls, or random selection, but not both. For the task of commenting on the voluntary poll on legalizing marijuana in Fig. 2.8, students are likely to say people could be lying or the sample size is too large but no further criticisms.

In terms of data representation at this stage, comments about the stacked dot plots shown in Figs. 3.20 and 3.21 are likely to be based on one summary statement that includes the context and perhaps one data reading comment, for example "most people have lived there less than 13 years" and "column three has 4 crosses." When asked to draw a sketch of a graph to illustrate the claim of Mr Robinson about heart deaths and car usage in the article in Fig. 3.6, students are likely to produce basic unlabelled graphs or labeled attempts that are unsuccessful in showing the association. Examples of such graphs are seen in Figs. 3.9 and 3.10, indicating that students can conceive of the task but not put all of the elements together for a complete graph. When asked about anything unusual in the graphs on boating deaths in Fig. 3.16 students are likely to focus on features that are indeed part of the graph but are not the salient unusual features. Responses, for example, may focus on labeling or on "unknown deaths." This is the response type that is found at the top of the Stage 3 cluster of items and may reflect a transition to the next stage in terms of interaction with an unfamiliar social context.

The concept of average continues to pose problems at Stage 3, with colloquial expressions used to describe "being average" or in the context of the newspaper article shown in Fig. 4.5. Given the support of a multiple-choice format as shown in Fig. 4.4, however, students are likely to be able to choose the appropriate alternative—associated with the total and working the mean algorithm backward—to explain 50 families having an average of 2.2 children.

At this stage students are likely to use qualitative language to describe chance outcomes; but while still describing equality of dice outcomes for a 1 and a 6, as in Fig. 5.6, in terms of "anything can happen," they are likely to determine that a girl's name is more likely to be drawn in the problem in Fig. 5.7, because there are "more girls' names in the hat." In relation to repeated spins of a 50-50 spinner, students are likely to translate the chance into half of the total number of spins but not acknowledge any possible variation from this value. Given a multiple-choice format, students are likely to interpret appropriately the "15% chance of getting a rash" expression used in Fig. 5.5. With a supportive environment the appropriate qualitative understanding of chance in a social context appears likely at this stage. For tasks dealing with conjunction events, such as those found in Fig. 5.13, students are likely to provide appropriately ordered frequencies describing men over 55, men having had one or more heart attacks, and both, and appropriately order probabilities for having a cold next year, missing a week of school next year, and both. It appears that straightforward contexts for displaying chance understanding are becoming accessible to students at this stage. A task requiring quantitative reasoning, such as the one involving coin tossing at a sporting match in Fig. 5.12, is a different matter, with responses greater than a half likely to be given for the probability of obtaining four tails in a row. Responses to the definition of "random" are likely to feature single elements such as "choosing something" or "random breath test" but may also attempt a simple definition with more than one element, such as "pick something by chance, like a lottery." Responses of the second type appear near the top of the cluster and may suggest transition to the next stage of statistical literacy reasoning.

Instances where inference is involved at this stage are rare indicating lack of engagement with more difficult tasks. When asked to select the better of the two stacked dot plots in Figs. 3.20 and 3.21 for telling the story of the number of years families have lived in a town, students are likely to make the appropriate choice, the scaled plot, but for vague reasons, such as "it is clearer," or to show indifference saying "they tell the same story."

Although variation is addressed by responses in chance contexts, examples are likely to be unrealistic. In the situation of repeated trials with a 50-50 spinner, the expectation of the same outcome is likely to occur again but this time with theoretical reasoning to back it up, such as "the chances are the same." In response to a request for the meaning of the term *variation* and an example of something that varies, attempts are likely to be vague and focus on single elements, such as "you get a choice" or "flavors of ice-cream." Improvement in appreciation of variation is only marginal at Stage 3.

At this stage students show more success in contexts where qualitative reasoning is adequate or the task involves recognizing the appropriate response from a list. At times when an appropriate response is selected, however, the accompanying justification is inadequate. Improved mathematical/statistical skills appear in the recognition, not the creation or the interpretation, of the mean and percent risk.

8.7   STAGE 4 OF STATISTICAL LITERACY—CONSISTENT NON-CRITICAL

The cluster of tasks appearing at Stage 4 indicates a consolidation of appropriate but non-critical engagement by students in various contexts. In terms of the Statistical Literacy Hierarchy, students appear to appreciate many contexts although they cannot go further to question claims. This is shown in appropriate responses in some contexts to tasks that do not require questioning and in partial responses reflecting context only to tasks that do have an expectation of critical questioning.

In terms of sampling students are likely to provide multiple elements in describing the concept, for example "you have a small piece of something." In suggesting methods of surveying a school in response to the task in Fig. 2.4, students are likely to present representative but not random ideas, such as "I'd choose 10 from each grade." In evaluating the proposed methods of the other parts of Fig. 2.4, students are again likely to single out peripheral features rather than critical ones for mention. For Shannon's random method in Part (a), responses of "good" justify this choice with reasons such as "there's lots of people" or "you pick evenly from a hat." They are however, also likely to choose Shannon's method as best, although perhaps in conjunction with Claire's voluntary scheme. For Adam's method of selecting 100 children in grade 1 in Part (c), students are likely to provide an appropriate justification for it being "bad," such as "there are not enough different age groups." Hence there is an indication of a transition into critical questioning in a familiar school-based social context. For the less familiar context of the media article about school students having access to guns in the United States in Figure 2.7, responses are likely to question the fact people could be lying, or say there are no criticisms because the whole of the United States would be the same. The non-representative nature of the sample is missed in these responses.

The context appears to play a role in student success on graphing tasks at this stage. For stacked dot plots, such as the one in Fig. 7.15, students are likely to be able to identify the highest data value and the range of the data, and to make appropriate qualitative descriptions of the shape of the graph. They are also likely to choose the statistically appropriate plot between Figs. 3.20 and 3.21 and give sound reasons for the choice, such as "you can see the difference between years more clearly and the graph is more spaced out." When asked in a media context to consider the unusual features of the pie graph that sums to 128.8% in Fig. 3.18, however, students are likely to single out peripheral rather than central ones for criticism, for example "other is a very large category." Similarly for the task to draw a graph to represent the causal claim in the article in Fig. 3.6 related to heart deaths and car usage, students produce graphs that show a partial association, such as those shown in Fig. 3.11.

For tasks based on average, students are likely to describe the mean algorithm or how to find the middle of a data set adequately if informally, and calculate correctly the mean of a small data set, although without recognition of the effect of an outlier.

Tasks in abstract chance settings are likely to be answered successfully at this stage for example with proportional reasoning to claim that Box A and Box B have the same chance of producing a blue marble for the question in Fig. 5.8. For the die question in Fig. 5.6, however, students are more likely to respond with a claim that a 1 and a 6 have the "same" chance rather than quantifying that chance. For chance tasks appearing in a media context, success is less likely. For the coin-tossing problem based on a media sporting report in Fig. 5.12, students are likely to identify correctly the chances of heads and tails on a single toss in Parts (b2) and (b3) but for four coins in Part (a) they are likely to suggest the same value. For the odds question in Fig. 5.15 again related to sports, the interpretation is likely to be based on chance language or predicted scores. In media contexts involving language rather than numerical calculations, engagement where critical questioning is not required is likely to be more successful. Students are likely to order the chance newspaper headlines in Fig. 5.3 appropriately, as well as interpret the conditional language found in Parts (a) and (b) of the article in Fig. 5.18 correctly by constructing "if . . . then . . ." statements such as "*if* smoke pack a day for more than 50 years *then* risk of wrinkles is 4.7 times greater." For Part (d) however, which involves embedded conditional statements, students are likely to be successful only with the simpler statement, which is interpreted as "*if* you smoke *then* you will be old and ugly before your time."

In terms of making inferences at this stage, students are likely to be inconsistent in recognizing central issues in forming judgments and predictions. As noted earlier for Stage 4, students are likely to choose the appropriately scaled stacked dot plot as telling a story better, with sound reasoning. In making predictions for whether a new student who came to school by car is a boy or a girl in Fig. 6.2 Part (b), students are likely to include data-based reasoning, for example to balance the boys or reflect a majority of girls. Responses however are unlikely to contain an element of uncertainty. Similarly the question on how Tom, absent from the graph, will come to school tomorrow in Part (d), is likely to be answered based on balancing or a majority. When suggesting questions for the researcher in relation to the media article in Fig. 3.6 about the association of heart deaths and car usage, students are likely to focus on questioning the data collection or on what the actual numbers are, rather than the cause–effect relationship. This indicates an appreciation of the context without critical questioning skills.

An appreciation of variation with respect to chance is likely to be shown at Stage 4, for example with the suggestion of variation as a reason for differences in repeated sets of trials with a 50-50 spinner. Realistic variation is also likely to be demonstrated in numerical predictions of outcomes for six sets of repeated trials and in predicting outcomes for 60 tosses of a die from the setting in Fig. 5.9. For the decision about which sets of spinner trials described in Fig. 7.16 are authentic, students are likely to choose the appropriate stacked dot plots and provide reasonable justifications for the choices. There is still difficulty however in the media context of the graphs of boating deaths shown in Fig. 3.16, where students are likely to focus on single columns in descriptions rather than comparisons across columns in describing features of the graphs. In discussing aspects of variation itself, students are likely to mention multiple relevant features, such as "variation means to change something" and "the weather is going to vary over the next few days."

The mathematical/statistical skills that are likely to be consolidated at this stage are associated with the mean, simple probabilities, and graph characteristics, all in straightforward settings. Variation is displayed appropriately in chance settings and most definitions are likely to reveal multiple aspects of the concept of interest. Appreciation is shown for features of many contexts indicating the application of the concepts reasonably, if not critically.

8.8   STAGE 5 OF STATISTICAL LITERACY—CRITICAL

The top two stages of the statistical literacy construct demonstrate similar critical thinking skills associated with the third tier goal of the Statistical Literacy Hierarchy. What distinguishes them is the level of mathematical skill required to engage in critical questioning. At Stage 5 sophisticated use of mathematics is not likely to appear but in some contexts, particularly familiar ones, students are likely otherwise to be successful.

For sampling tasks, students are likely to relate several elements together in describing a sample and its purpose. For the task of surveying a school in Fig. 2.4, they are likely to suggest random methods or random methods combined with representation, such as "10 from each grade, 5 boys and 5 girls picked at random." For three of the other suggested methods—Shannon's random method in Part (a), Raffi's choice of friends in Part (d), and Claire's booth for volunteers in Part (e)—appropriate decisions and statistical justifications are likely to be given. For the multiple-choice task of buying a car in Fig. 2.5, students are likely to make the appropriate choice of using the report on 800 cases. In terms of assessing the voluntary poll on legalizing marijuana described in the article in Fig. 2.8, responses are likely to focus on the central issues, for example, the type of listeners to the radio or that only motivated people telephone the station. For the article on access to guns by school students in the United States in Fig. 2.7, however, they are likely to recognize the non-representative nature of the sample only with the support of the additional question about other regions of the United States. Generally, however, in more familiar settings, students are likely to be successful in handling sampling issues at Stage 5.

In terms of graphing at this stage, students are likely to sketch appropriate representations for the claim in the article in Fig. 3.6 about the association of heart deaths and car usage, such as those in Figs. 3.12, 3.13, and 3.14. This represents the ability to handle two variables at the same time and show corresponding increases. For the task to comment on unusual features of the pie graph in Fig. 3.18 that sums to 128.8%, students are likely to focus appropriately on this inconsistency or the shapes of the segments of the graph in comparison to the percents they represent.

At this stage, for the idea of average, the ability to find the median and mean of a small data set is likely to be shown.

In relation to chance, appreciation of conditional language usage is likely to be consolidated with students providing appropriately ordered estimates for the probability a school teacher is a woman and the probability a woman is a school teacher (cf. Fig. 5.14) and giving appropriate "if . . . then . . ." statements for the last, embedded conditional statement on smoking and wrinkles found in Fig. 5.18. For multiple coin tosses as set in the con-

Every year, Susan selects about 5 young actors for the drama team who perform brilliantly at audition. Unfortunately, most of these kids turn out to be no better than the rest. Why do you suppose that Susan usually finds that they don't turn out to be as brilliant as she first thought?

- □(a) In her eagerness to find new talent, Susan may exaggerate the brilliance of the performances she sees at the audition.

- □(b) The actors probably just made some nice acts at the audition that were much better than usual for them.

- □(c) The actors probably coast on their talent alone without putting in the effort for a consistently excellent performance.

- □(d) The actors who did so well at the audition may find that the others are jealous, and so they slack off.

- □(e) The actors who did so well are likely to be students with other interests, so they don't put all their energies into acting after the audition.

FIG. 8.2.   Multiple-choice question about regression to the mean.

text of a sporting match in Figure 5.12, however, students are likely to give reasonable estimates that are qualitative rather than quantitative. Similarly for dealing with an odds statement from a newspaper headline, as seen in Figure 5.15, students are likely to be able to use ratio but not to determine the direction of the chances of winning appropriately.

There is little evidence of change in inference skills at this stage. For the multiple-choice item shown in Fig. 8.2,[14] students are likely to choose alternative (b) in accordance with an understanding of regression to the mean.

Appreciation of variation is likely to be shown in two types of tasks at Stage 5. In predicting the outcomes of spinning a 50-50 spinner repeatedly, students are likely spontaneously to use words like "about" or "probably" in suggesting numbers of successes or phrases such as "it will be close to half." Also in describing unusual features of the bar graphs in a report on boating deaths in Fig. 3.16, students are likely either to focus on an increase or change in the data over time or to acknowledge variation explicitly in the visual appearance of the graph.

8.9   STAGE 6 OF STATISTICAL LITERACY—
CRITICAL MATHEMATICAL

As noted previously, sophisticated mathematical skills are likely to be associated with success on many of the tasks that appear at Stage 6, particularly in chance or media contexts. As well, sensitivity to the need for uncertainty in making predictions and to subtle aspects of the language of tasks, appears to be associated with success.

In relation to sampling, students are likely to detect two flaws in the method proposed by Jake to survey a school in Part (b) of the task in Fig. 2.4, for example, "there are not enough people and they are selectively picked." They are likely to pick up the non-representative nature of the sample from Chicago in the article in Fig. 2.7, without any support. When asked for two methods to select children to lead a parade they are likely to suggest either two different random methods or a combination of random and representative methods.

In terms of graphing, it is likely that students are able to make two summary statements involving the context, rather than just data reading, for the stacked dot plots in Figs. 3.20 and 3.21. Terminology for the mode is recognized in relation to a stacked dot plot, which is likely to be associated with formal instruction in school. Errors in the bar graphs about boating deaths in Fig. 3.16 are likely to be identified and the rate calculations associated with the complex picto-bar graph in Fig. 3.17 completed correctly.

At this stage students are likely to take an outlier into account when calculating a mean and suggest the median as the appropriate measure of middle in relation to house prices in the context of the newspaper article in Fig. 4.5.

Quantitative reasoning is a focus of responses to chance tasks at the highest stage of statistical literacy. For straightforward questions such as those in Fig. 5.6 involving outcomes for a single die and Fig. 5.7 involving drawing names from a hat, students are likely to suggest numerical rather than qualitative descriptions such as "same" or "more" chance. For the classic fish-tagging question shown in Fig. 8.3,[15] students at this stage are likely to use proportional reasoning to obtain the solution of "2000." For the question from the media on explaining odds in Fig. 5.15, students are again likely to use proportional reasoning and suggest the correct direction for interpreting the result. For the article on tossing coins at the start of a cricket match in Fig. 5.12, independence is recognized and calculations are correct. Students are also likely to give integrated descriptions for the term random.

Inference at this stage is likely to reveal subtleties in thinking. Predictions for the pictograph on how children travel to school in Fig. 6.2 for example are likely to contain expressions of uncertainty. In predicting whether a new child who comes by car is a girl or boy in Part (b), a typical

A farmer wants to know how many fish there are in his dam. He took out 200 fish and tagged each of them, with a colored sign. He put the tagged fish back in the dam and let them get mixed with the others. On the second day, he took out 250 fish in a random manner, and found that 25 of them were tagged. Estimate how many fish are in the dam.

FIG. 8.3.   Proportional reasoning question.

response is "probably a girl—more girls get a car." For Part (c) on the empty row with a train, expressions use words like "can" or "might" to indicate varying possibilities, such as "you can get to school by it." In predicting how Tom in Part (d) will get to school tomorrow, again uncertainty is included with consideration of the data in the pictograph. In relation to the newspaper article about heart deaths and car usage found in Fig. 3.6 and discussed in terms of critical questioning in Section 6.6, students at Stage 6 are likely to ask the salient questions about a cause–effect relationship.

The mathematical/statistical skills that are likely to be displayed at the highest stage include proportional reasoning associated with ratio and appropriate part–whole interpretations, the ability to use rates in calculating costs, understanding of independence and its implications for calculating probabilities, an overall quantitative view of chance as probability, and a memory for terms such as "mode." This is combined with an ability to account for subtleties in language and context to produce the highest level of performance.

8.10   OVERALL OBSERVATIONS AND SUMMARY OF STATISTICAL LITERACY

The model of statistical literacy understanding presented in the previous six sections includes the interaction of many components besides the formal data and chance curriculum. The importance of appreciating the context within which a task is set, as well as the foundational mathematical skills required to achieve success, are seen. Although understanding of variation is displayed through the engagement with other topics in the curriculum, it is highlighted throughout the first five stages of the model to show continuing development with respect to it.

Although the six stages appear to be related in pairs to the lack of appreciation of context, the acknowledgment of context, and the critical interaction with context, the individual stages show a progression of difficulty of tasks with respect to student ability that can be useful in predicting student behaviors and outcomes in the classroom. From Stage 1 to Stage 2, for example, there is a tendency for students to focus less on idiosyncratic ideas and more on single relevant elements. Moving from Stage 3 to Stage 4, more consistency is seen in performance across tasks. From Stage 5 to Stage 6, there is more evidence of quantitative reasoning and appreciation of subtleties of language and context. Although there is no reason to hypothesize that all students will progress through these stages, there are signposts to suggest what might be seen and planned for in the classroom. It is then possible to return to earlier chapters for a more detailed account of what might be expected in relation to a specific topic or concept.

It is interesting to note that whereas the Statistical Literacy Hierarchy introduced in Chapter 1 suggests that Tier 1 involves the understanding of terminology before Tier 2, where terminology is interpreted in context, in the model of student understanding described here proficiency with definitions occurs at higher stages rather than lower ones. It is clear that understanding of complex concepts like random and variation takes time to develop and may be assisted by their application in various contexts. Also in terms of task format, it is likely to be more difficult to create a definition than to identify it in a multiple-choice setting. It is important for teachers to realize that writing a formal definition on the board is not a guarantee that it will be taken on board quickly and applied appropriately in context. The transition from the middle two to the top two stages of statistical literacy does, however, appear to be closely related to Tiers 2 and 3 of the Statistical Literacy Hierarchy. It is likely that critical questioning in context cannot be commenced until the context is understood.

In attempting to visualize the interactions taking place as the construct of statistical literacy develops, a picture of three intertwined strands emerges. These thick strands are associated with the structured development of the topics specific to the data and chance curriculum, with the increased facility to engage with context as it becomes more demanding of critical questioning, and with the general mathematical development that assists statistical reasoning. From the point of view of assessment, there is also a thinner strand related to the diminishing degree of support offered by the tasks that students are asked to complete.

8.11   BACK TO THE CLASSROOM

The newspaper article, "Beware the pushy fish-eater," which was presented at the beginning of Chapter 1,[16] is a fitting example with which to close the discussion of the growth and goals of statistical literacy. A number of questions that should come to the mind of the statistically literate reader, were posed in Section 1.1, ranging from interest in the relationship of the sponsor to the study, to concern about sample size and study methodology. The article provides the opportunity to review the premises underlying this book and illustrate the stages of development of statistical literacy suggested in this chapter. As the basis for a classroom task, the article about "the pushy fish-eater" could initiate general questions about the study that lay behind it or with added information from the actual report it could initiate a thorough investigation of the study.[17] Although the general questions are a good starting point, this section explores the potential when more information is available. Having an interesting, motivating task is a start in exploring the connections among topics in the school curriculum, in selling statistical literacy as an extension of school-based interests, and in illustrating the stages of statistical thinking associated with the statistical literacy construct.

The focus of this discussion is the first part of the second sentence in the article: "Seven in 10 men who frequently eat canned tuna, sardines, salmon, mackerel or kippers admit to being ambitious." The claim is based on the information presented in the horizontal bar graphs shown in Figs. 8.4 and 8.5.[18] It turns out that the survey was conducted with a sample of 250 people, 126 men and 124 women, evenly spread in three age groups, 15–30 years, 31–50 years, and 51–60+ years. There were four categories of fish consumption with "very frequent" representing three or more times a week.

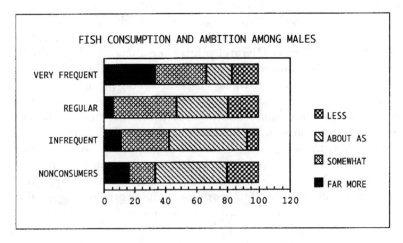

FIG. 8.4.   Fish consumption and ambition among males.

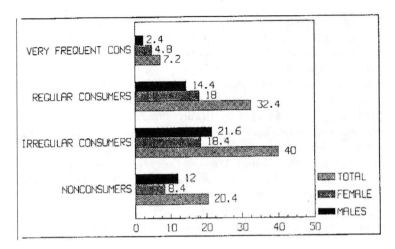

FIG. 8.5.   Frequency of fish consumption based on response total.

There were also four categories of ambitiousness: far more, somewhat more, about as, or less ambitious than most other people they knew. Hence each horizontal bar in Fig. 8.4 is the same length representing 100% of the men in each fish-eating category. "Far more" is shaded as one-third of the very frequent bar, as is "somewhat more." The graph in Fig. 8.5, however, represents the percent of the sample in each fish-eating category and it displays 2.4% for male very frequent consumers. Because 2.4% of 126 is 6, the claim in the article is hence based on 6 males who ate canned fish three or more times a week and 4 of whom thought they were far more or somewhat more ambitious than their peers.

All stages of a statistical investigation as suggested in the school curriculum are observed in the information available, from sampling to data representation and summary, with the inference interpretable in terms of a conditional statement that could be stated in probabilistic terms as P (ambitious man|frequent fish-eating man) = 0.7. It is also possible to suggest reactions to the article and the extra information that illustrate the six stages of statistical literacy discussed in this chapter.

A Stage 1 reaction would be likely to be based on belief of the claim and the cause–effect implication that goes with it. A comment like the following might be expected: "If wives want their husbands to be ambitious in their jobs, they should serve fish at least three times a week."

At Stage 2 it might be expected that students would react with "I don't know but it might be true because 70% is a big number and anything is possible." Another likely scenario at this stage is the repeating of anecdotal "sample of size one" stories: "I know a man who is running for mayor and he eats at my dad's fish and chip shop nearly every day."

Stage 3 reactions are likely to focus on some aspects of the information presented in the study but not retrieve the relevant features for an appropriate conclusion. A summary might read as follows: "It is good that they asked both men and women. Graph 1 (Fig. 8.4) shows 100% of each group, which is good. Graph 2 (Fig. 8.5) adds to 100%, which is also good." Such comments may provide a sequence of individual comments but there is no recognition of connections or contradictions among them.

At the next stage reactions are likely to perceive the conflict present in some of the information but not be able to resolve it. Hence a Stage 4 response might be the following: "Why did they ask both men and women but only report on men? Why are the two graphs presented in different forms? Maybe the company is trying to fool us."

Stage 5 reactions to the article are likely to report descriptively on the difficulties seen in the data collection and reporting in the graphs: "There aren't very many men (2.4%) who eat fish frequently and when you look at the other graph (Fig. 8.4), they combined the 'far more' and 'somewhat more' ambitious categories in order to get a bigger percent to report. This isn't many people." If students at Stage 5 calculate that 4 out of 6 frequent fish-eaters report being more ambitious than others, they are likely to report that the "7 out of 10" in the article is "wrong."

Reactions at Stage 6 are likely to extend the Stage 5 responses with an explanation of the representation of 4/6 as 0.67, the subsequent rounding to 0.7, and the misleading nature of reporting "7 out of 10" in the context of the data collected. Students at this stage are likely to be able to represent the claim as a conditional probability and suggest that the presentation of the two graphs in different ways may have been meant to hide the true nature of the data.

If one imagines classroom discussions or activities based on reactions in the previous paragraphs or on similar reactions to other stimuli, there is a suggestion from Iddo Gal for adults that can be easily adapted at the school level. Often one sees posters on classroom walls suggesting "Rules for Classroom Behavior" or even "Steps in Problem Solving." Iddo suggests a set of "Worry Questions" for the statistically literate in Fig. 8.6 that would make a very nice classroom poster.[19]

In planning to motivate discussion of the importance of statistical literacy beyond the use of media articles, there are links to quantitative literacy and numeracy that can be helpful. John Allen Paulos[20] in his books *Innumeracy* and *A Mathematician Reads the Newspaper* provides many examples that show fallacies in probabilistic or statistical thinking, as does A. K. Dewdney in *200% of Nothing*.[21] These books and others like them can be useful to teachers in providing motivating stories for topics across the mathematics curriculum. More specifically statistical is the classic book by Darrell Huff, *How to Lie with Statistics*.[22] Although dated it is still an interesting

> How reliable or accurate were the measures used to generate the reported data?
>
> If a sample was used, was it large enough? Could this sample serve as a reasonable basis for inferences about the whole population of interest?
>
> What is the shape of the underlying distribution of raw data (on which this reported statistic is based)? Could outliers cause a summary statistic to misrepresent the true picture?
>
> Is a given graph drawn appropriately, or does its scale distort trends in the data?
>
> Are the claims made sensible? Are they supported by the data? Is some information missing?

FIG. 8.6.   A sample of "Worry Questions" for adult statistical literacy devised by Iddo Gal.

short read. More recently Robert Hooke's *How to Tell the Liars from the Statisticians*[23] presents over 70 brief scenarios that can be linked directly to nearly all topics in the school data and chance curriculum. *Misused Statistics: Straight Talk for Twisted Numbers* by A. J. Jaffe and Herbert Spirer[24] takes a more structured approach with chapters generally conforming to the school curriculum and providing many well-documented examples. More generally Cynthia Crossen's *Tainted Truth: The Manipulation of Fact in America*[25] provides excellent case studies in relevant contexts that canvas issues beyond the strictly statistical but which need to be considered by students, such as knowing who sponsors particular research programs when interpreting the results. *Reckoning with Risk* by Gerd Gigerenzer[26] presents many intriguing examples and addresses some of the misunderstandings studied by the early psychologists who looked into probabilistic reasoning.[27] All of the sources provide ammunition for those, like the author, who believe that there must be a specific effort to move beyond a fact- and procedure-based approach to teaching data and chance in school. At almost every point from the middle school grades, it is possible to integrate scenarios that create awareness and motivation to become statistical detectives and not to be seduced by inappropriate interpretations of chance.

8.12   POSTSCRIPT

If the aims of writing this book have been met, what should happen next? It is my view that teachers are the next big frontier in bringing statistical literacy to all students to prepare them to leave school and enter society. We now have a good idea of students' starting points and potential growth over the middle school years. We do not have a good idea of teachers' starting points. Do teachers know what it is *they* know and do not know? Do teachers know what it is *their students* know and do not know—the students' idiosyncratic and partial understandings? Do teachers have experience with materials and tasks that can enhance understanding? In many cases I suspect the answer to these questions is "no."

Some of the other Tasmanian research has shown that it is possible to teach data and chance in such a way that performance improves; but with elementary grades it was necessary to provide a project teacher.[28] A large professional development effort is required to assist elementary and middle school teachers with their own understanding and understanding of their students' understanding. They also need experience with suitable tasks, trialed by themselves in their classrooms, to observe the outcomes. Starting points are provided in this book and many recent curriculum materials on the market. What is needed are people to lead programs, encourage and reward teachers, and monitor their progress and the progress of their students. It is only by showing the teachers measurable improvement in outcomes for their students that they will believe that statistical literacy is important and can be developed in their classrooms. This of course requires funding and it is to be hoped that those preaching the need for quantitative literacy will help support the cause.

NOTES

1. Cockroft (1982, para. 36).
2. National Council of Teachers of Mathematics (1989, p. 5).
3. National Council of Teachers of Mathematics (1989, p. 109).
4. National Council of Teachers of Mathematics (1989, p. 105).
5. Gal (2002).
6. Wallman (1993).
7. Gal (2002).
8. Freebody & Luke (2003); Luke & Freebody (1997).
9. Gal (2002).
10. Wild & Pfannkuch (1999).
11. Watson & Callingham (2004); Watson & Moritz (1998, 1999b, 2000b, 2002c, 2003a).
12. Bond & Fox (2001); Callingham & Watson (2005).
13. The summary presented in this chapter is based on the analysis carried out by Watson & Callingham (2003). Details of the Rasch analyses performed are given there.
14. Nisbett, Krantz, Jepson, & Kunda (1983).

15. Fischbein & Gazit (1984).
16. "Beware the pushy fish-eater" (1991).
17. Watson (1992).
18. Lewis (1991).
19. Gal (1997, 2002).
20. Paulos (1988, 1995).
21. Dewdney (1993).
22. Huff (1991).
23. Hooke (1983).
24. Jaffe & Spirer (1987).
25. Crossen (1994).
26. Gigerenzer (2002).
27. Kahneman & Tversky (1972); Tversky & Kahneman (1971, 1974, 1983).
28. Watson & Kelly (2002a, 2002c, 2002e).

Further Reading

Abelson, R. P. (1995). *Statistics as principled argument.* Hillsdale, NJ: Lawrence Erlbaum Associates.

Asp, G., Dowsey, J., & Hollingsworth, H. (1994). Students' understandings of pictographs and bar graphs. In G. Bell, B. Wright, N. Leeson, & G. Geake (Eds.), *Challenges in mathematics education: Constraints on construction* (Proceedings of the 17th annual conference of the Mathematics Education Research Group of Australasia, Vol. 1, pp. 57–65). Lismore, NSW: MERGA.

Bakker, A. (2004). Reasoning about shape as a pattern in variability. *Statistics Education Research Journal, 3*(2), 64–83.

Batanero, C., & Serrano, L. (1999). The meaning of randomness for secondary school students. *Journal for Research in Mathematics Education, 30,* 558–567.

Ben-Zvi, D. (2004). Reasoning about variability in comparing distributions. *Statistics Education Research Journal, 3*(2), 42–63.

Biehl, M., & Halpern-Felsher, B. L. (2001). Adolescents' and adults' understanding of probability expressions. *Journal of Adolescent Health, 28,* 30–35.

Bright, G. W., Harvey, J. G., & Wheeler, M. M. (1981). Fair games, unfair games. In A. P. Shulte (Ed.), *Teaching Statistics and Probability 1981 Yearbook* (pp. 49–59). Reston, VA: National Council of Teachers of Mathematics.

Bruine de Bruin, W., Fischhoff, B., Millstein, S. G., & Halpern-Felsher, B. L. (2000). Verbal and numerical expressions of probability: "It's a fifty-fifty chance." *Organizational Behavior and Human Decision Processes, 81*(1), 115–131.

Callingham, R. A., & Watson, J. M. (2002). *Implications of differential item function in statistical literacy: Is gender still an issue?* Refereed paper presented at the Measurement Special Interest Group of the Australian Association for Research in Education conference, Brisbane, December, 2002. Available at: http://www.aare.edu.au/02pap/cal02034.htm

Chick, H. L., & Hunt, D. (2001). Pre-service primary teachers' judgements about the probability of everyday events. In J. Bobis, B. Perry, & M. Mitchelmore (Eds.), *Numeracy and beyond* (Proceedings of the 24th annual conference of the Mathematics Education Research Group of Australasia, Vol. 1, pp. 147–154). Sydney, NSW: MERGA.

Curcio, F. R. (2001). *Developing data-graph comprehension in grades K–8* (2nd ed.). Reston, VA: National Council of Teachers of Mathematics.

Davidson, D. (1995). The representativeness heuristic and the conjunction fallacy effect in children's decision making. *Merrill-Palmer Quarterly, 41*, 328–346.

Derry, S. J., Levin, J. R., Osana, H. P., & Jones, M. S. (1998). Developing middle-school students' statistical reasoning abilities through simulation gaming. In S. P. Lajoie (Ed.), *Reflections on statistics: Learning, teaching and assessment in grades K–12* (pp. 175–195). Mahwah, NJ: Lawrence Erlbaum Associates.

Dessart, D. J. (1995). Randomness: A connection to reality. In P. A. House (Ed.), *Connecting mathematics across the curriculum. 1995 Yearbook* (pp. 177–181). Reston, VA: National Council of Teachers of Mathematics.

Economopoulos, K., & Wright, T. (1997). *How many pockets? How many teeth? Collecting and representing data. Investigations in Number, Data, and Space.* Palo Alto, CA: Dale Seymour.

Evans, J. St. B. T., & Dusoir, A. E. (1977). Proportionality and sample size as factors in intuitive statistical judgement. *Acta Psychologica, 41*, 129–137.

Finlay, E., & Lowe, I. (1993). *Chance and data: Exploring real data.* Melbourne: Curriculum Corporation.

Fischhoff, B., & Bruine de Bruin, W. (1999). Fifty-fifty = 50%? *Journal of Behavioral Decision Making, 12*, 149–163.

Friel, S. N. (1998). Teaching statistics: What's average? In L. J. Morrow (Ed.), *The teaching and learning of algorithms in school mathematics* (pp. 208–217). Reston, VA: National Council of Teachers of Mathematics.

Gal, I. (1995). Statistical tools and statistical literacy: The case of the average. *Teaching Statistics, 17*, 97–99.

Gal, I. (1998). Assessing statistical knowledge as it relates to students' interpretation of data. In S. P. Lajoie (Ed.), *Reflections on statistics: Learning, teaching and assessment in grades K–12* (pp. 275–295). Mahwah, NJ: Lawrence Erlbaum Associates.

Gal, I. (2000). Statistical literacy: Conceptual and instructional issues. In D. Coben, J. O'Donoghue, & G. E. Fitzsimons (Eds.), *Perspectives on adults learning mathematics: Research and practice* (pp. 135–150). Dordrecht: Kluwer.

Gal, I., & Garfield, J. (1997). Curricular goals and assessment challenges. In I. Gal & J. B. Garfield (Eds.), *The assessment challenge in statistics education* (pp. 1–13). Amsterdam: IOS Press & The International Statistical Institute.

Garfield, J., & Ahlgren, A. (1988). Difficulties in learning basic concepts in probability and statistics: Implications for research. *Journal for Research in Mathematics Education, 19*, 44–63.

Garfield, J., & Chance, B. (2000). Assessment in statistics education: Issues and challenges. *Mathematical Thinking and Learning, 2*(1&2), 99–125.

Garfield, J. B., & Gal, I. (1999). Assessment and statistics education: Current challenges and directions. *International Statistics Review, 67*, 1–12.

Gould, R. (2004). Variability: One statistician's view. *Statistics Education Research Journal, 3*(2), 7–16.

Horvath, J. K., & Lehrer, R. (1998). A model-based perspective on the development of children's understanding of chance and uncertainty. In S. P. Lajoie (Ed.), *Reflections on statistics: Learning, teaching and assessment in grades K–12* (pp. 121–148). Mahwah, NJ: Lawrence Erlbaum Associates.

Jackson, S. (1989). *An introduction to sample surveys.* Melbourne: Australian Bureau of Statistics.

Jones, G. A. (Ed.). (2005). *Exploring probability in school: Challenges for teaching and learning.* New York: Springer.

Jones, G. A., Langrall, C. W., Thornton, C. A., & Mogill, A. T. (1997). A framework for assessing young children's thinking in probability. *Educational Studies in Mathematics, 32*, 101–125.

Jones, G. A., Langrall, C. W., Thornton, C. A., & Mogill, A. T. (1999). Students' probabilistic thinking in instruction. *Journal for Research in Mathematics Education, 30*, 487–519.

Jones, G. A., Thornton, C. A., Langrall, C. W., Mooney, E. S., Perry, B., & Putt, I. J. (2000). A framework for characterizing children's statistical thinking. *Mathematical Thinking and Learning, 2*, 269–307.

Joram, E., Resnick, L. B., & Gabriele, A. J. (1995). Numeracy as cultural practice: An examination of numbers in magazines for children, teenagers, and adults. *Journal for Research in Mathematics Education, 26*, 346–361.

Kerslake, D. (1974). Some children's views on probability. *Mathematics in School, 3*(4), 22.

Konold, C., & Miller, C. (1994). *ProbSim* [Computer software]. Amherst, MA: University of Massachusetts.

Konold, C., & Pollatsek, A. (2002). Data analysis as the search for signals in noisy processes. *Journal for Research in Mathematics Education, 33*, 259–289.

Konold, C., Pollatsek, A., Well, A., & Gagnon, A. (1997). Students analyzing data: Research of critical barriers. In J. B. Garfield & G. Burrill (Eds.), *Research on the role of technology in teaching and learning statistics* (pp. 151–167). Voorburg, The Netherlands: International Statistical Institute.

Kuhn, K. M. (1997). Communicating uncertainty: Framing effects on responses to vague probabilities. *Organizational Behavior and Human Decision Processes, 71*(1), 55–83.

Lajoie, S. P. (1998). Reflections on a statistics agenda for K–12. In S. P. Lajoie (Ed.), *Reflections on statistics: Learning, teaching and assessment in grades K–12* (pp. 299–316). Mahwah, NJ: Lawrence Erlbaum Associates.

Lajoie, S. P., Lavinge, N. C., Munsie, S. D., & Wilkie, T. V. (1998). Monitoring student progress in statistics. In S. P. Lajoie (Ed.), *Reflections on statistics: Learning, teaching and assessment in grades K–12* (pp. 199–231). Mahwah, NJ: Lawrence Erlbaum Associates.

Landwehr, J. M., & Watkins, A. E. (1986). *Exploring data: Quantitative literacy series*. Palo Alto, CA: Dale Seymour.

Lee, C. (Ed.). (2003). *Reasoning about variability: Proceedings of the Third International Research Forum on Statistical Reasoning, Thinking, and Literacy* [CD-ROM]. Mt. Pleasant, MI: Central Michigan University.

Lidster, S. T., Pereira-Mendoza, L., Watson, J. M., & Collis, K. F. (1995, November). *What's Fair for Grade 6?* Paper presented at the annual conference of the Australian Association for Research in Education, Hobart. Available at: http://www.aare.edu.au/95pap/lidss95306.txt

Lidster, S. T., Watson, J. M., Collis, K. F., & Pereira-Mendoza, L. (1996). The relationship of the concept of fair to the construction of probabilistic understanding. In P. C. Clarkson (Ed.), *Technology in mathematics education* (Proceedings of the 19th annual conference of the Mathematics Education Research Group of Australasia, pp. 352–359). Melbourne: MERGA.

Lovitt, C., & Lowe, I. (1993). *Chance and Data Investigations, Volumes 1 and 2*. Melbourne: Curriculum Corporation.

Makar, K., & Confry, J. (2005). "Variation-talk": Articulating meaning in statistics. *Statistics Education Research Journal, 4*(1), 27–54.

Metz, K. E. (1997). Dimensions in the assessment of students' understanding and application of chance. In I. Gal & J. B. Garfield (Eds.), *The assessment challenge in statistics education* (pp. 223–238). Amsterdam: IOS Press & The International Statistical Institute.

Metz, K. E. (1998a). Emergent ideas of chance and probability in primary-grade children. In S. P. Lajoie (Ed.), *Reflections on statistics: Learning, teaching and assessment in grades K–12* (pp. 149–174). Mahwah, NJ: Lawrence Erlbaum Associates.

Metz, K. E. (1998b). Emergent understanding and attribution of randomness: Comparative analysis of the reasoning of primary grade children and undergraduates. *Cognition and Instruction, 16*, 285–365.

Mevarech, Z. R., & Kramarsky, B. (1997). From verbal descriptions to graphic representations: Stability and change in students' alternative conceptions. *Educational Studies in Mathematics, 32,* 229–263.

Meyer, R. A., Browning, C., & Channell, D. (1995). Expanding students' conceptions of the arithmetic mean. *School Science and Mathematics, 95,* 114–117.

Mooney, E. S. (2002). A framework for characterizing middle school students' statistical thinking. *Mathematical Thinking and Learning, 4*(1), 23–63.

Moritz, J. B. (2000). Graphical representations of statistical associations by upper primary students. In J. Bana & A. Chapman (Eds.), *Mathematics education beyond 2000* (Proceedings of the 23rd annual conference of the Mathematics Education Research Group of Australasia, Vol. 2, pp. 440–447). Perth, WA: MERGA.

Moritz, J. B. (2002). Study times and test scores: What students' graphs show. *Australian Primary Mathematics Classroom, 7*(1), 24–31.

Mosteller, F., & Youtz, C. (1990). Quantifying probabilistic expressions. *Statistical Science, 5,* 2–34.

Moxley, L. M., & Sanford, A. J. (2000). Communicating quantities: A review of psycholinguistic evidence of how expressions determine perspectives. *Applied Cognitive Psychology, 14,* 237–255.

Noelting, G. (1980a). The development of proportional reasoning and the ratio concept: Part I—The determination of stages. *Educational Studies in Mathematics, 11,* 217–253.

Noelting, G. (1980b). The development of proportional reasoning and the ratio concept: Part II—Problem-structure at successive stages: Problem-solving strategies and the mechanism of adaptive restructuring. *Educational Studies in Mathematics, 11,* 331–363.

Pendlebury, C., & Robinson, F. E. (1928). *New school arithmetic.* London: G. Bell & Sons.

Petrosino, A. J., Lehrer, R., & Schauble, L. (2003). Structuring error and experimental variation as distribution in the fourth grade. *Mathematical Thinking and Learning, 5*(2&3), 131–156.

Pfannkuch, M. (2005). Thinking tools and variation. *Statistics Education Research Journal, 4*(1), 83–91.

Rangecroft, M. (1991). Graphwork—Developing a progression. Part 1—The early stages. *Teaching Statistics, 13*(2), 44–46.

Reading, C. (2004). Student description of variation while working with weather data. *Statistics Education Research Journal, 3*(2), 84–105.

Reading, C., & Pegg, J. (1995). Teaching statistics: Background and implications. In L. Grimison & J. Pegg (Eds.), *Teaching secondary school mathematics: Theory into practice* (pp. 140–163). Sydney: Harcourt-Brace.

Ritson, R. (2000). A question of choice. *Australian Primary Mathematics Classroom, 5*(3), 10–14.

Rubin, A., & Mokros, J. (1990). *Data: Kids, cats, and ads: Statistics.* Menlo Park, CA: Dale Seymour.

Russell, S. J., & Mokros, J. (1996). What do children understand about average? *Teaching Children Mathematics, 2,* 360–364.

Russell, S. J., Schifter, D., & Bastable, V. (2002). *Developing mathematical ideas: Collecting, representing, and analyzing data.* Parsippany, NJ: Dale Seymour.

Shaughnessy, J. M., Ciancetta, M., & Canada, D. (2004). Types of student reasoning on sampling tasks. In M. Johnsen-Høines & A. B. Fuglestad (Eds.), *Proceedings of the 28th annual conference of the International Study Group for the Psychology of Mathematics Education* (Vol. 4, pp. 177–184). Bergen, Norway: PME.

Singer, M., Konold, C., & Rubin, A. (1996). *Between never and always: Probability. Investigations in number, data, and space.* Palo Alto, CA: Dale Seymour.

Streefland, L. (1991). *Fractions in realistic mathematics education: A paradigm of developmental research.* Dordrecht: Kluwer.

Teigen, K. H. (2001). When equal chances = good chances: Verbal probabilities and the equiprobability effect. *Organizational Behavior and Human Decision Processes, 85*(1), 77–108.

Teigen, K. H., & Brun, W. (1999). The directionality of verbal probability expressions: Effects on decisions, predictions, and probabilistic reasoning. *Organizational Behavior and Human Decision Processes, 80*(2), 155–190.

Teigen, K. H., & Brun, W. (2000). Ambiguous probabilities: When does $p = 0.3$ reflect a possibility and when does it express a doubt? *Journal of Behavioral Decision Making, 13*, 345–362.

Torok, R. (2000). Putting the variation into chance and data. *Australian Mathematics Teacher, 56*(2), 25–31.

Tufte, E. R. (1990). *Envisioning information*. Cheshire, CT: Graphics Press.

Tufte, E. R. (1997). *Visual explanations: Images and quantities, evidence and narrative*. Cheshire, CT: Graphics Press.

Wallsten, K. K., Fillenbaum, S., & Cox, J. A. (1986). Base rate effects on the interpretations of probability and frequency expressions. *Journal of Memory and Language, 25*, 571–587.

Watson, J. M. (1995a). Conditional probability: Its place in the mathematics curriculum. *Mathematics Teacher, 88*, 12–17.

Watson, J. M. (1995b). Statistical literacy: A link between mathematics and society. In A. Richards, G. Gillman, K. Milton, & J. Oliver (Eds.), *Flair: Forging links and integrating resources* (Proceedings of the 15th biennial conference of the Australian Association of Mathematics Teachers, pp. 12–28). Adelaide, SA: AAMT.

Watson, J. M. (1998). Statistical literacy: What's the chance? *Reflections, 23*(1), 6–14.

Watson, J. M. (2002a). Discussion: Statistical literacy before adulthood. *International Statistical Review, 70*, 26–30.

Watson, J. M. (2002b). Doing research in statistics: More than just data. [Keynote Address]. In B. Phillips (Ed.), *Developing a statistically literate society? Proceedings of the Sixth International Conference on Teaching Statistics, Cape Town* [CD-ROM]. Voorburg, The Netherlands: International Statistical Institute.

Watson, J. M. (2002c). Lessons from variation research I: Student understanding. In M. Goos & T. Spencer (Eds.), *Mathematics—Making waves*. (Proceedings of the 19th biennial conference of the Australian Association of Mathematics Teachers Inc., Brisbane, pp. 261–268). Adelaide, SA: AAMT.

Watson, J. M., & Kelly, B. A. (2005). The winds are variable: Student intuitions about variation. *School Science and Mathematics, 105*, 252–269.

Watson, J. M., & Moritz, J. B. (1997). Teachers' views of sampling. In N. Scott & H. Hollingsworth (Eds.), *Mathematics creating the future* (Proceedings of the 16th biennial conference of the Australian Association of Mathematics Teachers Inc., pp. 345–353). Adelaide, SA: AAMT.

Watson, J. M., & Moritz, J. B. (2002a). Developing concepts of sampling for statistical literacy. In J. Sowder & B. Schappelle (Eds.), *Lessons learned from research* (pp. 117–124). Reston, VA: National Council of Teachers of Mathematics.

Watson, J. M., & Moritz, J. B. (2002b). Quantitative literacy for pre-service teachers via the internet. *Mathematics Teacher Education and Development, 4*, 43–56.

Well, A. D., Pollatsek, A., & Boyce, S. J. (1990). Understanding the effects of sample size on the variability of the mean. *Organizational Behavior and Human Decision Processes, 47*, 289–312.

Winkler, R. L. (1990). Comment: Representing and communicating uncertainty. *Statistical Science, 5*, 26–30.

References

Amir, G. S., & Williams, J. S. (1999). Cultural influences on children's probabilistic thinking. *Journal of Mathematical Behavior, 18,* 85–107.

Aussies living for longer, ABS says. (1994, January 29). *The Mercury* (Hobart, Tasmania), p. 8.

Australia hotting up. (1997, January 11). *The Mercury* (Hobart, Tasmania), p. 11.

Australian Education Council. (1991). *A national statement on mathematics for Australian schools.* Melbourne: Author.

Australian Education Council. (1994a). *Mathematics—A curriculum profile for Australian schools.* Melbourne: Curriculum Corporation.

Australian Education Council. (1994b). *A statement on health and physical education for Australian schools.* Melbourne: Curriculum Corporation.

Barbella, P., Kepner, J., & Schaeffer, R. L. (1994). *Exploring measurements.* [Quantitative Literacy Series] Palo Alto, CA: Dale Seymour.

Batanero, C., Estepa, A., Godino, J. D., & Green, D. R. (1996). Intuitive strategies and preconceptions about association in contingency tables. *Journal for Research in Mathematics Education, 27,* 151–169.

Batanero, C., Serrano, L., & Garfield, J. B. (1996). Heuristics and biases in secondary school students' reasoning about probability. In L. Puig & A. Gutiérres (Eds.), *Proceedings of the 20th annual conference of the International Group for the Psychology of Mathematics Education* (Vol. 2, pp. 43–50). Valencia, Spain: PME.

Beer gets blame for violent crime rate. (1994, August 23). *The Mercury* (Hobart, Tasmania), p. 8.

Beichner, R. J. (1994). Testing student interpretation of kinematics graphs. *American Journal of Physics, 62,* 750–762.

Bereska, C., Bolster, C. H., Bolster, L. C., & Scheaffer, R. (1998). *Exploring statistics in the elementary grades. Book One (K–6).* White Plains, NY: Dale Seymour.

Bereska, C., Bolster, C. H., Bolster, L. C., & Scheaffer, R. (1999). *Exploring statistics in the elementary grades. Book Two (grades 4–8).* White Plains, NY: Dale Seymour.

Bernstein, P. L. (1996). *Against the gods: The remarkable story of risk.* New York: Wiley.

Beware the pushy fish-eater. (1991, May 7). *The Mercury* (Hobart, Tasmania).

Biggs, J. B. (1992). Modes of learning, forms of knowing, and ways of schooling. In A. Demetriou, M. Shayer, & A. Efklides (Eds.), *Neo-Piagetian theories of cognitive development: Implications and applications for education* (pp. 31–51). London: Routledge.

Biggs, J. B., & Collis, K. F. (1982). *Evaluating the quality of learning: The SOLO taxonomy*. New York: Academic Press.

Biggs, J. B., & Collis, K. F. (1991). Multimodal learning and the quality of intelligent behavior. In H. A. H. Rowe (Ed.), *Intelligence: Reconceptualization and measurement* (pp. 57–76). Hillsdale, NJ: Lawrence Erlbaum Associates.

Bond, T. G., & Fox, C. M. (2001). *Applying the Rasch Model: Fundamental measurement in the human sciences*. Mahwah, NJ: Lawrence Erlbaum Associates.

Borovcnik, M., & Bentz, H. J. (1991). Empirical research in understanding probability. In R. Kapadia & M. Borovcnik (Eds.), *Chance encounters: Probability in education* (pp. 73–105). Dordrecht: Kluwer.

Brasell, H. M., & Rowe, M. B. (1993). Graphing skills among high school physics students. *School Science and Mathematics, 93*(2), 63–70.

Bright, G. W., & Friel, S. N. (1998). Graphical representations: Helping students interpret data. In S. P. Lajoie (Ed.), *Reflections on statistics: Learning, teaching, and assessment in grades K–12* (pp. 63–88). Mahwah, NJ: Lawrence Erlbaum Associates.

Bryant, P. E., & Somerville, S. C. (1986). The spatial demands of graphs. *British Journal of Psychology, 77*, 187–197.

Burrill, G., & Romberg, T. A. (1998). Statistics and probability for the middle grades: Examples from *Mathematics in Context*. In S. P. Lajoie (Ed.), *Reflections on statistics: Learning, teaching and assessment in grades K–12* (pp. 33–59). Mahwah, NJ: Lawrence Erlbaum Associates.

Cai, J. (1995). Beyond the computational algorithm: Students' understanding of the arithmetic average concept. In L. Meira & D. Carraher (Eds.), *Proceedings of the 19th Psychology of Mathematics Education Conference* (Vol. 3, pp. 144–151). São Paulo, Brazil: PME Program Committee.

Cai, J. (1998). Exploring students' conceptual understanding of the averaging algorithm. *School Science and Mathematics, 98*, 93–98.

Callingham, R., & Watson, J. M. (2005). Measuring statistical literacy. *Journal of Applied Measurement, 6*(1), 19–47.

Cañizares, M. J., & Batanero, C. (1998, June). *A study on the stability of equiprobability bias in 10–14 year-old children*. Poster paper presented at the Fifth International Conference on Teaching Statistics, Singapore.

Capel, A. D. (1885). *Catch questions in arithmetic & mensuration and how to solve them*. London: Joseph Hughes.

Carpenter, T. P., & Moser, J. M. (1984). The acquisition of addition and subtraction concepts in grades one through three. *Journal for Research in Mathematics Education, 15*, 179–202.

Case, R. (1988). Neo-Piagetian theory: Retrospect and prospect. In A. Demetriou (Ed.), *The neo-Piagetian theories of cognitive development: Toward an Integration* (pp. 267–285). Amsterdam: Elsevier.

Cats get bad press: Survey. (1994, June 30). *The Mercury* (Hobart, Tasmania), p. 9.

Chick, H. L., & Watson, J. M. (2001). Data representation and interpretation by primary school students working in groups. *Mathematics Education Research Journal, 13*, 91–111.

Chick, H. L., & Watson, J. M. (2002). Collaborative influences on emergent statistical thinking—A case study. *Journal of Mathematical Behavior, 21*, 371–400.

Cockcroft, W. H. (1982). *Mathematics counts: Report of the committee of inquiry into the teaching of mathematics in schools*. London: HMSO.

Corwin, R. B., & Friel, S. N. (1990). *Statistics: Prediction and sampling: A unit of study for grades 5–6*. [Used numbers: Real data in the classroom] Palo Alto, CA: Dale Seymour.

Corwin, R. B., & Russell, S. J. (1990). *Measuring: From paces to feet: A unit of study for grades 3–4*. [Used numbers: Real data in the classroom] Palo Alto, CA: Dale Seymour.

Crawford, W. (1991, June 11). Family car is killing us, says Tasmanian researcher. *The Mercury* (Hobart, Tasmania), p. 2.

Crossen, C. (1994). *Tainted truth: The manipulation of fact in America.* New York: Touchstone.

Curcio, F. R. (1987). Comprehension of mathematical relationships expressed in graphs. *Journal for Research in Mathematics Education, 18*, 382–393.

Curcio, F. R. (1989). *Developing graph comprehension.* Reston, VA: National Council of Teachers of Mathematics.

De Cesare, J. (1996, May 14). $5.6m bill. *The Mercury* (Hobart, Tasmania), p. 1.

Decriminalise drug use: poll. (1992, September 26). *The Mercury* (Hobart, Tasmania), p. 3.

Delbridge, A., & Bernard, J. R. L. (1998). *The Macquarie concise dictionary* (3rd ed., rev.). Sydney: The Macquarie Library, Pty. Ltd.

Department for Education (England & Wales). (1995). *Mathematics in the national curriculum.* London: Author.

Department of Education Tasmania. (2002). *Essential learnings framework 1.* Hobart: Author.

Dewdney, A. K. (1993). *200% of nothing: An eye-opening tour through the twists and turns of math abuse and innumeracy.* New York: Wiley.

Doerr, H. M., & English, L. D. (2003). A modeling perspective on students' mathematical reasoning about data. *Journal for Research in Mathematics, 34*, 110–136.

Dossey, J. A. (1997). National indicators of quantitative literacy. In L. A. Steen (Ed.), *Why numbers count: Quantitative literacy for tomorrow's America* (pp. 45–59). New York: College Entrance Examination Board.

Dossey, J. A., Giordano, F. R., McCrone, S., & Weir, M. D. (2002). *Mathematics methods and modeling for today's mathematics classroom: A contemporary approach to teaching grades 7–12.* Pacific Grove, CA: Brooks/Cole.

Dunkels, A. (1988). EDA in the primary classroom—Graphing and concept formation combined. In R. Davidson & J. Swift (Eds.), *Proceedings of the Second International Conference on Teaching Statistics* (pp. 61–66). Victoria, BC: The Organizing Committee, ICOTS2.

Education Queensland. (2000). *New Basics Project technical paper.* Retrieved 11 January 2002 from http://education.qld.gov.au/corporate/newbasics/html/library.html

Ernest, P. (1984). Introducing the concept of probability. *Mathematics Teacher, 77*, 524–525.

Estepa, A., Batanero, C., & Sanchez, F. T. (1999). Students' intuitive strategies in judging association when comparing two samples. *Hiroshima Journal of Mathematics Education, 7*, 17–30.

Falk, R. (1983a). Experimental models for resolving probabilistic ambiguities. In R. Hershkowitz (Ed.), *Proceedings of the annual conference of the International Group for the Psychology of Mathematics Education* (pp. 319–325). Rehovot, Israel: Weizmann Institute of Science.

Falk, R. (1983b). Probabilistic reasoning as an extension of commonsense thinking. In M. Zweng, T. Green, J. Kilpatrick, H. Pollak, & M. Suydam (Eds.), *Proceedings of the Fourth International Congress on Mathematical Education* (pp. 190–195). Boston: Birkhäuser.

Farouque, F. (1994, July 27). Cancer deaths on rise, but heart still the top killer. *The Age* (Melbourne, Victoria), p. 4.

Fathom [Computer software]. (2002). Emeryville, CA: Key Curriculum Press.

Fenton, P., & Watson, J. (2001). Triangular numbers: Fact or fiction? *Australian Primary Mathematics Classroom, 6*(1), 10–14.

Fischbein, E. (1975). *The intuitive sources of probabilistic thinking in children.* Dordrecht: D. Reidel.

Fischbein, E., & Gazit, A. (1984). Does the teaching of probability improve probabilistic intuitions? An exploratory research study. *Educational Studies in Mathematics, 15*, 1–24.

Fischbein, E., Nello, M. S., & Marino, M. S. (1991). Factors affecting probability judgements in children and adolescents. *Educational Studies in Mathematics, 22*, 523–549.

Fischbein, E., & Schnarch, D. (1997). The evolution with age of probabilistic, intuitively based misconceptions. *Journal for Research in Mathematical Education, 28*, 96–105.

Fong, G. T., Krantz, D. H., & Nisbett, R. E. (1986). The effects of statistical training on thinking about everyday problems. *Cognitive Psychology, 18,* 253–292.

Freebody, P., & Luke, A. (2003). Literacy as engaging with new forms of life: The 'four roles' model. In G. Bull & M. Anstey (Eds.), *The literacy lexicon* (2nd ed., pp. 51–65). Frenchs Forest, NSW: Prentice Hall, Pearson Education Australia.

Friel, S. N., & Bright, G. W. (1998). Teach-Stat: A model for professional development in data analysis and statistics for teachers K–6. In S. P. Lajoie (Ed.), *Reflections on statistics: Learning, teaching, and assessment in grades K–12* (pp. 89–117). Mahwah, NJ: Lawrence Erlbaum Associates.

Friel, S. N., Bright, G. W., & Curcio, F. R. (1997). Understanding students' understanding of graphs. *Mathematics Teaching in the Middle School, 3,* 224–227.

Friel, S. N., Curcio, F. R., & Bright, G. W. (2001). Making sense of graphs: Critical factors influencing comprehension and instructional implications. *Journal for Research in Mathematics Education, 32,* 124–158.

Friel, S., & Joyner, J. (Eds.). (1997). *Teach-Stat for teachers: Professional development manual.* Palo Alto, CA: Dale Seymour.

Friel, S. N., Mokros, J. R., & Russell, S. J. (1992). *Statistics: Middles, means, and in-betweens: A unit of study for grades 5–6.* [Used numbers: Real data in the classroom] Palo Alto, CA: Dale Seymour.

Gal, I. (1997). On developing statistically literate adults. In G. E. FitzSimons (Ed.), *Adults returning to study mathematics: Papers from Working Group 18: Eighth International Congress on Mathematical Education* (pp. 49–53). Adelaide: Australian Association of Mathematics Teachers, Inc.

Gal, I. (2002). Adults' statistical literacy: Meanings, components, responsibilities. *International Statistical Review, 70,* 1–51.

Gal, I., Rothschild, K., & Wagner, D. A. (1989, April). *Which group is better?: The development of statistical reasoning in elementary school children.* Paper presented at the meeting of the Society for Research in Child Development, Kansas City, MO.

Gal, I., Rothschild, K., & Wagner, D. A. (1990, April). *Statistical concepts and statistical reasoning in school children: Convergence or divergence?* Paper presented at the meeting of the American Educational Research Association, Boston.

Gal, I., & Wagner, D. A. (1992). *Project STARC: Statistical reasoning in the classroom* (Annual Report No. 2). Philadelphia, PA: University of Pennsylvania, Literacy Research Center.

Garfield, J., & delMas, R. (1991). Students' conceptions of probability. In D. Vere-Jones (Ed.), *Proceedings of the Third International Conference on Teaching Statistics. Vol. 1. School and general issues* (pp. 340–349). Voorburg, The Netherlands: International Statistical Institute.

Garfield, J., & Gal, I. (1999). Teaching and assessing statistical reasoning. In L. V. Stiff & F. R. Curcio (Eds.), *Developing mathematical reasoning in grades K–12 (1999 Yearbook)* (pp. 207–219). Reston, VA: National Council of Teachers of Mathematics.

Gigerenzer, G. (2002). *Reckoning with risk: Learning to live with uncertainty.* London: Penguin.

Gigerenzer, G., & Hoffrage, U. (1995). How to improve Bayesian reasoning without instruction: Frequency formats. *Psychological Review, 102,* 684–704.

Gnanadeskin, M., Scheaffer, R. L., & Swift, J. (1987). *The art and techniques of simulation.* [Quantitative Literacy Series] Palo Alto, CA: Dale Seymour.

Golf most popular sport. (1995, June 21). *The Mercury* (Hobart, Tasmania), p. 63.

Goodchild, S. (1988). School pupils' understanding of average. *Teaching Statistics, 10,* 77–81.

Green, D. (1983a). Shaking a six. *Mathematics in Schools, 12*(5), 29–32.

Green, D. R. (1983b). A survey of probability concepts in 3000 pupils aged 11–16 years. In D. R. Grey, P. Holmes, V. Barnett, & G. M. Constable (Eds.), *Proceedings of the First International Conference on Teaching Statistics* (Vol. 2, pp. 766–783). Sheffield, England: Teaching Statistics Trust.

Green, D. R. (1984). Talking of probability . . . *Bulletin of the Institute of Mathematics and its Applications, 20*(9/10), 145–149.

Green, D. R. (1986). Children's understanding of randomness: Report of a survey of 1600 children aged 7–11 years. In R. Davidson & J. Swift (Eds.), *Proceedings of the Second International Conference on Teaching Statistics* (pp. 287–291). Victoria, BC: The Organizing Committee, ICOTS2.

Green, D. (1991). A longitudinal study of pupils' probability concepts. In D. Vere-Jones (Ed.), *Proceedings of the Third International Conference on Teaching Statistics. Vol. 1. School and general issues* (pp. 320–328). Voorburg, The Netherlands: International Statistical Institute.

Green, D. (1993). Data analysis: What research do we need? In L. Pereira-Mendoza (Ed.), *Introducing data analysis in the schools: Who should teach it?* (pp. 219–239). Voorburg, The Netherlands: International Statistical Institute.

Haley, M. (2000, March 30). Boaties' safety failure. *The Mercury* (Hobart, Tasmania), p. 7.

Hardiman, P. T., Well, A. D., & Pollatsek, A. (1984). Usefulness of a balance model in understanding the mean. *Journal of Educational Psychology, 76*(5), 792–801.

Hart, K. M. (Ed.). (1981). *Children's understanding of mathematics: 11–16.* London: John Murray.

Hart, W. L. (1953). *College algebra* (4th ed.). Boston: D.C. Heath.

Hawkins, A. S., & Kapadia, R. (1984). Children's conception of probability—A psychological and pedagogical review. *Educational Studies in Mathematics, 15,* 349–377.

Holmes, P. (1980). *Teaching statistics 11–16.* Slough, UK: Schools Council and Foulsham Educational.

Holmes, P. (1986). A statistics course for all students aged 11–16. In R. Davidson & J. Swift (Eds.), *Proceedings of the Second International Conference on Teaching Statistics* (pp. 194–196). Victoria, BC: The Organizing Committee, ICOTS2.

Hooke, R. (1983). *How to tell the liars from the statisticians.* New York: Marcel Dekker.

Huff, D. (1991). *How to lie with statistics.* London: Penguin. (Original work published 1954)

Jacobs, V. R. (1997, March). *Children's understanding of sampling in surveys.* Paper presented at the annual meeting of the American Educational Research Association, Chicago.

Jacobs, V. R. (1999). How do students think about statistical sampling before instruction? *Mathematics in the Middle School, 5*(4), 240–263.

Jaffe, A. J., & Spirer, H. F. (1987). *Misused statistics: Straight talk for twisted numbers.* New York: Marcel Dekker.

Jones, A. (Ed.). (1996). *Chambers Dictionary of Quotations.* New York: Larousse Kingfisher Chambers, Inc.

Kahneman, D., & Tversky, A. (1972). Subjective Probability: A judgement of representativeness. *Cognitive Psychology, 3,* 430–454.

Kelly, B. A., & Watson, J. M. (2002). Variation in a chance sampling setting: The lollies task. In B. Barton, K. C. Irwin, M. Pfannkuch, & M. O. J. Thomas (Eds.), *Mathematics education in the South Pacific* (Proceedings of the 26th annual conference of the Mathematics Education Research Group of Australasia, Vol. 2, pp. 366–373). Sydney, NSW: MERGA.

Kilpatrick, J., Martin, W. G., & Schifter, D. (Eds.). (2003). *A research companion to Principles and Standards for School Mathematics.* Reston, VA: National Council of Teachers of Mathematics.

Kirkby, D., & Short, G. (1991). *Maths investigations through games: Book 2.* Melbourne: Longman Cheshire.

Konold, C. (1989). Informal conceptions of probability. *Cognition and Instruction, 6,* 59–98.

Konold, C., & Garfield, J. (1992). *Statistical reasoning assessment: Part 1. Intuitive Thinking.* Amherst, MA: Scientific Reasoning Research Institute, University of Massachusetts.

Konold, C., & Higgins, T. L. (2002). Working with data: Highlights related to research. In S. J. Russell, D. Schifter, & V. Bastable (Eds.), *Developing mathematical ideas: Collecting, representing, and analyzing data* (pp. 165–201). Parsippany, NJ: Dale Seymour.

Konold, C., & Higgins, T. L. (2003). Reasoning about data. In J. Kilpatrick, W. G. Martin, & D. Schifter (Eds.), *A research companion to Principles and Standards for School Mathematics* (pp. 193–215). Reston, VA: National Council of Teachers of Mathematics.

Konold, C., & Miller, C. D. (2005). *Tinkerplots: Dynamic data exploration* [Computer software]. Emeryville, CA: Key Curriculum Press.

Konold, C., Pollatsek, A., Well, A., Lohmeier, J., & Lipson, A. (1993). Inconsistencies in students' reasoning about probability. *Journal for Research in Mathematics Education, 24,* 392–414.

Konold, C., Robinson, A., Khalil, K., Pollatsek, A., Well, A., Wing, R., & Mayr, S. (2002). Students' use of modal clumps to summarize data. In B. Phillips (Ed.), *Developing a statistically literate society? Proceedings of the Sixth International Conference on Teaching Statistics, Cape Town* [CD-ROM]. Voorburg, The Netherlands: International Statistical Institute.

Landwehr, J. M., Swift, J., & Watkins, A. E. (1987). *Exploring surveys and information from samples.* Palo Alto, CA: Dale Seymour.

Lappan, G., Fey, J. T., Fitzgerald, W. M., Friel, S. N., & Phillips, E. D. (1997a). *Comparing and scaling: Ratio, proportion, and percent.* Palo Alto, CA: Dale Seymour.

Lappan, G., Fey, J. T., Fitzgerald, W. M., Friel, S. N., & Phillips, E. D. (1997b). *Data around us: Number sense.* [Teacher's edition]. Menlo Park, CA: Dale Seymour.

Lappan, G., Fey, J. T., Fitzgerald, W. M., Friel, S. N., & Phillips, E. D. (1997c). *Samples and populations: Data and statistics.* [Teacher's edition]. Menlo Park, CA: Dale Seymour.

Lappan, G., Fey, J. T., Fitzgerald, W. M., Friel, S. N., & Phillips, E. D. (1997d). *What do you expect? Probability and expected value.* [Teacher's edition]. Menlo Park, CA: Dale Seymour.

Lappan, G., Fey, J. T., Fitzgerald, W. M., Friel, S. N., & Phillips, E. D. (1998a). *Clever counting: Combinatorics.* [Teacher's edition]. Menlo Park, CA: Dale Seymour.

Lappan, G., Fey, J. T., Fitzgerald, W. M., Friel, S. N., & Phillips, E. D. (1998b). *Data about us: Statistics.* [Teacher's edition]. Menlo Park, CA: Dale Seymour.

Lappan, G., Fey, J. T., Fitzgerald, W. M., Friel, S. N., & Phillips, E. D. (1998c). *How likely is it? Probability.* [Teacher's edition]. Menlo Park, CA: Dale Seymour.

Lappan, G., Fey, J. T., Fitzgerald, W. M., Friel, S. N., & Phillips, E. D. (1998d). *Samples and populations: Data and statistics.* [Teacher's edition]. Menlo Park, CA: Dale Seymour.

Lecoutre, M.-P. (1992). Cognitive models and problem spaces in "purely random" situations. *Educational Studies in Mathematics, 23,* 557–568.

Lehrer, R., & Romberg, T. (1996). Exploring children's data modeling. *Cognition and Instruction, 14*(1), 69–108.

Lehrer, R., & Schauble, L. (2000). Modeling in mathematics and science. In R. Glaser (Ed.), *Advances in instructional psychology* (Vol. 5, pp. 101–159). Mahwah, NJ: Lawrence Erlbaum Associates.

Leinhardt, G., Zaslavsky, O., & Stein, M. K. (1990). Functions, graphs and graphing: Tasks, learning and teaching. *Review of Educational Research, 60*(1), 1–64.

Leon, M. R., & Zawojewski, J. S. (1991). Use of the arithmetic mean: An investigation of four properties, issues and preliminary results. In D. Vere-Jones (Ed.), *Proceedings of the Third International Conference on Teaching Statistics: Vol. 1. School and general issues* (pp. 302–306). Voorburg, The Netherlands: International Statistical Institute.

Let someone else drive, bridge commuters told. (1994, February 27). *The Mercury* (Hobart, Tasmania), p. 3.

Lewis, D. (1991). *Survey characteristics of oily fish consumers at different levels of consumption frequency* (Report prepared for John West Fish and Wearne Public Relations). London: Author.

Li, J., & Pereira-Mendoza, L. (2002). Misconceptions in probability. In B. Phillips (Ed.), *Developing a statistically literate society? Proceedings of the Sixth International Conference on Teaching Statistics, Cape Town* [CD-ROM]. Voorburg, The Netherlands: International Statistical Institute.

Lokan, J., Ford, P., & Greenwood, L. (1996). *Maths and science on the line: Australian junior secondary students' performance in the Third International Mathematics and Science Study.* Melbourne: Australian Council for Educational Research.

The longer your overseas call, the cheaper the rate. (1993, July 22). *The Mercury* (Hobart, Tasmania), p. 17.

Lovitt, C., & Lowe, I. (1993). "What's in the bag?" In *Chance and data investigations* (Vol. 2, pp. 400–407). Melbourne: Curriculum Corporation.

Luke, A., & Freebody, P. (1997). Shaping the social practices of reading. In S. Musprati, A. Luke, & P. Freebody (Eds.), *Constructing critical literacies: Teaching and learning textual practice* (pp. 185–225). St. Leonards, NSW: Allen & Unwin.

Madison, B. L. (2002). Educating for numeracy: A challenging responsibility. *Notices of the American Mathematical Society*, February, 2000, p. 181. Available at http://www.ams.org/notices/200202/commentary.pdf

Madison, B. L., & Steen, L. A. (2003). *Quantitative literacy: Why numeracy matters for schools and colleges*. Princeton, NJ: The National Council on Education and the Disciplines.

Maher, C. (1998). Is this game fair? The emergence of statistical reasoning in young children. In L. Pereira-Mendoza, L. S. Kea, T. W. Kee, & W. Wong (Eds.), *Statistical education—Expanding the network. Proceedings of the Fifth International Conference on Teaching of Statistics* (Vol. 1, pp. 53–59). Voorburg, The Netherlands: International Statistical Institute.

Malone, J., & Miller, D. (1993). Communicating mathematical terms in writing: Some influential variables. In M. Stephens, A. Waywood, D. Clarke, & J. Izard (Eds.), *Communicating mathematics: Perspectives from classroom practice and current research* (pp. 177–190). Melbourne: Australian Council for Educational Research.

Mann, R., Harmoni, R., & Power, C. (1989). Adolescent decision making: The development of competence. *Journal of Adolescence, 12*, 56–69.

McLennan, W. (1997). *Aspects of literacy: Assessed skill levels Australia 1996*. Canberra: Commonwealth of Australia.

Megalogenis, G. (1990, May 7). Hobart defies homes trend. *The Mercury* (Hobart, Tasmania), p. 3.

Meletiou-Mavrotheris, M., & Lee, C. (2002). Teaching students the stochastic nature of statistical concepts in an introductory statistics course. *Statistics Education Research Journal, 1*(2), 22–37.

Metz, K. E. (1999). Why sampling works or why it can't: Ideas of young children engaged in research of their own design. In F. Hitt & M. Santos (Eds.), *Proceedings of the 21st annual meeting of the North American Chapter of the International Group for the Psychology of Mathematics Education* (Vol. 2, pp. 492–499). Cuernavaca, Mexico: PME.

Mevarech, Z. (1983). A deep structure model of students' statistical misconceptions. *Educational Studies in Mathematics, 14*, 415–429.

Miller, L. D. (1993). Making the connection with language. *Arithmetic Teacher, 40*, 311–316.

Ministry of Education. (1992). *Mathematics in the New Zealand curriculum*. Wellington, NZ: Author.

Mokros, J., & Russell, S. J. (1995). Children's concepts of average and representativeness. *Journal for Research in Mathematics Education, 26*, 20–39.

Moore, D. S. (1990). Uncertainty. In L. S. Steen (Ed.), *On the shoulders of giants: New approaches to numeracy* (pp. 95–137). Washington, DC: National Academy Press.

Moore, D. S. (1991a). *Statistics: Concepts and controversies* (3rd ed.). New York: Freeman.

Moore, D. S. (1991b). Statistics for all: Why, what, and how? In D. Vere-Jones (Ed.), *Proceedings of the Third International Conference on Teaching Statistics. Vol. 1. School and general issues* (pp. 423–428). Voorburg, The Netherlands: International Statistical Institute.

Moore, D. S. (1997). New pedagogy and new content: The case of statistics. *International Statistical Review, 65*, 123–165.

Moore, D. S., & McCabe, G. P. (1993). *Introduction to the practice of statistics* (3rd ed.). New York: W.H. Freeman.

Moritz, J. B. (1998). Long odds: Longitudinal development of student understanding of odds. In C. Kanes, M. Goos, & E. Warren (Eds.), *Teaching mathematics in new times* (Proceedings of the 21st annual conference of the Mathematics Education Research Group of Australasia, Vol. 2, pp. 373–380). Gold Coast: MERGA.

Moritz, J. B. (1999). Graphing data: Relating representation and interpretation. In K. Baldwin & J. Roberts (Eds.), *Mathematics—The next millennium* (Proceedings of the 17th biennial conference of the Australian Association of Mathematics Teachers Inc., pp. 90–99). Adelaide, SA: AAMT.

Moritz, J. B., & Watson, J. M. (1997a). Graphs: Communication lines to students? In F. Biddulph & K. Carr (Eds.), *People in mathematics education* (Proceedings of the 20th annual conference of the Mathematics Education Research Group of Australasia, Vol. 2, pp. 344–351). Waikato, NZ: MERGA.

Moritz, J. B., & Watson, J. M. (1997b). Pictograph representation: Telling the story. In N. Scott & H. Hollingsworth (Eds.), *Mathematics creating the future* (Proceedings of the 16th biennial conference of the Australian Association of Mathematics Teachers Inc., pp. 222–231). Adelaide, SA: AAMT.

Moritz, J. B., & Watson, J. M. (2000). Reasoning and expressing probability in students' judgements of coin tossing. In J. Bana & A. Chapman (Eds.), *Mathematics education beyond 2000* (Proceedings of the 23rd annual conference of the Mathematics Education Research Group of Australasia, Vol. 2, pp. 448–455). Perth, WA: MERGA.

Moritz, J. B., Watson, J. M., & Collis, K. F. (1996). Odds: Chance measurement in three contexts. In P. C. Clarkson (Ed.), *Technology in mathematics education* (Proceedings of the 19th annual conference of the Mathematics Education Research Group of Australasia, pp. 390–397). Melbourne, VIC: MERGA.

Moritz, J. B., Watson, J. M., & Pereira-Mendoza, L. (1996, November). *The language of statistical understanding: An investigation in two countries.* A paper presented at the Joint ERA/AARE Conference, Singapore. Available at: http://www.aare.edu.au/96pap/morij96280.txt

National Council of Teachers of Mathematics. (1989). *Curriculum and evaluation standards for school mathematics.* Reston, VA: Author.

National Council of Teachers of Mathematics. (2000). *Principles and standards for school mathematics.* Reston, VA: Author.

Neumann, H. (1966). *Probability.* Canberra: Canberra Mathematical Association.

Newman, C. M., Obremski, T. E., & Scheaffer, R. L. (1987). *Exploring probability.* [Quantitative Literacy Series] Palo Alto, CA: Dale Seymour.

Nisbett, R. E., Krantz, D. H., Jepson, C., & Kunda, Z. (1983). The use of statistical heuristics in everyday inductive reasoning. *Psychological Review, 90,* 339–363.

O'Keefe, J. J. (1997). The human scatterplot. *Mathematics Teaching in the Middle School, 3,* 208–209.

Orr, D. B. (1995). *Fundamentals of applied statistics and surveys.* New York: Chapman & Hall.

Outhred, L., & Shaw, P. F. (1999). Visual representations in first year statistics. In J. M. Truran & K. M. Truran (Eds.), *Making the difference* (Proceedings of the 22nd annual conference of the Mathematics Education Research Group of Australasia Incorporated, pp. 411–417), Sydney: MERGA.

Palmer, C. I., & Krathwohl, W. C. (1921). *Analytic geometry with introductory chapter on the calculus.* New York: McGraw-Hill.

Paulos, J. A. (1988). *Innumeracy: Mathematical illiteracy and its consequences.* New York: Random House.

Paulos, J. A. (1995). *A mathematician reads the newspaper.* New York: Basic Books.

Pegg, J. E. (2002a). Assessment in mathematics: A developmental approach. In J. M. Royer (Ed.), *Mathematical cognition* (pp. 227–259). Greenwich, CT: Information Age Publishing.

Pegg, J. E. (2002b). Fundamental cycles of cognitive growth. In A. Cockburn & E. Nardi (Eds.), *Proceedings of the 26th Conference of the International Group for the Psychology of Mathematics Education* (Vol. 4, pp. 41–48). Norwich, UK: University of East Anglia.

Pereira-Mendoza, L. (1995). Graphing in the primary school: Algorithm versus comprehension. *Teaching Statistics, 17*(1), 2–6.

Pereira-Mendoza, L., & Mellor, J. (1991). Students' concepts of bar graphs—Some preliminary findings. In D. Vere-Jones (Ed.), *Proceedings of the Third International Conference on Teaching Statistics: Vol. 1. School and general issues* (pp. 150–157). Voorburg, The Netherlands: International Statistical Institute.

Pfeffer, C. R. (Ed.). (1989). *Suicide among youth: Perspectives on risk and prevention.* Washington, DC: American Psychiatric Press.

Plant, M., & Plant, M. (1992). *Risk takers: Alcohol, drugs, sex and youth.* London: Routledge.

Pollatsek, A., Lima, S., & Well, A. D. (1981). Concept or computation: Students' understanding of the mean. *Educational Studies in Mathematics, 12,* 191–204.

Pollatsek, A., Well, A. D., Konold, C., Hardiman, P., & Cobb, G. (1987). Understanding conditional probabilities. *Organizational Behavior and Human Decision Processes, 40,* 255–269.

Pratt, D. (2000). Making sense of the total of two dice. *Journal for Research in Mathematics Education, 31,* 602–625.

Rao, C. R. (1975). Teaching of statistics at the secondary level: An interdisciplinary approach. *International Journal of Mathematical Education in Science and Technology, 6,* 151–162.

Reading, C., & Shaughnessy, M. (2000). Student perceptions of variation in a sampling situation. In T. Nakahara & M. Koyama (Eds.), *Proceedings of the 24th annual conference of the International Group for the Psychology of Mathematics Education* (Vol. 4, pp. 89–96). Hiroshima, Japan: Hiroshima University.

Reed, S. K. (1984). Estimating answers to algebra word problems. *Journal of Experimental Psychology: Learning, Memory and Cognition, 10,* 778–790.

Rosato, D. (2002, September 15). Worried about corporate numbers? How about the charts? *The New York Times,* p. BU7.

Roscoe, B., & Kruger, T. L. (1990). AIDS: Late adolescents' knowledge and its influence on sexual behaviour. *Adolescence, 25*(97), 39–48.

Rose, M. (1994, June 27). Needle to make parents do the right thing. *The Mercury* (Hobart, Tasmania), p. 1.

Ross, J. A., & Cousins, J. B. (1993a). Enhancing secondary school students' acquisition of correlational reasoning skills. *Research in Science and Technological Education, 11,* 191–205.

Ross, J. A., & Cousins, J. B. (1993b). Patterns of student growth in reasoning about correlational problems. *Journal of Educational Psychology, 85,* 49–65.

Roth, W. M., & McGinn, M. K. (1997). Graphing: Cognitive ability or practice? *Science Education, 81*(1), 91–106.

Rubin, A. (2005, Spring). Math that matters: The case for replacing the algebra/calculus track with data literacy—a critical skill for modern life. *Threshold: Exploring the Future of Education,* pp. 22–25, 31.

Rubin, A., Bruce, B., & Tenney, Y. (1991). Learning about sampling: Trouble at the core of statistics. In D. Vere-Jones (Ed.), *Proceedings of the Third International Conference on Teaching Statistics: Vol. 1. School and general issues* (pp. 314–319). Voorburg, The Netherlands: International Statistical Institute.

Russell, S. J., & Corwin, R. B. (1989). *The shape of the data: A unit of study for grades 4–6.* [Used numbers: Real data in the classroom] Palo Alto, CA: Dale Seymour.

Russell, S. J., & Corwin, R. B. (1990). *Sorting: Groups and graphs: A unit of study for grades 2–3.* [Used numbers: Real data in the classroom] Palo Alto, CA: Dale Seymour.

Salsburg, D. (2001). *The lady tasting tea: How statistics revolutionized science in the twentieth century.* New York: Henry Holt.

Scheaffer, R. L. (2003). Statistics and quantitative literacy. In B. L. Madison & L. A. Steen (Eds.), *Quantitative literacy: Why numeracy matters for schools and colleges* (pp. 145–152). Princeton, NJ: The National Council on Education and the Disciplines.

Scheaffer, R. L., Watkins, A. E., & Landwehr, J. M. (1998). What every high-school graduate should know about statistics. In S. P. Lajoie (Ed.), *Reflections on statistics: Learning, teaching and assessment in grades K–12* (pp. 3–31). Mahwah, NJ: Lawrence Erlbaum Associates.

Schoolgirls are smokers, drinkers. (1994, December 1). *The Mercury* (Hobart, Tasmania), p. 11.

Schwartz, D. L., & Goldman, S. R. (1996). Why people are not like marbles in an urn: An effect of context on statistical reasoning. *Applied Cognitive Psychology, 10,* S99–S112.

Schwartz, D. L., Goldman, S. R., Vye, N. J., Barron, B. J., & The Cognition and Technology Group at Vanderbilt. (1998). Aligning everyday and mathematical reasoning: The case of sampling assumptions. In S. P. Lajoie (Ed.), *Reflections on statistics: Learning, teaching and assessment in grades K–12* (pp. 233–273). Mahwah, NJ: Lawrence Erlbaum Associates.

Scott, J. (1997, July 12–13). Bands must learn the art of business. *The Weekend Australian,* p. 2.

Shaughnessy, J. M. (1992). Research in probability and statistics: Reflections and directions. In D. A. Grouws (Ed.), *Handbook of research on mathematics teaching and learning* (pp. 465–494). New York: National Council of Teachers of Mathematics & Macmillan.

Shaughnessy, J. M. (1997). Missed opportunities in research on the teaching and learning of data and chance. In F. Biddulph & K. Carr (Eds.), *People in mathematics education* (Proceedings of the 20th annual conference of the Mathematics Education Research Group of Australasia, Vol. 1, pp. 6–22), Waikato, NZ: MERGA.

Shaughnessy, J. M. (2003). Research on students' understandings of probability. In J. Kilpatrick, W. G. Martin, & D. Schifter (Eds.), *A research companion to Principles and Standards for School Mathematics* (pp. 216–226). Reston, VA: National Council of Teachers of Mathematics.

Shaughnessy, J. M., Canada, D., & Ciancetta, M. (2003). Middle school students' thinking about variability in repeated trials: A cross-task comparison. In N. A. Pateman, B. J. Dougherty, & J. T. Zilliox (Eds.), *Proceedings of the 27th annual conference of the International Group for the Psychology of Mathematics Education held jointly with the 25th conference of PME-NA* (Vol. 4, pp. 159–165). Honolulu, HI: Center for Research and Development Group, University of Hawaii.

Shaughnessy, M., & Ciancetta, M. (2002). Students' understanding of variability in a probability environment. In B. Phillips (Ed.), *Developing a statistically literate society? Proceedings of the Sixth International Conference on Teaching Statistics, Cape Town* [CD-ROM]. Voorburg, The Netherlands: International Statistical Institute.

Shaughnessy, J. M., Watson, J., Moritz, J., & Reading, C. (1999, April). School mathematics students' acknowledgment of statistical variation. In C. Maher (Chair), *There's more to life than centers.* Presession Research Symposium, 77th Annual National Council of Teachers of Mathematics Conference, San Francisco, CA.

Shaughnessy, J. M., & Zawojewski, J. S. (1999). Secondary students' performance on data and chance in the 1996 NAEP. *The Mathematics Teacher, 92,* 713–718.

Skalicky, J. (2005). Assessing multiple objectives with a single task in statistics. In P. Clarkson, A. Downton, D. Gronn, M. Horne, A. McDonough, R. Pierce, & A. Roche (Eds.), *Building connections: Theory, research and practice* (Proceedings of the 28th annual conference of the Mathematics Education Research Group of Australasia, Melbourne, pp. 688–695). Sydney: MERGA.

Speiser, B., & Walter, C. (1998). Two dice, two sample spaces. In L. Pereira-Mendoza, L. S. Kea, T. W. Kee, & W. Wong (Eds.), *Statistical education—Expanding the network. Proceedings of the Fifth International Conference on the Teaching of Statistics* (Vol. 1, pp. 61–66). Voorburg, The Netherlands: International Statistical Institute.

Spending a penny in supermarkets. (1996, October 2). *The Mercury* (Hobart, Tasmania), p. 5.

Statistics Canada and Organisation for Economic Cooperation and Development (OECD). (1996). *Literacy, economy, and society: First results from the International Adult Literacy Survey.* Ottawa: Author.

Steen, L. A. (Ed.). (1990). *On the shoulders of giants: New approaches to numeracy.* Washington, DC: National Academy Press.

Steen, L. A. (Ed.). (1997). *Why numbers count: Quantitative literacy for tomorrow's America.* New York: College Entrance Examination Board.

Steen, L. A. (Ed.). (2001). *Mathematics and democracy: The case for quantitative literacy.* Washington, DC: Woodrow Wilson National Fellowship Foundation.

Steen, L. A. (2002). Quantitative literacy: Why numeracy matters for schools and colleges. *Focus, Newsletter of the Mathematical Association of America/MAA Online.* Vol. 22, No. 2, pp. 8–9. Available at http://www.maa.org/features/OL.html

Steinle, V., Stacey, K., & Chambers, D. (2002). *Teaching and learning about decimals. Version 2.1* [CD-ROM]. Melbourne: University of Melbourne.

Stone, A., & Russell, S. J. (1990). *Counting: Ourselves and our families: A unit of study for grades K–1.* [Used numbers: Real data in the classroom] Palo Alto, CA: Dale Seymour.

Strauss, S., & Bichler, E. (1988). The development of children's concept of the arithmetic average. *Journal for Research in Mathematics Education, 19,* 64–80.

Tarr, J. E. (2002). Confounding effects of the phrase "50-50 chance" in making conditional probability judgments. *Focus on Learning Problems in Mathematics, 24*(4), 35–53.

Tarr, J. E., & Jones, G. A. (1997). A framework for assessing middle school students' thinking in conditional probability and independence. *Mathematics Education Research Journal, 9,* 39–59.

That's life. (1993, July 21). *The Mercury* (Hobart, Tasmania), p. 17.

Thin thighs don't come in jars. (1995, March 22). *The Mercury* (Hobart, Tasmania), p. 16.

Thompson, C. J. (1991). The role of statistics in achieving numeracy for all. In D. Vere-Jones (Ed.), *Proceedings of the Third International Conference on Teaching Statistics. Vol. 1. School and general issues* (pp. 429–432). Voorburg, The Netherlands: International Statistical Institute.

Torok, R., & Watson, J. (2000). Development of the concept of statistical variation: An exploratory study. *Mathematics Education Research Journal, 12,* 147–169.

Truran, J. (1985). Children's understanding of symmetry. *Teaching Statistics, 7*(3), 69–74.

Truran, K. (1995). Animism: A view of probability behaviour. In B. Atweh & S. Flavel (Eds.), *Galtha* (Proceedings of the 18th annual conference of the Mathematics Education Research Group of Australasia, pp. 537–542). Darwin, NT: MERGA.

Tufte, E. R. (1983). *The visual display of quantitative information.* Cheshire, CT: Graphics Press.

Tversky, A., & Kahneman, D. (1971). Belief in the law of small numbers. *Psychological Bulletin, 76*(2), 105–110.

Tversky, A., & Kahneman, D. (1974). Judgement under uncertainty: Heuristics and biases. *Science, 185,* 1124–1131.

Tversky, A., & Kahneman, D. (1980). Causal schemas in judgements under uncertainty. In M. Fishbein (Ed.), *Progress in social psychology* (Vol. 1, pp. 49–72). Hillsdale, NJ: Lawrence Erlbaum Associates.

Tversky, A., & Kahneman, D. (1983). Extensional versus intuitive reasoning: The conjunction fallacy in probability judgement. *Psychological Review, 90,* 293–315.

Utts, J. M. (1999). *Seeing through statistics.* (2nd ed.). Pacific Grove, CA: Duxbury Press.

Varga, T. (1983). Statistics in the curriculum for everybody—How young children and how their teachers react. In D. R. Grey, P. Holmes, V. Barnett, & G. M. Constable (Eds.), *Proceedings of the First International Conference on the Teaching Statistics* (Vol. 2, pp. 71–80). Sheffield, UK: Teaching Statistics Trust.

Vidakovic, D., Berenson, S., & Brandsma, J. (1998). Children's intuition of probabilistic concepts emerging from fair play. In L. Pereira-Mendoza, L. S. Kea, T. W. Kee, & W. Wong (Eds.), *Statistical education—Expanding the network. Proceedings of the Fifth International Conference on the Teaching of Statistics* (Vol. 1, pp. 67–73). Voorburg, The Netherlands: International Statistical Institute.

Wagner, D. A., & Gal, I. (1991). *Project STARC: Acquisition of statistical reasoning in children* (Annual Report No. 1). Philadelphia, PA: University of Pennsylvania, Literacy Research Center.

Wainer, H., & Velleman, P. F. (2001). Statistical graphics: Mapping the pathways of science. *Annual Review of Psychology, 52,* 305–335.

Walker, H. M. (1931). Mathematics and statistics. In W. D. Reeve (Ed.), *National Council of Teachers of Mathematics, The sixth yearbook: Mathematics in modern life* (pp. 111–135). New York: Teachers' College, Columbia University.

Wallman, K. K. (1993). Enhancing statistical literacy: Enriching our society. *Journal of the American Statistical Association, 88,* No. 421, 1–8.

Watson, J. M. (1978). A current event for the mathematics classroom. *Mathematics Teacher, 71,* 658–663.

Watson, J. M. (1980). A resource for teaching conditional probability. *Australian Mathematics Teacher, 36*(3), 21–23.

Watson, J. M. (1991). Building probability models in a differential equations course. *International Journal of Mathematical Education in Science and Technology, 22,* 507–517.

Watson, J. M. (1992). Fishy statistics. *Teaching Statistics, 14*(3), 17–21.

Watson, J. M. (1993). Introducing the language of probability through the media. In M. Stephens, A. Wayward, D. Clarke, & J. Izard (Eds.), *Communicating mathematics—Perspectives from current research and classroom practice in Australia* (pp. 119–139). Melbourne: Australian Council for Educational Research.

Watson, J. M. (1994a). Instruments to assess statistical concepts in the school curriculum. In National Organizing Committee (Ed.), *Proceedings of the Fourth International Conference on Teaching Statistics* (Vol. 1, pp. 73–80). Rabat, Morocco: National Institute of Statistics and Applied Economics.

Watson, J. (1994b). *Maths works: Teaching and learning chance and data* (assisted by W. Ransley). Adelaide, SA: Australian Association of Mathematics Teachers.

Watson, J. M. (1996). Reflections on videoconferencing and hypertext as media for professional development. In R. Zevenbergen (Ed.), *Mathematics education in changing times: Reactive or proactive* (pp. 165–176). Melbourne, VIC: Mathematics Education Lecturers' Association.

Watson, J. M. (1997a). Assessing statistical literacy using the media. In I. Gal & J. B. Garfield (Eds.), *The assessment challenge in statistics education* (pp. 107–121). Amsterdam: IOS Press & The International Statistical Institute.

Watson, J. M. (1997b). Chance and data for luddites. *Australian Mathematics Teacher, 53*(3), 24–29.

Watson, J. M. (1998a). Assessment of statistical understanding in a media context. In L. Pereira-Mendoza, L. S. Kea, T. W. Kee, & W. Wong (Eds.), *Statistical education—Expanding the network. Proceedings of the Fifth International Conference on Teaching Statistics* (Vol. 2, pp. 793–799). Voorburg, The Netherlands: International Statistical Institute.

Watson, J. M. (1998b). Numeracy benchmarks for years 3 and 5: What about chance and data? In C. Kanes, M. Goos, & E. Warren (Eds.), *Teaching mathematics in new times* (Proceedings of the 21st annual conference of the Mathematics Education Research Group of Australasia, Vol. 2, pp. 669–676). Brisbane, QLD: MERGA.

Watson, J. M. (1998c). Professional development for teachers of probability and statistics: Into an era of technology. *International Statistical Review, 66,* 271–289.

Watson, J. M. (1998d). Professional development of teachers using CD-ROM technology. In L. Pereira-Mendoza, L. S. Kea, T. W. Kee, & W. Wong (Eds.), *Statistical education—Expanding the network. Proceedings of the Fifth International Conference on Teaching Statistics* (Vol. 2, pp. 921–927). Voorburg, The Netherlands: International Statistical Institute.

Watson, J. M. (1998e). The role of statistical literacy in decisions about risk: Where to start. *For the Learning of Mathematics, 18*(3), 25–27.

Watson, J. M. (1999). The media, technology and statistical literacy for all. In Z. Usiskin (Ed.), *Developments in school mathematics education around the world. Volume 4* (pp. 308–322). Reston, VA: National Council of Teachers of Mathematics.

Watson, J. M. (2000a). Preservice mathematics teachers' understanding of sampling: Intuition or mathematics. *Mathematics Teacher Education and Development, 2*, 121–135.

Watson, J. M. (2000b). Statistics in context. *Mathematics Teacher, 93*, 54–58.

Watson, J. M. (2001). Longitudinal development of inferential reasoning by school students. *Educational Studies in Mathematics, 47*, 337–372.

Watson, J. M. (2002a). Creating cognitive conflict in a controlled research setting: Sampling. In B. Phillips (Ed.), *Developing a statistically literate society? Proceedings of the Sixth International Conference on Teaching Statistics, Cape Town* [CD-ROM]. Voorburg, The Netherlands: International Statistical Institute.

Watson, J. M. (2002b). Inferential reasoning and the influence of cognitive conflict. *Educational Studies in Mathematics, 51*, 225–256.

Watson, J. M. (2002c). Lessons from variation research II: For the classroom. In M. Goos & T. Spencer (Eds.), *Mathematics—Making waves* (Proceedings of the 19th biennial conference of the Australian Association of Mathematics Teachers Inc., Brisbane, pp. 424–432). Adelaide, SA: AAMT.

Watson, J. M. (2002d). When 2 + 2 ≠ 4 and 6 + 6 ≠ 12 in data and chance. *New England Mathematics Journal, 34*(2), 56–68.

Watson, J. M. (2004a). Developing reasoning about samples. In J. Garfield & D. Ben-Zvi (Eds.), *The challenge of developing statistical literacy, reasoning, and thinking* (pp. 277–294). Dordrecht: Kluwer.

Watson, J. M. (2004b). *The role of cognitive conflict in developing students' understanding of average.* Manuscript submitted for publication.

Watson, J. M. (2005). The probabilistic reasoning of middle school students. In G. A. Jones (Ed.), *Exploring probability in school: Challenges for teaching and learning* (pp. 145–169). New York: Springer.

Watson, J. M., & Baxter, J. P. (1997). Learning the unlikely at distance as an information technology enterprise: Development and research. In J. B. Garfield & G. Burrill (Eds.), *Research on the role of technology in teaching and learning statistics* (pp. 285–299). Voorburg, The Netherlands: International Statistical Institute.

Watson, J. M., Baxter, J. P., Olssen, K. H., & Lovitt, C. (1996). Professional development at distance as an information technology enterprise. *Asia Pacific Journal of Teacher Education, 24*, 139–146.

Watson, J. M., & Callingham, R. A. (1997). Data cards: An introduction to higher order processes in data handling. *Teaching Statistics, 19*, 12–16.

Watson, J. M., & Callingham, R. A. (2003). Statistical literacy: A complex hierarchical construct. *Statistics Education Research Journal, 2*(2), 3–46.

Watson, J. M., & Callingham, R. A. (2004, June). *Statistical literacy: From idiosyncratic to critical thinking.* Paper presented at the International Association for Statistical Education Roundtable, "Curricular Development in Statistics Education," Lund, Sweden.

Watson, J. M., & Caney, A. (2005). Student understanding of the concept of random. *Focus on Learning Problems in Mathematics, 27*(4), 1–42.

Watson, J. M., & Chick, H. L. (2001a). Does help help?: Collaboration during mathematical problem solving. *Hiroshima Journal of Mathematics Education, 9*, 33–73.

Watson, J. M., & Chick, H. L. (2001b). Factors influencing the outcomes of collaborative mathematics problem solving—An introduction. *Mathematical Thinking and Learning, 3*(2&3), 125–173.

Watson, J. M., & Chick, H. L. (2004). What is unusual? The case of a media graph. In M. Johnsen-Høines & A. B. Fuglestad (Eds.), *Proceedings of the 28th annual conference of the Inter-*

national Group for the Psychology of Mathematics Education (Vol. 2, pp. 207–214), Bergen, Norway: PME.

Watson, J. M., & Chick, H. L. (2005). Collaborative statistical investigations in diverse settings. *International Journal of Mathematical Education in Science and Technology, 36*, 573–600.

Watson, J. M., & Collis, K. F. (1994). Multimodal functioning in understanding chance and data concepts. In J. P. da Ponte & J. F. Matos (Eds.), *Proceedings of the 18th annual conference of the International Group for the Psychology of Mathematics Education* (Vol. 4, pp. 369–376). Lisbon: PME.

Watson, J. M., Collis, K. F., Callingham, R. A., & Moritz, J. B. (1995). A model for assessing higher order thinking in statistics. *Educational Research and Evaluation, 1*, 247–275.

Watson, J. M., Collis, K. F., & Moritz, J. B. (1994). Assessing statistical understanding in Grades 3, 6 and 9 using a short answer questionnaire. In G. Bell, B. Wright, N. Leeson, & G. Geake (Eds.), *Challenges in mathematics education: Constraints on construction* (Proceedings of the 17th annual conference of the Mathematics Education Research Group of Australasia, pp. 675–682). Lismore, NSW: MERGA.

Watson, J. M., Collis, K. F., & Moritz, J. B. (1995a). Children's understanding of luck. In B. Atweh & S. Flavel (Eds.), *Galtha* (Proceedings of the 18th annual conference of the Mathematics Education Research Group of Australasia, pp. 550–556). Darwin, NT: MERGA.

Watson, J. M., Collis, K. F., & Moritz, J. B. (1995b, November). *The development of concepts associated with sampling in grades 3, 5, 7 and 9*. A paper presented at the annual conference of the Australian Association for Research in Education, Hobart, Tasmania. Available at: http://www.aare.edu.au/95pap/watsj95475.txt

Watson, J. M., Collis, K. F., & Moritz, J. B. (1997). The development of chance measurement. *Mathematics Education Research Journal, 9*, 60–82.

Watson, J. M., & Kelly, B. A. (2002a). Can grade 3 students learn about variation? In B. Phillips (Ed.), *Developing a statistically literate society? Proceedings of the Sixth International Conference on Teaching Statistics, Cape Town* [CD-ROM]. Voorburg, The Netherlands: International Statistical Institute.

Watson, J. M., & Kelly, B. A. (2002b). Emerging concepts in chance and data. *Australian Journal of Early Childhood, 27*(4), 24–28.

Watson, J. M., & Kelly, B. A. (2002c). Grade 5 students' appreciation of variation. In A. Cockburn & E. Nardi (Eds.), *Proceedings of the 26th annual conference of the International Group for the Psychology of Mathematics Education* (Vol. 4, pp. 385–392). Norwich, UK: University of East Anglia.

Watson, J. M., & Kelly, B. A. (2002d, December). *School students' understanding of stacked dot (line) plots*. Refereed paper presented at the Australian Association for Research in Education conference, Brisbane. Available at: http://www.aare.edu.au/02pap/wat02243.htm

Watson, J. M., & Kelly, B. A. (2002e). Variation as part of chance and data in grades 7 and 9. In B. Barton, K. C. Irwin, M. Pfannkuch, & M. O. J. Thomas (Eds.), *Mathematics education in the South Pacific* (Proceedings of the 26th annual conference of the Mathematics Education Research Group of Australasia, Vol. 2, pp. 682–289). Sydney: MERGA.

Watson, J. M., & Kelly, B. A. (2003a). Developing intuitions about variation: The weather. In C. Lee (Ed.), *Reasoning about variability: Proceedings of the Third International Research Forum on Statistical Reasoning, Thinking, and Literacy* [CD-ROM]. Mt. Pleasant, MI: Central Michigan University.

Watson, J. M., & Kelly, B. A. (2003b). Inference from a pictograph: Statistical literacy in action. In L. Bragg, C. Campbell, G. Herbert, & J. Mousley (Eds.), *Mathematics education research: Innovation, networking, opportunity* (Proceedings of the 26th annual conference of the Mathematics Education Research Group of Australasia, Geelong, pp. 720–727). Sydney, NSW: MERGA.

Watson, J. M., & Kelly, B. A. (2003c). Predicting dice outcomes: The dilemma of expectation versus variation. In L. Bragg, C. Campbell, G. Herbert, & J. Mousley (Eds.), *Mathematics edu-*

cation research: Innovation, networking, opportunity (Proceedings of the 26th annual conference of the Mathematics Education Research Group of Australasia, Geelong, pp. 728–735). Sydney, NSW: MERGA.

Watson, J. M., & Kelly, B. A. (2003d). The vocabulary of statistical literacy. In *Educational research, risks, & dilemmas: Proceedings of the joint conferences of the New Zealand Association for Research in Education and the Australian Association for Research in Education* [CD-ROM]. Auckland, New Zealand, December, 2003. Available at: http://www.aare.edu.au/03pap/alpha.htm

Watson, J. M., & Kelly, B. A. (2004a). Expectation versus variation: Students' decision making in a chance environment. *Canadian Journal of Science, Mathematics and Technology Education, 4*, 371–396.

Watson, J. M., & Kelly, B. A. (2004b). *Longitudinal development of student understanding of outcomes involving two or more dice.* Manuscript submitted for publication.

Watson, J. M., & Kelly, B. A. (2004c). Statistical variation in a chance setting: A two-year study. *Educational Studies in Mathematics, 57*, 121–144.

Watson, J. M., & Kelly, B. A. (2005). Cognition and instruction: Reasoning about bias in sampling. *Mathematics Education Research Journal, 17*(1), 24–57.

Watson, J. M., & Kelly, B. A. (in press). Expectation versus variation: Decision making in a sampling environment. *Canadian Journal of Science, Mathematics and Technology Eduaction.*

Watson, J. M., Kelly, B. A., Callingham, R. A., & Shaughnessy, J. M. (2003). The measurement of school students' understanding of statistical variation. *International Journal of Mathematical Education in Science and Technology, 34*, 1–29.

Watson, J. M., & Moritz, J. B. (1998). Longitudinal development of chance measurement. *Mathematics Education Research Journal, 10*(2), 103–127.

Watson, J. M., & Moritz, J. B. (1999a). The beginning of statistical inference: Comparing two data sets. *Educational Studies in Mathematics, 37*, 145–168.

Watson, J. M., & Moritz, J. B. (1999b). The development of the concept of average. *Focus on Learning Problems in Mathematics, 21*(4), 15–39.

Watson, J. M., & Moritz, J. B. (1999c). Interpreting and predicting from bar graphs. *Australian Journal of Early Childhood, 24*(2), 22–27.

Watson, J. M., & Moritz, J. B. (2000a). Developing concepts of sampling. *Journal for Research in Mathematics Education, 31*, 44–70.

Watson, J. M., & Moritz, J. B. (2000b). Development of understanding of sampling for statistical literacy. *Journal of Mathematical Behavior, 19*, 109–136.

Watson, J. M., & Moritz, J. B. (2000c). The longitudinal development of understanding of average. *Mathematical Thinking and Learning, 2*(1&2), 11–50.

Watson, J. M., & Moritz, J. B. (2001a). Development of reasoning associated with pictographs: Representing, interpreting, and predicting. *Educational Studies in Mathematics, 48*, 47–81.

Watson, J. M., & Moritz, J. B. (2001b). The role of cognitive conflict in developing students' understanding of chance measurement. In J. Bobis, B. Perry, & M. Mitchelmore (Eds.), *Numeracy and beyond* (Proceedings of the 24th annual conference of the Mathematics Education Research Group of Australasia, Vol. 2, pp. 523–530). Sydney, NSW: MERGA.

Watson, J. M., & Moritz, J. B. (2002). School students' reasoning about conjunction and conditional events. *International Journal of Mathematical Education in Science and Technology, 33*, 59–84.

Watson, J. M., & Moritz, J. B. (2003a). The development of comprehension of chance language: Evaluation and interpretation. *School Science and Mathematics, 103*, 65–80.

Watson, J. M., & Moritz, J. B. (2003b). Fairness of dice: A longitudinal study of students' beliefs and strategies for making judgments. *Journal for Research in Mathematics Education, 34*, 270–304.

Watson, J. M., Moritz, J. B., & Pereira-Mendoza, L. (1998). Interpreting a graph in a social context. *The Mathematics Educator, 3*(1), 61–71.

Watson, J. M., & Pereira-Mendoza, L. (1996). Reading and predicting from bar graphs. *Australian Journal of Language and Literacy, 19*, 244–258.

Watson, J. M., & Shaughnessy, J. M. (2004). Proportional reasoning: Lessons from research in data and chance. *Mathematics Teaching in the Middle School, 10*, 104–109.

Webb, R., O'Meara, M., & Brown, B. (1993, January 28). Coles Myer accelerates retail purge. *The Australian Financial Review*, p. 1.

Wells, H. G. (1994). *World brain.* London: Adamantine Press. (Original work published 1938)

Wild, C. J., & Pfannkuch, M. (1999). Statistical thinking in empirical enquiry. *International Statistical Review, 67*, 223–265.

Wrinkles ultimate smoking deterrent. (1991, May 16). *The Mercury* (Hobart, Tasmania), p. 1.

Zawojewski, J. S., & Shaughnessy, J. M. (2000). Data and chance. In E. A. Silver & P. A. Kenney (Eds.), *Results from the seventh mathematics assessment of the National Assessment of Educational Progress* (pp. 235–268). Reston, VA: National Council of Teachers of Mathematics.

Author Index

Subject Index